Lecture Notes in Computer Science   9550

Commenced Publication in 1973
Founding and Former Series Editors:
Gerhard Goos, Juris Hartmanis, and Jan van Leeuwen

Marina L. Gavrilova · C.J. Kenneth Tan
Andrés Iglesias · Mikio Shinya
Akemi Galvez · Alexei Sourin (Eds.)

Transactions on Computational Science XXVI

Special Issue on Cyberworlds and Cybersecurity

Springer

ISSN 0302-9743   ISSN 1611-3349 (electronic)
Lecture Notes in Computer Science
ISBN 978-3-662-49246-8   ISBN 978-3-662-49247-5 (eBook)
DOI 10.1007/978-3-662-49247-5

Library of Congress Control Number: 2015960432

This Springer imprint is published by SpringerNature
The registered company is Springer-Verlag GmbH Berlin Heidelberg

LNCS Transactions on Computational Science

Computational science, an emerging and increasingly vital field, is now widely recognized as an integral part of scientific and technical investigations, affecting researchers and practitioners in areas ranging from aerospace and automotive research to biochemistry, electronics, geosciences, mathematics, and physics. Computer systems research and the exploitation of applied research naturally complement each other. The increased complexity of many challenges in computational science demands the use of supercomputing, parallel processing, sophisticated algorithms, and advanced system software and architecture. It is therefore invaluable to have input by systems research experts in applied computational science research.

Transactions on Computational Science focuses on original high-quality research in the realm of computational science in parallel and distributed environments, also encompassing the underlying theoretical foundations and the applications of large-scale computation.

The journal offers practitioners and researchers the opportunity to share computational techniques and solutions in this area, to identify new issues, and to shape future directions for research, and it enables industrial users to apply leading-edge, large-scale, high-performance computational methods.

In addition to addressing various research and application issues, the journal aims to present material that is validated – crucial to the application and advancement of the research conducted in academic and industrial settings. In this spirit, the journal focuses on publications that present results and computational techniques that are verifiable.

Scope

The scope of the journal includes, but is not limited to, the following computational methods and applications:

- Aeronautics and Aerospace
- Astrophysics
- Big Data Analytics
- Bioinformatics
- Biometric Technologies
- Climate and Weather Modeling
- Communication and Data Networks
- Compilers and Operating Systems
- Computer Graphics
- Computational Biology
- Computational Chemistry
- Computational Finance and Econometrics

- Computational Fluid Dynamics
- Computational Geometry
- Computational Number Theory
- Data Representation and Storage
- Data Mining and Data Warehousing
- Information and Online Security
- Grid Computing
- Hardware/Software Co-design
- High-Performance Computing
- Image and Video Processing
- Information Systems
- Information Retrieval
- Modeling and Simulations
- Mobile Computing
- Numerical and Scientific Computing
- Parallel and Distributed Computing
- Robotics and Navigation
- Supercomputing
- System-on-Chip Design and Engineering
- Virtual Reality and Cyberworlds
- Visualization

Editorial

The *Transactions on Computational Science* journal is part of the Springer series *Lecture Notes in Computer Science*, and is devoted to the gamut of computational science issues, from theoretical aspects to application-dependent studies and the validation of emerging technologies.

The journal focuses on original high-quality research in the realm of computational science in parallel and distributed environments, encompassing the facilitating theoretical foundations and the applications of large-scale computations and massive data processing. Practitioners and researchers share computational techniques and solutions in the area, identify new issues, shape future directions for research, and enable industrial users to apply the presented techniques.

The current volume is devoted to the topic of cyber-community and cyber-security. It comprises ten extended versions of selected papers from the International Conference on CyberWorlds 2014, held in June 2014 in Santander, Spain. The topics covered include areas of virtual reality, games, social networks, haptic modeling, cybersecurity, and applications in education and arts.

We would like to extend our sincere appreciation to the special issue guest editors, Andrés Iglesias, Mikio Shinya, Akemi Galvez, and Alexei Sourin, for their dedication and hard work in preparing this high-quality special issue. We would also like to thank all of the authors for submitting their papers to the special issue and the associate editors and reviewers for their valuable work.

It is our hope that this collection of ten papers presented in this special issue will be a valuable resource for *Transactions on Computational Science* readers and will stimulate further research into the vibrant area of cyberwords and their applications.

November 2015

Marina L. Gavrilova
C.J. Kenneth Tan

Preface to the Special Issue on Cyberworlds 2014

This special issue includes the extended versions of high-quality papers selected from the Cyberworlds 2014 conference, held in Santander, Spain, during October 6–8, 2014 (for details, see: http://www.cw2014.unican.es). The International Conference on Cyberworlds, organized annually since 2002 in cooperation with the EURO-GRAPHICS Association and the IFIP Workgroup 5.10 - Computer Graphics and Virtual Worlds, is the premier conference focused on cyberworlds and all related issues, including (but not limited to) computer graphics, shape modeling, user interfaces, virtual worlds, multimodal interaction and rendering, computer vision for augmented and mixed reality, multiplayer online games, social and affective computing, and cognitive informatics. The ten selected papers reflect the great diversity of topics covered by the Cyberworlds 2014 conference as well as the excellent level of its scientific contributions.

The first paper, "Image-Based Virtual Try-On System with Garment Reshaping and Color Correction," by Yoshihiro Kanamori, Hiroki Yamada, Masaki Hirose, Jun Mitani, and Yukio Fukui, proposes an image-based virtual try-on system for garments in order to reproduce the appearance of try-on during online shopping. The primary goal is to avoid the unnatural images usually obtained from naive compositing in virtual fitting, where typically the garment is simply superimposed onto the customer image. The contribution consists of the entire design of a novel virtual fitting system including remarkable features such as garment image reshaping based on wearers' body shapes, automatic color correction using facial colors, and automatic retouching of protrusions behind garments. A user test is also conducted to validate the system. It confirms that the virtual fitting results are natural looking and visually appealing.

The second paper, "Constructive Roofs from Solid Building Primitives," by Johannes Edelsbrunner, Ulrich Krispel, Sven Havemann, Alexei Sourin, and Dieter W. Fellner, presents a new method for abstract building specification that allows one to specify complex buildings from simpler parts with an emphasis on assisting the blending of roofs. The importance of this topic comes from the observation that procedural modeling requires less effort than the manual 3D modeling typically required as post-processing in mesh-based automatic reconstruction of buildings. In procedural modeling, a coarse outline of the building is represented via a number of parts, while rules further refine the resulting geometry. However, nesting or Boolean union of parts are not fully suitable for structures such as roofs. This method aims at solving this problem. A prototype implementation of the system was evaluated by modeling three scenes with interesting roof structures from aerial images: the royal palace of Milan, part of the city of Graz, and the royal palace of Magdalena in Santander (Cyberworlds 2014 conference venue). Our readers are kindly invited to take a look at the pictures in the paper to appreciate the good performance of this approach.

The third paper, "Isometric Shape Correspondence Based on the Geodesic Structure," by Taorui Jia, Kang Wang, Zhongke Wu, Junli Zhao, Pengfei Xu, Cuiting Liu, and Mingquan Zhou, proposes a novel and computationally efficient approach to find the correspondence between two (nearly) isometric shapes represented as manifold triangle meshes. The method is based on the geodesic structure of the shape and minimum cost flow. The motivation is that, even for the same rigid object, it is difficult to get two perfectly isometric shapes (because of the triangulation process and geometry discretization errors). Thus, the goal is to find a shape-correspondence method minimizing the isometric deviation in a k dimensional Euclidean space that is built through geodesics from the same-base vertices, where the two (nearly) isometric shapes are nearly at the same position and have approximately a similar surface. Some correspondence examples are also discussed. They show that this method yields correct matches for a number of shapes.

The fourth paper "Individual Theta/Beta-Based Algorithm for Neurofeedback Games to Improve Cognitive Abilities," by Yisi Liu, Xiyuan Hou, Olga Sourina, and Olga Bazanova, proposes and implements a neurofeedback system integrating an individual theta/beta-based neurofeedback algorithm in a shooting game. The system computes the individual alpha peak frequency, individual alpha band width, and individual theta/beta ratio, which make the neurofeedback training more effective. An experiment with five subjects was carried out to assess the effectiveness of the neurofeedback training system. The results show that all subjects overall have higher individual alpha peak frequency values right after the training or the next day, a clear indication of an enhancement of the subjects' cognitive abilities related to features such as attention and memory.

The fifth paper, "Scale-Invariant Heat Kernel Mapping for Shape Analysis," by Kang Wang, Zhongke Wu, Sajid Ali, Junli Zhao, Taorui Jia, Wuyang Shui, and Mingquan Zhou, presents a new shape analysis method with the scale-invariant property aimed at removing the effects of scale ambiguity. The method, called scale-invariant heat kernel mapping, is based on the heat diffusion process on shapes. This mapping procedure is an automatic scale adaptation method that allows the user to perform shape analysis without being confused by the scaling factors. Some experiments performed on the TOSCA dataset and reported in the paper demonstrate that the method achieves good robustness and effectiveness and it is suitable for situations of scaling transformation only, isometric deformation and scaling, and local scaling on shapes.

The sixth paper, "A Community-Built Virtual Heritage Collection," by Helen C. Miles, Andrew T. Wilson, Frédéric Labrosse, Bernard Tiddeman, and Jonathan C. Roberts, describes a Web platform developed for the HeritageTogether project through which members of the public can upload their own photographs of heritage assets to be processed into 3D models using an automated structure-to-motion work flow. These 3D models are displayed online using a lightbox-style gallery and a virtual museum, while the large amounts of additional data produced are stored in an online archive. The Web platform is part of a larger project that aims to capture, create, and archive digital heritage assets in conjunction with local communities in Wales, UK, with a focus on megalithic monuments. The ultimate goal is to inspire local communities to learn more about their heritage and to help to preserve it using computer tools such as a digital community and community-built archive and museum of heritage data. Our readers are kindly invited to visit the Web platform and (why not?) even become enthusiastic contributors of this exciting and valuable project.

The seventh paper "Identifying Users from Online Interactions in Twitter," by Madeena Sultana, Padma Polash Paul, and Marina Gavrilova, focuses on the potential of the analysis of online interactions for user identification. This is a very hot topic of research closely related to the exponential growth of online social networks. The main goal of this paper is to determine how online interactions of individuals can be effectively used as biometric information. To this aim, the paper analyzes how such online interactions retain the behavioral patterns of users and their consistency over time. As a result, it proposes a novel method to identify users from online interactions in Twitter. Experiments conducted on a database of 50 Twitter users over five different periods of time show very promising results that demonstrate the potential of online interactions for the authentication process of social network users.

The eighth paper, "Applying Geometric Function on Sensors 3D Gait Data for Human Identification," by Sajid Ali, Zhongke Wu, Xulong Li, Nighat Saeed, Dong Wang, and Mingquan Zhou, proposes a novel approach for human identification based on sensor data acquired by means of an optical system. The basic idea is to process 3D motion data of gait joints through the straight-walking view. Three joints of the human body (hip, knee, and ankle) are selected to compute the gait movement in this algorithm. The method extracts suitable 3D static and dynamic joint features from data and applies parametric Bézier curves on these features to derive the strong correlation between joint movements. The control points of the curve are used to build the triangles of each walking pose, which are then used to compute the area with transfer features from the 3D to 1D space of each pose. Then, statistical techniques are used to obtain a unique direct relationship between gait joints, called gait signature, which can be further used to perform human identification from a database containing recorded motion subjects, each walking at different speed, and performing several direction changes. Experimental results show that the method exhibits outstanding human identification capabilities.

The ninth paper, "The Influences of Online Gaming on Leadership Development," by Tinnawat Nuangjumnong, seeks to identify the effects of gameplay on leadership behaviors and determine how video games can be used as a didactic tool for leadership development. Through contingency leadership theory, and using a large set of self-report questionnaires, this study finds that the continuous practice of specific game roles (such as carry, support, or ganker) in MOBAs (multiplayer online battle arena games) promotes the development of real-world leadership styles. Effects of gameplay on leadership behaviors are estimated using propensity score matching and doubly robust estimation. The empirical analysis reveals that game players who predominantly play a specific role in games exhibit stronger real-world behaviors of the corresponding leadership style.

The tenth and last paper, "An Efficient Pose-Tolerant Face Recognition Approach," by Refik Samet, Ghulam Sakhi Shokouh, and Kemal Batuhan Baskurt, addresses the problem of pose in face recognition for biometric identification. Pose is one of the most critical problems in face recognition, because the face appearance changes drastically with changes in facial pose due to misalignment and hiding of many facial features.

This paper proposes a novel pose-tolerant face-recognition approach that includes feature extraction, pose transformation learning, and recognition stages. In the first stage, 2D PCA (principal component analysis) is used as a robust feature extraction technique. Then, linear regression is used as an efficient and accurate transformation learning technique to create a frontal face image from different posed face images in the second stage. In the last stage, Mahalanobis distance is used for recognition. Experiments on FERET and FEI face databases demonstrate that this method outperforms other traditional approaches for these benchmarks.

We are deeply grateful to the editor-in-chief of *Transactions on Computational Science*, Prof. Marina Gavrilova, and all journal editorial staff for their continuing help and assistance during the whole process of preparing these papers. We also wish to thank the authors for their high-quality contributions and their great cooperation in preparing this special issue. We owe special thanks to the conference program vice-chairs, Profs. Norimasa Yoshida (Nihon University, Japan) and Michio Shiraishi (Toho University, Japan), and the Program Committee members and reviewers for their hard work in reviewing the papers and making constructive comments and suggestions, which have substantially contributed to improving all the papers. They undoubtely did a great job!

We also thank the Computer Science Research Program of the Spanish Ministry of Economy and Competitiveness, Project TIN2012-30768, the University of Cantabria (Santander, Spain), and Toho University (Funabashi, Japan) for their support and all the facilities given to produce this special issue. Last, but certainly not least, we wish to thank the readers for their interest in this special issue and for supporting the *Transactions on Computational Science* journal. Many thanks to all of them!

December 2015

Andrés Iglesias
Mikio Shinya
Akemi Galvez
Alexei Sourin

LNCS Transactions on Computational Science – Editorial Board

Contents

Image-Based Virtual Try-On System with Garment Reshaping and Color Correction

Yoshihiro Kanamori[✉], Hiroki Yamada, Masaki Hirose, Jun Mitani, and Yukio Fukui

University of Tsukuba, Tsukuba, Japan
{kanamori,mitani,fukui}@cs.tsukuba.ac.jp,
{yamada,hirose}@npal.cs.tsukuba.ac.jp
http://www.npal.cs.tsukuba.ac.jp/

Abstract. We propose an image-based virtual try-on system for garments in order to reproduce the appearance of try-on during online shopping. Given whole-body images of a fashion model and a customer, we cut out a garment image from the fashion model image and reshape it so that it fits to the body shape of the customer. The reshaping function is estimated automatically from the body contours of the fashion model and the customer. The fitting result is refined further by automatic color correction with reference to the facial regions and a method of retouching parts that protrude from the rear of the garment image. We verified the effectiveness of our system through a user test.

Keywords: Image-based virtual fitting · Image warping · Color constancy

1 Introduction

The number of users shopping online for garments has tended to increase recently, and this is expanding widely as means of enjoying shopping comfortably from customers' own homes. However, there is a problem that we cannot try on clothes because we cannot handle real garments, unlike shopping in a real bricks-and-mortar store. Since fit is such an important criterion when buying garments, this is one reason impeding the spread of online shopping. To address this problem, there have been proposals for virtual fitting systems that implement fitting online in a virtual manner. For example, the online virtual fitting service *Awaseba* [6] composites a whole-body image of a registered customer (hereafter called a *"customer image"*) with an image of a garment from a catalog (hereafter called a *"garment image"*), and presents an image of the customer apparently wearing the garment. However, typical online services just provide virtual fitting by naïve compositing.

Virtual fitting by naïve compositing often produces unnatural images (Fig. 1, right). Whereas this is partially because of the differences in brightness between the images, the large cause is that the shape of the garment image does not

© Springer-Verlag Berlin Heidelberg 2016
M.L. Gavrilova et al. (Eds.): Trans. on Comput. Sci. XXVI, LNCS 9550, pp. 1–16, 2016.
DOI: 10.1007/978-3-662-49247-5_1

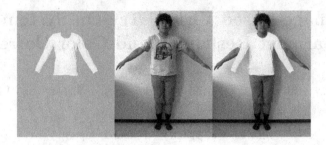

Fig. 1. Virtual fitting by a naïve superimposing. From left, the garment image, the customer image, and the fitting result. Naïve superimposition results in an unnatural image mainly because the garment does not match the body shape.

match the body shape of the customer. For example, in Fig. 1, the garment is neither matched to the positions of the arms nor the width of the trunk.

We therefore introduce an image-based virtual fitting system that suppresses the unnaturalness of the virtual fitting image. In our system, the garment image to be fitted is cut out from an image of it being worn by a fashion model, and then is warped according to a warping function with which the body shape of the fashion model matches that of the customer. This can be considered as warping in the literature of *deformation transfer* [18], where deformation is transferred from a source 3D mesh onto another target mesh. The body shapes are automatically estimated from the contours of each human body and can be retouched if necessary. The brightness differences between the garment image and the customer image are adjusted automatically by color correction based on facial colors. Finally, our system automatically retouches protrusion from the rear of the composite garment image.

Our contribution lies in the entire design of a novel virtual fitting system with the following features:

1. garment image reshaping based on wearers' body shapes,
2. automatic color correction using facial colors, and
3. automatic retouching of protrusion behind garments.

We confirm the effectiveness of our system by conducting a user test.

2   Related Work

Existing virtual fitting approaches can be divided into two main groups, i.e., 3D model-based and 2D image-based methods.

There have been proposed 3D virtual try-on systems [4,5,15] that can produce compelling fitting results using measured 3D human models and cloth simulation based on physical parameters of garments. Recent dressing simulations [3,10,20,22] can reproduce detailed drapes or folds of garments fitted on various different body shapes. Whereas these simulations often use a 3D avatar

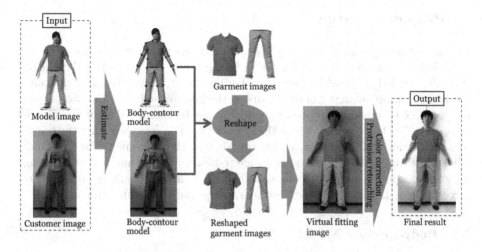

Fig. 2. Overview of our system. Our system first estimates the body-contour models both for the fashion model and the customer, and then warps the garment cut out from the fashion model's image so that the garment matches to the customer's body shape. The fitting result is refined further by automatic color correction and automatic protrusion retouching.

as a 3D human model, customer's own 3D model can be generated using depth camera, e.g., Microsoft Kinect, for whole-body scan [11,19].

Despite these progress, providing an experience as if the customer him- or herself wore a specific garment is still difficult because photorealistic rendering of 3D human models as well as garments is not handy even now. Additionally, preparing a huge number of detailed 3D models for garments in online shops is currently impractical.

Compared to 3D model-based approaches, 2D image-based methods have advantages that collecting data and photorealistic rendering are relatively easy. As such, there are example-based approaches that use a pre-recorded database and find the best matching dataset to provide a virtual fitting result. The system by Ehara and Saito [8] used a database of marker-attached T-shirt images in different poses. Zhou et al. [24] prepared a database of animating garments in different poses and achieved a real-time virtual fitting by superimposing a garment fitted onto a person captured using Kinect. Hilsmann et al. [12] reproduced the shapes of garments with detailed folds by interpolating images of garments worn in different poses. These example-based approaches, however, are hardly applicable in real apparel websites because of the costly database; for example, for an apparel website [17], photographs of more than ten thousand items are taken everyday. In contrast, we reduce the load of preparation beforehand, by inputting only one 2D image for creating data for one garment.

3   Proposed System

The flow of our system is shown in Fig. 2. The inputs to our system are a whole-body image of a fashion model wearing the garment to be used in the fitting (hereafter called a *"model image"*) and a customer image. We first estimate the body-contour models from contours of the human bodies in the both input images. The estimated body-contour models can be retouched by user input if necessary. We then determine how the garment is to be reshaped from the body-contour model of the fashion model and that of the customer. The customer adjusts the position of the garment image to be composited and a virtual fitting image is output. Finally, a more natural virtual fitting result is obtained by correcting the brightness of the customer image and retouching protrusions.

3.1   Body-Contour Model

In our system, contours of human bodies are used to reshape garments accord-ing to the differences of physique shapes between the fashion model and the customer. Ideally, we should know the underlying naked body shapes hidden by clothes, as done by Guan et al. [9]. Their method trains a parametric 2D contour model using a database of parametric 3D human models with differ-ent proportions and different poses [1], which requires highly-costly preparation. Our system instead uses a simple heuristics to estimate a simple 2D shape model while restricting the input poses in which the arms and feet are slightly spread to avoid occlusions of body contours (Fig. 3). Our 2D shape model, called a *body-contour model*, is specific to our system and can be estimated with less calculation. Our estimation is of course error-prone, but the user can modify the estimated model easily and quickly, as demonstrated in our user test.

The body-contour model consists of body-feature points and body-feature edges, as shown in Fig. 3. The number of body-feature points was determined through experiments regarding estimation easiness and quality of image reshap-ing. Consequently, we selected a total of 27 points at the neck, shoulder, arm, wrist, armpits, trunk, hips, leg, and ankle on the left and right sides plus one at the crotch, as shown by from $\mathbf{p}_0$ to $\mathbf{p}_{26}$ in Fig. 3.

Heuristic Estimation of Body-Contour Model. The positions of body-feature points are estimated under an assumption that proportional lengths of the body parts are common to human bodies even though there are individual differences. For example, the position of the arm joint can be predicted as being at a position about one-third of the length from shoulder to fingertips (Fig. 4, left). Our heuristics is thus to find noticeable points such as necks and shoulders first, and then apply pre-defined proportions to determine remaining points.

We first extract a person's contour by tracing the boundary of a pre-defined mask, and sample the contour at M equidistant points (we use $M = 200$). Of the points on this contour, we take the uppermost one (with the maximum y-coordinate) to be the point $\mathbf{v}_0$ at the top of the head and number the rest

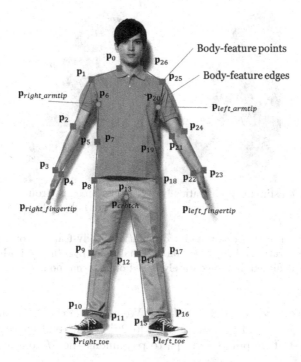

Fig. 3. Body-contour model. It is a 2D shape that consists of 27 body-feature points (from p_0 to p_{26}, red squares) and body-feature edges that connect the points. The blue circles indicate the reference points used to determine body-feature points (Color figure online).

Right side			
P	A	B	$PA : PB$
Arm p_2	Shoulder p_1	Fingertip $p_{right\_fingertip}$	1 : 2
Wrist p_3	Arm p_2	Fingertip $p_{right\_fingertip}$	2 : 1
Hip p_8	Armpit p_6	Toe p_{right_toe}	1 : 2
Trunk p_7	Armpit p_6	Hip p_8	1 : 1
Leg p_9	Hip p_8	Toe p_{right_toe}	2 : 1
Ankle p_{10}	Leg p_9	Toe p_{right_toe}	2 : 1
Left side			
P	A	B	$PA : PB$
Arm p_{24}	Shoulder p_{25}	Fingertip $p_{left\_fingertip}$	1 : 2
Wrist p_{23}	Arm p_{24}	Fingertip $p_{left\_fingertip}$	2 : 1
Hip p_{18}	Armpit p_{20}	Toe p_{left_toe}	1 : 2
Trunk p_{19}	Armpit p_{20}	Hip p_{18}	1 : 1
Leg p_{17}	Hip p_{18}	Toe p_{right_toe}	2 : 1
Ankle p_{16}	Leg p_{17}	Toe p_{right_toe}	2 : 1

Fig. 4. Ratios used to determine body-feature points. body-feature point P is determined by the ratio of lengths PA and PB along the contour. The left image shows an example for body-feature point p_2 for the right arm. In the left image, the squares are body-feature points and the circle is a reference point.

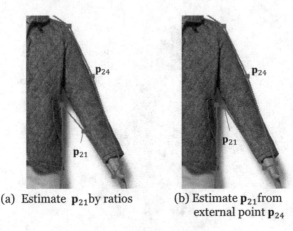

(a) Estimate $\mathbf{p}_{21}$ by ratios   (b) Estimate $\mathbf{p}_{21}$ from
                                                 external point $\mathbf{p}_{24}$

Fig. 5. Comparison of the feature-point calculation. Body-feature point $\mathbf{p}_{24}$ is calculated (a) by length ratio and (b) based on external point $\mathbf{p}_{24}$. In (b), both $\mathbf{p}_{24}$ and the wrist point are calculated more accurately based on external points.

counterclockwise as $\mathbf{v}_i$ $(i = 0, 1, ..., M-1)$. We also take the angle subtended by the vertices $\mathbf{v}_{i-1}$, $\mathbf{v}_i$ and $\mathbf{v}_{i+1}$ to be $\theta_i \in [0, 2\pi]$ (counterclockwise is positive). We select body-feature points from $\mathbf{p}_0$ to $\mathbf{p}_{26}$ among the M contour points.

Search for Neck and Shoulder Points. We extract the neck and shoulder points as the points that give the greatest and smallest values of the angle θ_i when counting along a given number of contour points from the top-of-the-head point $\mathbf{v}_0$. The neck point $\mathbf{p}_0$ on the left side is the point at which the angle θ_i is smallest within the range of l points (we use $l = 10$) in sequence counterclockwise from $\mathbf{v}_0$. Next, the shoulder point $\mathbf{p}_1$ on the left side is the point at which the angle θ_i is greatest within the range of m points (we use $m = 10$) counterclockwise from $\mathbf{p}_0$. We search in a similar manner clockwise from $\mathbf{v}_0$ for the neck and shoulder points $\mathbf{p}_{26}$ and $\mathbf{p}_{25}$ on the right side.

Search for Fingertips, Armpits and Others. We then detect noticeable points such as fingertips and armpits among the contour points by reversals in the y coordinate, which we use these points as reference when obtaining the body-feature points by length ratios, and thus we call them *"reference points"*. Note that we do not use the top-of-the-head point as a reference point. The reference points in our system are the following seven points (Fig. 3): the fingertips, armpits, and toetips on the left and right sides, plus the crotch. Regarding notations, the left and right fingertips are $\mathbf{p}_{left\_fingertip}$ and $\mathbf{p}_{right\_fingertip}$, the left and right armpits $\mathbf{p}_{left\_armpit}$ and $\mathbf{p}_{right\_armpit}$, the left and right toetips $\mathbf{p}_{left\_toe}$ and $\mathbf{p}_{right\_toe}$, and the crotch $\mathbf{p}_{crotch}$.

The body-feature points for armpits and crotch are selected from reference points: $\mathbf{p}_6 = \mathbf{p}_{right\_armpit}$, $\mathbf{p}_{20} = \mathbf{p}_{left\_armpit}$ and $\mathbf{p}_{13} = \mathbf{p}_{crotch}$. For the remaining body-feature points for the arms and stomach, we determine the positions

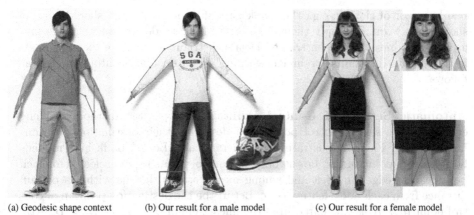

(a) Geodesic shape context   (b) Our result for a male model   (c) Our result for a female model

Fig. 6. Comparison of body-contour model (red polylines) estimation. (a) Result obtained using geodesic shape context [13] and (b)(c) our results. The failure regions enclosed by red rectangles in (b)(c) are magnified (Color figure online).

Table 1. Pairings of internal and external body-feature points.

Positions	Right side		Left side	
	Internal	External	Internal	External
Arms	p_5	p_2	p_{21}	p_{24}
Wrists	p_4	p_3	p_{22}	p_{23}
Legs	p_{12}	p_9	p_{14}	p_{17}
Ankles	p_{11}	p_{10}	p_{15}	p_{16}

according to the pre-defined length ratio between each pair of certain points, as listed in Fig. 4.

Regarding the internal points at the arm and leg parts, we also tried the ratio-based approach but often failed because of accumulated errors. We thus instead find these points from the corresponding external points at opposite sides according to the contour normals (Fig. 5). The pairings of the internal and external points are shown in Table 1.

Figure 6 shows a comparison of estimation for body-contour models using the geodesic shape context [13] and our method. The geodesic shape context might produce erroneous results as shown in Fig. 6(a). Our results shown in Fig. 6(b)(c) have less errors, and the user can manually correct them quickly.

3.2 Garment Image Reshaping

Using the body-contour models, the garment image is reshaped to fit the customer's body shape. We used the 2D mesh warping of Weng et al. [21] for reshaping the garment image. Their method suppresses excessive distortions while trying to keep the area of the input mesh, which seems beneficial for emulating the real behavior of clothes; e.g., the trunk part of a too-small shirt should become short when worn. To apply their method, we first divide a garment image into a triangular mesh using constrained Delaunay triangulation. We then automatically set control points for image warping based on body-contour models as follows.

Automatic Setting of Control Points. To apply the method of Weng et al. [21], we select control points and designate their destination positions for reshaping. Figure 7 illustrates this schematically. Let $\mathbf{p}_n^s$ be fashion model's body-feature point and $\mathbf{p}_n^t$ be customer's. Control points $\mathbf{m}_j^s$ are selected for each body-feature edge, and selected among mesh vertices that lie within a certain distance from each body-feature edge. Let $\mathbf{m}_j^t$ be the destination position of control point $\mathbf{m}_j^s$. $\mathbf{m}_j^t$ is calculated from the linear sum of the vectors $\mathbf{w}_n = \mathbf{p}_n^t - \mathbf{p}_n^s$ and $\mathbf{w}_{n+1} = \mathbf{p}_{n+1}^t - \mathbf{p}_{n+1}^s$ as follows:

$$\mathbf{m}_j^t = \mathbf{m}_j^s + (1 - \alpha)\mathbf{w}_n + \alpha\mathbf{w}_{n+1},$$
$$\alpha = \frac{(\mathbf{p}_{n+1}^s - \mathbf{p}_n^s) \cdot (\mathbf{m}_j^s - \mathbf{p}_n^s)}{\left|\mathbf{p}_{n+1}^s - \mathbf{p}_n^s\right|^2}. \tag{1}$$

Note that, if the same mesh vertex is selected as control points for multiple body-feature edges, the vertex is used as the control point only for the nearest body-feature edge.

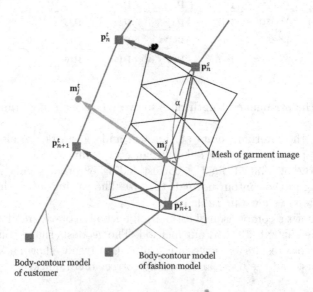

Fig. 7. Illustration of the calculation of control points from the body-contour model. The red curve indicates fashion model's contour while the blue curve the customer's. Control point $\mathbf{m}_j^s$ is selected as the mesh vertex that is the closest from fashion model's feature edge (Color figure online).

3.3   Brightness Correction Based on Facial Regions

We perform automatic color correction to suppress the brightness differences between the garment image and the customer image. This is based on *color constancy* on facial colors, i.e., an assumption that the facial colors of the fashion model and the customer are the same, and the strangeness is caused solely by the difference of the photographic environments. Recently, Bianco et al. [2] also proposed a method for estimating illumination based on facial colors. Their method learns a database consisting of each pair of a neutral-color reference card (used to know the ground truth) and a facial color. Our method is much simpler; we just adjust the brightness only from a pair of images without using such database.

Our method works as follows. First, facial regions are extracted automatically using *Active Shape Model* [7] both from the model image and the customer image. Here we assume that the fashion model is photographed under an ideal illumination while the customer under an unknown illumination, and the facial color of the fashion model $\mathbf{f}_m$ and that of the customer $\mathbf{f}_c$ have the following relationship based on the von Kries model [14]:

$$\mathbf{f}_m = D_{c,m}\,\mathbf{f}_c, \qquad (2)$$

where $D_{c,m}$ is a diagonal matrix that converts colors under the customer's illumination into those under the ideal (i.e., fashion model's) illumination. $D_{c,m}$ is then estimated as follows.

$$D_{c,m} = diag(\mathbf{f}_c)^{-1}\,\mathbf{f}_m, \qquad (3)$$

where $diag(\mathbf{x})$ represents a diagonal matrix consisting of the three components of vector $\mathbf{x}$. We then apply matrix $D_{c,m}$ to the customer image. We confirmed that the Lab color space yields good results by experiments.

In case that the colors of the fashion model and the customer are largely different, our system lets the customer choose the most appropriate facial color from face examples with different colors.

3.4   Protrusion Retouching

Local Reshaping of Image to Reduce Protrusions. To prevent customer's cloth from protruding from the garment image (Fig. 8, left), we warp the customer image locally (Fig. 8, right). For this, we use the method of Schaefer et al. [16] to provide faster feedback. In the following, we describe how to automatically set control points used for the image warping.

Control Point Setting. Control points are assigned automatically along image boundaries and customer's body contour (Fig. 11). For image boundaries, 20 control points are set equidistantly for each vertical and horizontal boundary. For customer's body contour, 200 control points are set in the same way as the contour points in Sect. 3.1.

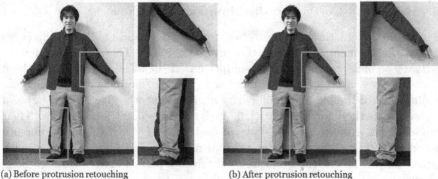

(a) Before protrusion retouching   (b) After protrusion retouching

Fig. 8. Example of protrusion retouching. (a) Before and (b) after the retouching. The red regions in each image are magnified. The protrusions from the rears of garments are retouched naturally (Color figure online).

Closed−margin edges

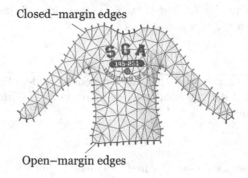

Open−margin edges

Fig. 9. Open-margin edges (blue) and closed-margin edges (red) of a garment image. Edges that permit protrusions, e.g., sleeves and neck, are configured as open-margin edges (Color figure online).

Addition of Boundary Information to Garment Image. Control points along customer's contour are not necessarily displaced; some parts of the garment contour, e.g., the throat and cuffs, permit protrusions of customer's cloth, and thus control points around such parts do not have to be moved. We call such edges of the garment contour as *"open-margin edges"*. Conversely, edges around shoulders forbid protrusions and we call such edges of the garment contour as *"closed-margin edges"*. Figure 9 shows an example. By default, all the edges of the garment contour are set as closed-margin, and we let the user manually mark open-margin edges.

Control points around closed-margin edges are to be displaced, and are searched within a trapezoidal region formed by extensions in contour normal directions from both endpoints of each closed-margin edge (Fig. 10). If control points are found within the search region and are outside of the garment image, they are registered as to be displaced.

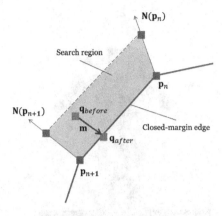

Fig. 10. Illustration of control point's destination. For each closed-margin edge, control points are searched and moved onto their closed-margin edge.

Displacement of Control Points. Figure 10 illustrates how to determine the destination positions of the control points. For each control point, we first find its belonging closed-margin edge. Let $\mathbf{m}$ be the displacement direction vector of the control point, then $\mathbf{m}$ is calculated by linear interpolation of two normals at both endpoints of the closed-margin edge:

$$\mathbf{m} = -(1 - \alpha)\,\mathbf{N}(\mathbf{p}_n) - \alpha\,\mathbf{N}(\mathbf{p}_{n+1})$$

$$\alpha = \frac{(\mathbf{p}_n - \mathbf{q}_{before}) \times \mathbf{N}(\mathbf{p}_n)}{(\mathbf{p}_n - \mathbf{q}_{before}) \times \mathbf{N}(\mathbf{p}_n) + (\mathbf{q}_{before} - \mathbf{p}_{n+1}) \times \mathbf{N}(\mathbf{p}_{n+1})} \tag{4}$$

where $\mathbf{N}(\mathbf{p}_n)$ denotes the normal at $\mathbf{p}_n$ and is calculated as an unit vector orthogonal to the vector $\mathbf{p}_{n+1} - \mathbf{p}_{n-1}$. $\times$ denotes a 2D vector operation, i.e., $\mathbf{a} \times \mathbf{b} = (a_x, a_y) \times (b_x, b_y) = a_x\,b_y - a_y\,b_x$. $\mathbf{q}_{before}$ is the position of the control point before displacement. Its destination $\mathbf{q}_{after}$ is determined by moving $\mathbf{q}_{before}$ onto the closed-margin edge along vector $\mathbf{m}$ (Fig. 10).

4 Results

Our prototype system was written in C++ using OpenGL and wxWidgets. The execution environment was a PC with an Intel Core i7-2600 CPU (3.40 GHz), and 4 GB main memory, with an NVIDIA GeForce GTX460 GPU.

4.1 Virtual Fitting Results

Figure 13 shows virtual fitting images using our system. Without garment image reshaping (Fig. 13(c)), the result looks unnatural because the garment image does not conform to the arm and leg positions. With reshaping (Fig. 13(d)), the result becomes better. In Fig. 13(e), color correction reduces the brightness difference caused by the illumination differences, and the protrusion retouching makes

Fig. 11. Control points (green) and mesh (blue) for the customer image. Control points are assigned equidistantly along the customer's contour and the image boundary (Color figure online).

Fig. 12. Composition of garments onto posed customers. Garment images can be warped according to posed body shapes thanks to the underlying meshes.

the result look closer to real fitting results. Color correction is especially useful because customers often take photographs under un-calibrated lights whereas the fashion model are taken under studio-adjusted lights. The result in the fifth row demonstrates that our method also works well with a loosely-fitted garment, without introducing unexpected distortion to the garment.

As an application, we can also composite garments onto posed customer images as shown in Fig. 12. Garment images can be warped according to posed body shapes thanks to the underlying meshes. While these results were obtained

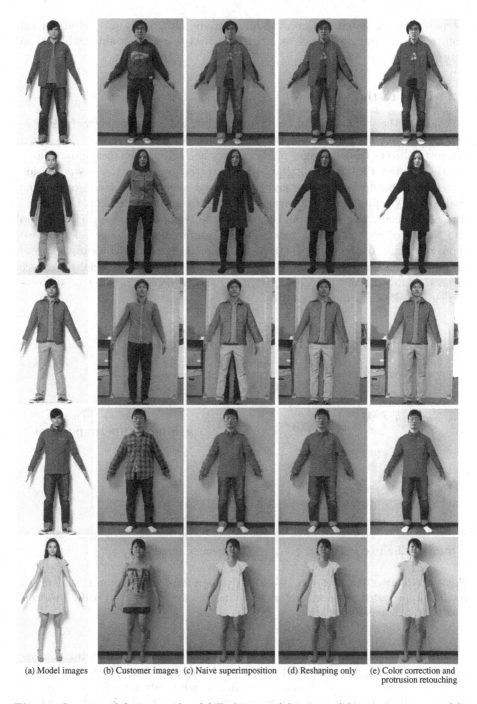

(a) Model images   (b) Customer images (c) Naive superimposition   (d) Reshaping only   (e) Color correction and
                                                                                              protrusion retouching

Fig. 13. Our virtual fitting results. (a) Fashion model images, (b) customer images, (c) naïve superimposition, (d) our virtual fitting results, and (e) results with protrusion retouching as well as color correction. While naïve superimposition in (c) cannot match garments to the positions of arms or legs, our system successfully reshapes garments as shown in (d) and yields more natural fitting results as in (e).

by quick manual manipulation of mesh contours, integrating a pose estimation from a human image as well as skeleton-driven warping would enable us to automate this process.

4.2   User Testing

To evaluate the validity of our results, we conducted experiments with ten students majoring in computer science (six males and four females). We asked the test subjects to use images of themselves as customer images and evaluate whether or not the virtual fitting images created by using the customer-side system were natural composite images. We used a five-point Likert scale in the evaluation. We prepared four garment sets as the garment data for the virtual fitting: (A) coat, (B) T-shirt and jeans, (C) jacket and jeans, and (D) poncho and skirt. For each of the garment sets, we commissioned the creation of two types of virtual fitting image: virtual fitting images obtained by simple superimpositions and images created using our system. The male test subjects were given the three garment sets (A), (B), and (C) while the female test subjects were given all of the four sets.

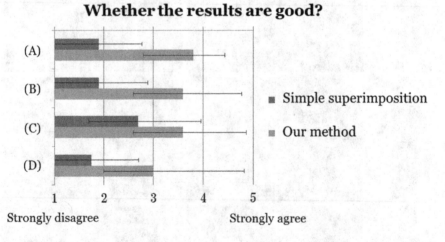

Fig. 14. Result of the user test. We asked the subjects whether the virtual fitting results by our system were satisfactory or not using a five-point Likert scale. The error bars indicate standard deviations.

Figure 14 shows the results. The virtual fitting images created using our system were more highly evaluated than those obtained by simple superimposition, making it clear that natural composite images are produced using our system. However, there were also comments by test subjects who did not score as high as 5, *"the thinning of the clothing conforming to the body shape is unnatural"* and *"the center lines of the body and the garment image are skew."*

Regarding the time for modifying automatically-estimated body-contour models, test subjects took 72 s on average. Since this operation need only be done once for each customer, we believe the time is sufficiently short.

5 Conclusions and Future Work

We have introduced an image-based virtual fitting system that (1) reshapes the garment image based on wearers body shapes, (2) automatically adjusts brightness differences between the garment image and the customer image based on facial colors, and (3) automatically retouches protrusions of customer's cloth behind garments. For reshaping, we proposed a simple body-contour model and its heuristic estimation method. Garment images are warped so that fashion model's body-contour model matches customer's body-contour model. We confirmed that out virtual fitting results were sufficiently natural-looking by conducting a user test.

Future challenges include more advanced virtual try-on by fitting a parametric 3D human model [23] to the customer's image. That will allow us handle more realistic 3D effects such as shading changes and cloth deformation.

References

1. Anguelov, D., Srinivasan, P., Koller, D., Thrun, S., Rodgers, J., Davis, J.: SCAPE: shape completion and animation of people. In: ACM SIGGRAPH 2005 Papers, pp. 408–416 (2005)
2. Bianco, S., Schettini, R.: Color constancy using faces. In: 2012 IEEE Conference on Computer Vision and Pattern Recognition (CVPR), pp. 65–72 (2012)
3. Brouet, R., Sheffer, A., Boissieux, L., Cani, M.P.: Design preserving garment transfer. ACM Trans. Graph. **31**(4), 36:1–36:11 (2012)
4. Cordier, F., Lee, W., Seo, H., Magnenat-Thalmann, N.: From 2D photos of yourself to virtual try-on dress on the web. In: Blandford, A., Vanderdonckt, J., Gray, P. (eds.) People and Computers XV—Interaction Without Frontiers, pp. 31–46. Springer, London (2001)
5. Cordier, F., Seo, H., Magnenat-Thalmann, N.: Made-to-measure technologies for an online clothing store. IEEE Comput. Graph. Appl. **23**(1), 38–48 (2003)
6. Avielan Corporation: Awaseba. www.awaseba.com/
7. Edwards, G.J., Taylor, C.J., Cootes, T.F.: Interpreting face images using active appearance models. In: Proceedings of Third IEEE International Conference on Automatic Face and Gesture Recognition, pp. 300–305 (1998)
8. Ehara, J., Saito, H.: Texture overlay for virtual clothing based on PCA of silhouettes. In: Proceedings of the 5th IEEE and ACM International Symposium on Mixed and Augmented Reality, ISMAR 2006, pp. 139–142. IEEE Computer Society (2006)
9. Guan, P., Freifeld, O., Black, M.J.: A 2D human body model dressed in eigen clothing. In: Daniilidis, K., Maragos, P., Paragios, N. (eds.) ECCV 2010, Part I. LNCS, vol. 6311, pp. 285–298. Springer, Heidelberg (2010)
10. Guan, P., Reiss, L., Hirshberg, D.A., Weiss, A., Black, M.J.: DRAPE: DRessing Any PErson. ACM Trans. Graph. **31**(4), 35:1–35:10 (2012)

11. Hauswiesner, S., Straka, M., Reitmayr, G.: Free viewpoint virtual try-on with commodity depth cameras. In: Proceedings of the 10th International Conference on Virtual Reality Continuum and Its Applications in Industry, VRCAI 2011, pp. 23–30 (2011)
12. Hilsmann, A., Fechteler, P., Eisert, P.: Pose space image based rendering. Comput. Graph. Forum **32**(2), 265–274 (2013). Proceedings of Eurographics
13. Jain, V., Zhang, H.: Robust 2D shape correspondence using geodesic shape context. In: Proceedings of Pacific Graphics, pp. 121–124 (2005)
14. von Kries, J.: Influence of adaptation on the effects produced by luminous stimuli. In: MacAdam, D. (ed.) Sources of Color Science, pp. 109–119. MIT Press, Cambridge (1970)
15. Protopsaltou, D., Luible, C., Arevalo-Poizat, M., Magnenat-Thalmann, N.: A body and garment creation method for an internet based virtual fitting room. In: Proceedings of Computer Graphics International (CGI 2002), pp. 105–122. Springer (2002)
16. Schaefer, S., McPhail, T., Warren, J.: Image deformation using moving least squares. In: ACM SIGGRAPH 2006 Papers, pp. 533–540. ACM, New York (2006)
17. STARTTODAY CO., LTD.: ZOZOTOWN. http://zozo.jp/
18. Sumner, R.W., Popović, J.: Deformation transfer for triangle meshes. ACM Trans. Graph. **23**(3), 399–405 (2004). Proceedings of SIGGRAPH 2004
19. Tong, J., Zhou, J., Liu, L., Pan, Z., Yan, H.: Scanning 3D full human bodies using kinects. IEEE Trans. Visual. Comput. Graph. **18**(4), 643–650 (2012). Proceedings of IEEE Virtual Reality
20. Wang, H., Hecht, F., Ramamoorthi, R., O'Brien, J.: Example-based wrinkle synthesis for clothing animation. In: ACM SIGGRAPH 2010 Papers, pp. 107:1–107:8 (2010)
21. Weng, Y., Xu, W., Wu, Y., Zhou, K., Guo, B.: 2D shape deformation using nonlinear least squares optimization. Vis. Comput. **22**(9), 653–660 (2006)
22. Xu, W., Umentani, N., Chao, Q., Mao, J., Jin, X., Tong, X.: Sensitivity-optimized rigging for example-based real-time clothing synthesis. In: ACM Transactions on Graphics (Proceedings of SIGGRAPH 2014), vol. 33, no. 4, August 2014
23. Zhou, S., Fu, H., Liu, L., Cohen-Or, D., Han, X.: Parametric reshaping of human bodies in images. In: ACM SIGGRAPH 2010 Papers, pp. 126:1–126:10 (2010)
24. Zhou, Z., Shu, B., Zhuo, S., Deng, X., Tan, P., Lin, S.: Image-based clothes animation for virtual fitting. In: SIGGRAPH Asia 2012 Technical Briefs, pp. 33:1–33:4 (2012)

Constructive Roofs from Solid Building Primitives

Johannes Edelsbrunner[1]([✉]), Ulrich Krispel[1,2], Sven Havemann[1],
Alexei Sourin[3], and Dieter W. Fellner[1,4]

[1] Institute for Computer Graphics and Knowledge Visualization (CGV),
Graz University of Technology, Graz, Austria
{j.edelsbrunner,s.havemann}@cgv.tugraz.at
[2] Fraunhofer Austria Research GmbH, Graz, Austria
ulrich.krispel@fraunhofer.at
[3] School of Computer Engineering,
Nanyang Technological University, Singapore, Singapore
assourin@ntu.edu.sg
[4] GRIS, TU Darmstadt & Fraunhofer IGD, Darmstadt, Germany
d.fellner@igd.fraunhofer.de

Abstract. The creation of building models has high importance, due to
the demand for detailed buildings in virtual worlds, games, movies and
geo information systems. Due to the high complexity of such models,
especially in the urban context, their creation is often very demanding
in resources. Procedural methods have been introduced to lessen these
costs, and allow to specify a building (or a class of buildings) by a higher
level approach, and leave the geometry generation to the system. While
these systems allow to specify buildings in immense detail, roofs still
pose a problem. Fully automatic roof generation algorithms might not
yield desired results (especially for reconstruction purposes), and complete manual specification can get very tedious due to complex geometric
configurations. We present a new method for an abstract building specification, that allows to specify complex buildings from simpler parts with
an emphasis on assisting the blending of roofs.

Keywords: 3D-modeling · Procedural modeling · Architectural models

1 Introduction

With the growing popularity of virtual 3D worlds in games and movies, various
VR simulations and 3D street walk-throughs of todays cities or cultural heritage
scenes, attention of researchers shifts towards quick and flexible ways of modeling
or reconstructing large numbers of buildings.

While manually generated models typically yield the highest visual quality,
the effort to produce such results is immense. The research addressed at this
problem can be grouped into two approaches: automatic reconstruction from
measurement data, and automatic generation using procedural modeling.

© Springer-Verlag Berlin Heidelberg 2016
M.L. Gavrilova et al. (Eds.): Trans. on Comput. Sci. XXVI, LNCS 9550, pp. 17–40, 2016.
DOI: 10.1007/978-3-662-49247-5_2

Fig. 1. Modeling a building by parametrizable parts greatly reduces the necessary effort. A simple union of parts might lead to undesirable results (left). Therefore, we introduce automatic roof *trimming* for solid building primitives. The resulting model can be further refined using existing procedural approaches (right).

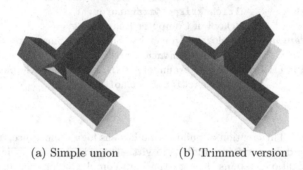

(a) Simple union   (b) Trimmed version

Fig. 2. A simple union of building parts with roof does not produce a desirable result (a). The influence of parts can be non-local, in this example the bounding plane of the roof geometry of the smaller building trims the roof geometry of the higher building and induces a small triangular roof area (b).

While automatic reconstruction might produce a faithful appearance of the original object, the result is often a (possibly dense) 3D mesh. This results in serious limitations to the modifiability of such models, as manual effort is required to change such models.

On the contrary, procedural modeling is an abstract representation of the building process of a model. Changing the procedural description typically requires less effort than manual 3D modeling, however the procedural system has to keep the balance between automation (lessen manual effort) and expressiveness of the system (which types of models can be created).

Current procedural modeling methods use mass modeling to define the coarse outline of a building by representing it via a number of parts. Rules further refine the geometry of these parts. Basic interaction between parts is possible via occlusion queries. Automatic roof synthesis can be done, but does not reflect all possible roof configurations present in real buildings.

Especially buildings in historic cities can often be modeled by simple parts, but achieving the final roof geometry is not possible by simple nesting or boolean union of the parts. The problem here is that the roof of one part can be influenced by the roof of another part (see Figs. 1 and 2). Depending on the constellation of the parts, different topological connections arise (see Fig. 3). These problems can increase with growing irregularity of the building. Figure 4 shows a view of the city of Graz, Austria. Merging and influencing roof parts form a complex roof landscape. Still, blending of roof faces follows some consistent rules which we formalize in this paper.

The goal of this paper is to present a method that will allow representing a big variety of coarse building structures with roofs using a concise declarative approach. The structure is modeled by parts and their geometric influence to each other. The resulting structure can be input for a rule-based system that refines the geometry of the building parts. We show an example of both techniques combined in Figs. 1 and 21.

Fig. 3. Complex roof shapes. At (1, 2, 3, 4) the geometry has different topologies, depending on how roof-parts merge together. At (1) four roof-faces meet in one vertex, which is a special constraint since in general four planes do not intersect in one point.

We make the following Research contributions in this paper:

1. We present an *abstract building model* specification, that facilitates a concise description of a building assembled of several parts.
2. We introduce a method for automatic geometric trimming of adjacent building parts that influence each other.

2   Related Work

Shape grammars have been introduced by Stiny et al. [22] in order to generate paintings using rule systems. In [29] the concept was extended to split grammars in order to model 3-dimensional structures, especially building facades. The concept was further refined by [21]. Several other works were built on this principles, extending it to interconnected structures [14], extended systems of rule application [15], or more general split rules [27]. These systems can use the aforementioned mass modeling approach to generate rough geometry. While

Fig. 4. Aerial image of the inner city of Graz, Austria. Different roof parts merge and form a complex roof landscape. There are many implicit dependencies of parameters of roof faces like slope, height of eave, etc. This roof landscape is not easily created with existing modeling tools. Imagery ©2015 Google, Map data ©2015 Google.

most of these systems support basic roof generation, complex roof structures are either fully automatic (using a straight skeleton approach), limiting the number of possible roof structures, or the roof structures have to be modeled in detail for each part, resulting in a complex description.

3D construction of building roofs is an often covered topic in literature. Most papers are however concerned with reconstruction of roofs from image or scan data [2,9,13,25,28]. A good overview is given in [8]. The aforementioned methods usually use variants of plane fitting. The work of Milde et al. [19,20] and Dorschlag et al. [4] use additional grammar and graph based approaches to further aid the reconstruction process. The method presented by Fischer et al. [7] uses an approach with connectors to align the extracted planes.

While they can produce good results, the output is often only a polygon mesh without semantic information. This is not very suitable for scenarios where a modifiable model is needed (e.g., urban planning), which is why recent methods use primitive fitting (with simple convex houses and gabled, hipped, flat, etc. roofs) where the primitives could be seen as semantic units [10,11].

When models of non-existing objects have to be built (e.g., for movies, video games, etc.) none of the mentioned methods is applicable. There are many papers which deal with the 3D construction of buildings, however, the roof is most of the time only a small part of the solution and often modeled in a primitive and simple way. For example,

- [5, 6, 17, 21, 23, 24] use simple roof-primitives with often convex ground shape plans and gabled, hipped, flat, etc. roofs, and combine them to generate their roofs,
- [26] has a special specification for Asian roofs,
- [16, 18] use the famous straight skeleton algorithm [1] to generate the roof.

The methods with simple roof-primitives can yield good results for very regular buildings, but when the roof gets more complex and irregular, these methods are not able to fully reproduce the shape. Special specifications, like in the case for Asian roofs, are very suitable for the domain, but lack the possibility to describe a broad spectrum of roofs.

The straight skeleton algorithm is very suitable for generating general roofs, as its resulting skeleton corresponds to the edges of a roof on the building. Using it, a roof on an arbitrary simple ground polygon can be created. The downside is that the generated roof is only one of many possible roofs, and there is no way to get another roof. Here, an extension to the straight skeleton, called the weighted straight skeleton [3], brings greater flexibility. The work of Kelly et al. [12] uses the weighted straight skeleton to model not only arbitrary roof-shapes, but also the whole outer shell of a building. One drawback of this method is that straight skeleton algorithms (even more in the weighted case) are hard to implement due to algorithmic problems when numerical errors arise.

The problem of roof modeling also arises in geographic information systems. Open street map[1] is a project that lets volunteers all over the world collaborate in creating mapping data for streets, buildings, borders, etc. In order to model roofs, they have built a large categorization table of roofs. Each category has its own set of parameters. So a large class of buildings can be declaratively modeled by specifying the category and the corresponding parameters. Also, the straight skeleton method is contained in the categorization. Additionally, a method proposed for open street map is roof-line modeling. Here, the modeler traces roof lines on an aerial image (from top-down view) of the building and provides additional information, e.g. a type (ridge, edge, apex, ...), or height.

What is mostly missing is the accurate handling of merging roof faces of neighboring houses. In historic cities, houses that are adjacent often have the same roof. Depending on how the houses connect, the roof parts merge in different ways. While automatic reconstruction via plane fitting might reproduce the situation correctly (depending how good the algorithm is), methods that work with mass modeling primitives have difficulties, because for the merging the primitives must be changed. The weighted straight skeleton is capable of modeling these connections, but it might become unhandy when big roof regions with multiple roof part connections are modeled, because the whole roof must be modeled as one piece to ensure correct geometry at interconnections.

---

[1] http://www.openstreetmap.org.

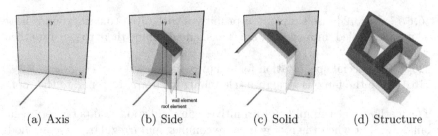

| (a) Axis | (b) Side | (c) Solid | (d) Structure |

Fig. 5. The components of our abstract building model. An *axis* is given for orientation. Relative to an axis, a *side* is defined. A side has wall and roof elements. Multiple sides form a *solid*, which is the basic building block for a *structure*.

3   Solid Building Primitives

In this section we give an overview of the building abstraction, and specify the individual components of our system.

The core abstraction in our system is the assembling of a building by separately defined parts, which are called *solids*. As most buildings are composed of planar walls, each solid is composed of several planar *side* parts, which represent a cross-sectional profile of the corresponding wall and roof part. Each side part corresponds to a line segment of the ground polygon of a solid. The geometry of a solid is obtained by intersection of half-spaces that correspond to the profile line segments of each side part.

A simple union of solids defined in this way might lead to undesirable results (see Fig. 2). However, we have observed that in many situations the correct result can be obtained by trimming solids by corresponding half-spaces of side parts of adjacent solids.

3.1   Basic Components

Our abstract building model is composed of several components. We will now give a explanation of the basic components in a bottom-up manner (see Fig. 5):

Axis
> is a directed line segment in the ground plane, defined by a start- and an endpoint.

Side
> corresponds to a planar building part consisting of a wall and a roof element. These elements are specified as line segments of the cross-sectional profile of the part, with respect to a reference axis that corresponds to the direction of a line segment of the ground polygon. Various parameters define the shape of the side (see Fig. 6).

Solid
> is composed of multiple side components whose wall elements correspond to a convex ground polygon. Each line segment of the cross-sectional profile of a side corresponds to a half-space in 3D.

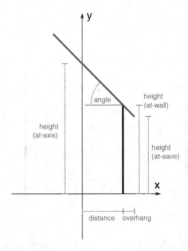

Fig. 6. Cross section view of a side. A side in our abstract building model consists of wall and roof elements. Here we show one possible parameterization (parameters in gray) from which the wall (black) and roof (red) elements are derived (Color figure online).

Structure

is the combination (grouping) of several solids. Structures can be nested, e.g. for representing dormers.

3.2   Parametrized Sides and Solids

Our definition of the side component allows to model a rich variation of different roof types and building parts. It is however relatively low-level, therefore we introduce parametrizations for sides and solids, that allow us to reduce the necessary effort to describe a building that is composed of similar parts. For example, if a building is modeled from aerial photographs, it is practical to define sides relative to ridge lines of roofs. When using ground polygons from a GIS (geographic information system) database, sides should be relative to the ground polygon. Different parametrizations for sides can be seen in Fig. 7.

The parametrization includes an *overhang*, as roofs often extend over walls in order to prevent rain falling on walls.

3.3   Automatic Generation of Sides for Solids

As described, the user can specify axis in the system. This can be done i.e. by tracing of aerial images. Subsequently a side is assigned to this axis. In order to reduce the amount of work needed, all sides of a solid can automatically be generated from this one given side. In the standard case of a rectangular solid this

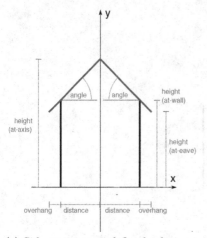

(a) Side parameters defined relative to one axis.

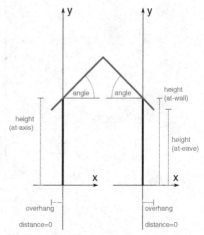

(b) Side parameters defined relative to two axes.

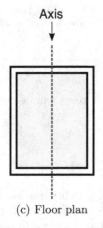

(c) Floor plan

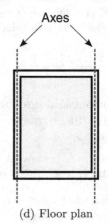

(d) Floor plan

Fig. 7. A solid is composed of multiple *side* components which can be parametrized arbitrarily. In (a, c) *side* components are specified with respect to the ridge (both *side* components use the same reference-axis and coordinate-system). (b, d) *side* components are specified with respect to the walls (*side* components use different reference-axes and coordinate-systems).

would be four sides generated from one given side, but also n-gon constellations are possible (see Fig. 8).

The parameters from the original side are automatically copied to the newly generated sides. But this process can also be modified. For example, when the ridge of a hipped house is traced, the copying of all parameters is useful since the roof has the same properties on all sides (slope, eave height, etc.) (see Fig. 8(c)). However, for a gabled house the start and end sides are different (see Fig. 8(c)). Here we tell the generation process to change the parameters for the start and

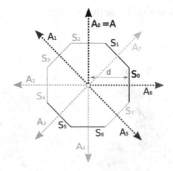

(a) Axis defined by start- and
endpoint and its side.

(b) Generation of an octagonal
footprint.

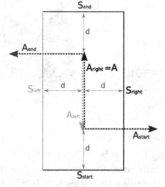
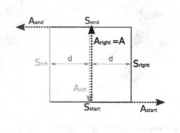

(c) Generation of a rectangular
footprint. The parameters for
each side are copied.

(d) Generation of a rectangular
footprint. The parameters for
start and end and for left and
right are copied differently.

Fig. 8. Automatic generation of sides for solids. Based on an axis A, given by two
points P_{start} and P_{end} and its according side S (a) additional sides for a complete solid
can be generated. The axis are denoted A_i and the according sides S_i. Each side has
parameters, the distance is here denoted with d. Different copy mechanisms allow for
shapes in rectangular (c, d) or circular arrangement (b). The original parameters of
the side are either copied for all parts (b, c) or modified while copying (d).

end sides. The distance is set to 0, and the roof components of this sides are
removed.

3.4   Automatic Trimming of Solids

When multiple *solids* are combined using a simple union, unwanted configurations can occur like in Fig. 2(a). Therefore, we introduce *trimming* between
solids: the geometry of one solid should be truncated by parts of the geometry

of another solid. In order to specify which parts get trimmed, a direction has to be specified.

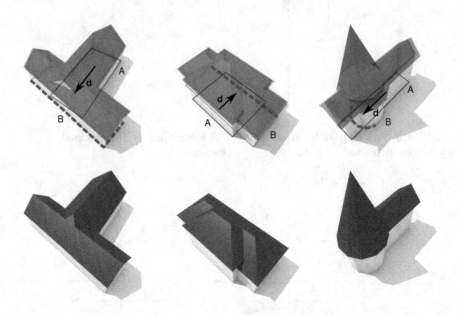

Fig. 9. We demonstrate the concept of trimming for solids by interactions of different building parts (top row). The user specifies an influence direction for each connecting solid (black arrow), the system automatically identifies the sides which will influence the result geometrically (green dashed lines on the ground polygon). Only sides corresponding to green segments will be used for the trimming (bottom row) (Color figure online).

Recall that each side of a solid consists of wall and roof elements, which correspond to half-spaces in 3D. Assume having two solids A and B. We specify that A gets trimmed by B according to the direction d (see Fig. 9). Then, for each side s of B there is a test whether the outward facing normal vector of the wall component of s and d form a positive scalar-product. If yes (green segments in Fig. 9), the wall sub-solid of A is intersected by the half-space formed by the wall component of s and the roof sub-solid is intersected by the half-space formed by the roof component of s.

A trimming connection is directed, as one solid gets trimmed by another. Therefore, two solids yield four different possibilities of trimming variations between each other (see Fig. 10).

Using this method of trimming we can ensure that the influence between solids adapts correctly to changes in the parametrization. As an example, Fig. 11 shows the results of automatic trimming under varying roof angles for one solid.

Fig. 10. Two connected solids A and B can influence each other in four possible ways: No trimming (top left), A trimming B (top right), B trimming A (bottom left), and both solids trimming each other (bottom right). Note that different combinations would be possible by changing the influence directions.

Fig. 11. A building that consists of two solids is evaluated with different parametrizations of the sides. In this example, only the slope of the roof of the right solid was gradually incremented from the first to the last image and the model was re-evaluated. It can be observed that the roof geometry adapts accordingly to the situation.

3.5   Roof Shapes

Up to now, we assumed the roof element of a side to be a single planar element. However, Mansard roofs have two or more slopes on their sides. We account for this by introducing side parametrizations that generate more than one roof element, which is called *profile-polygon* component in our specification. We show examples of a few roofs with profile polygons in Fig. 12.

Automatic trimming is performed in the same manner, although the case in which neighboring solids influence each other in a way that introduces additional geometry (compare to the small triangular area that emerges in Fig. 2(a)) might not be well defined. This, however, is not of practical importance, as we did not encounter such situations in real roof configurations, where these roofs usually have the same ridge height.

Fig. 12. Some roof shapes consist of more than one planar element, e.g. mansard roofs. We account for such types by a general profile-polygon type. The last two examples show solids with non-rectangular ground polygons.

4   Specification of the Building

In order to model a building we have to parameterize and combine multiple solids. We developed a specification with which this can be done in a structured fashion for one building.

4.1   Structure of Specification

Figure 14 shows the elements of a structuring language we have developed. A building is represented as a structure, which consists of multiple solids. Each solid has at least one side, and a side has a parametrization (as already covered in Sect. 3.1).

To achieve the correct influence of solids as described in Sect. 3.4, a solid can contain multiple trimmings. A trimming references to the influencing solid and an axis that specifies the direction.

Additionally, a solid can also have dormers (see Fig. 13). A dormer is a structure, which is put on the solid and where appropriate cutting of roof faces is done on the solid. For repetition of the same dormer multiple times along an axis, we provide the dormer-pattern construct, where a repetition pattern must be provided. These patterns are formed in analogy to repetition or subdivision patterns in shape grammars.

This specification can easily be extended for further building and roof elements (e.g. chimneys, ..) or different side parametrization.

Fig. 13. Dormers on a solid. They are structures which are places on a solid, either individually or according to a pattern.

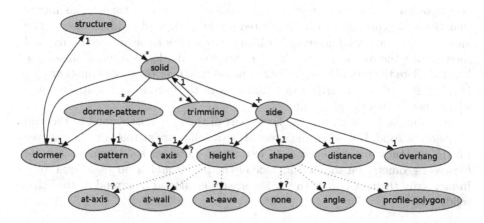

Fig. 14. Our abstract building model: The coarse structure is specified by solids and their influence to each other. Nodes of the graph show elements, arrows show their relationships (in a classical *has-a* notation). The quantifiers show the number of subelements (? ... zero or one, 1 ... one, * ... zero or multiple, + ... one or multiple).eps

4.2   Geometry Operators

The geometry of roofs must often fulfill certain criteria. Important properties for the roof can be for example:

- Faces are planar (all vertices of a face must be co-planar - this can be a problem when a face has more than three vertices).
- Faces intersect in one common vertex (for more than three faces this can be a problem).
- Ridges are horizontal (often means that the to the ridge adjacent building sides must be exactly parallel).
- Faces merge over multiple building parts (this often means that the corresponding walls must be co-linear).

These properties form parameter dependencies, and they are a problem for the input format, since there must be a way to avoid over-specification of parameters (and therefore violation of the dependencies). Because of that, we included geometry operators in the language. They operate on the axis element and can produce new axis elements that allow for fulfilling the requirements stated above. The operators are for example translation, rotation, parallel-translation, and line-intersection.

5 Implementation

5.1 Double-Covered Areas

The geometry of a roof can be described as a 2-dimensional manifold where every possible vertical ray intersects the roof exactly 0 or 1 times. This means that the roof geometry can be generated as the surface of solid geometry. The idea is to generate solid geometry (which easily allows Boolean operations) and then extract the roof faces from it. The exception are double-covered areas (see Fig. 15). Here the roof of one part of the house rises over the roof of another part (see Fig. 15(b)), and a vertical ray can intersect the overall roof multiple times, which complicates the algorithm.

At a double-covered area, the lower part of the roof must extend to the wall of the other solid. But when the eaves of both solids are at the same height (see Fig. 15(a)), they are not allowed to extend to the other solids wall, otherwise incorrect geometry on the bottom side of the roof would occur (see Fig. 15(c)). In fact, only the roof part with the lower eave is allowed to extend to the other solids wall.

5.2 Organization of the Components

In order to extract the geometry we generate convex polyhedra for each side and perform Boolean operations on them. Figure 16 shows the *inner* and *outer side geometry* for various sides. They are both identical, except that the outer one extends the amount of overhang farther outward from the wall. Through this, we will later be able to generate the geometry for overhangs and double-covered areas.

The geometry for a solid is generated by intersection of the geometry of all sides. Taking either the inner or outer side geometry, this yields the *inner* and

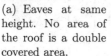

(a) Eaves at same height. No area of the roof is a double covered area.

(b) Eaves at different height. A double covered area is formed.

(c) Same height - wrong result if the roof geometry extends to the adjacent wall.

(d) Different height - wrong result if the roof geometry does not extends to the adjacent wall.

Fig. 15. Eaves and double-covered areas. Eaves are a challenge for the geometry generation. Eaves with the same height (a) need a different geometry generation than eaves with different heights (b). We show two examples (c, d) where simple algorithms yield wrong results.

outer sub-solids as shown in Fig. 17. The inner sub-solid is used for the extraction of the geometry for the walls, and the outer sub-solid is used for the extraction of the geometry of the roof. An exception are roofs with double-covered areas. Here the roof of one solid is covered by the roof of another solid. So for each side of a solid, depending on the situation, the inner or outer side geometry needs to be taken. Then an individual sub-solid is formed by the intersection of the side geometries.

5.3 Trimming

As already described, a solid can be trimmed by another solid. Which sides of the other solid are selected for the trimming is described in Sect. 3.4. For the geometry extraction this means that the selected sides of the other solid are simply added as sides to the trimmed solid. This way, the solid gets automatically cut because its geometry is determined by the intersection of the geometry of its sides.

5.4 Geometry Extraction

The geometry of the walls can be obtained by performing a Boolean union of the inner sub-solids (see Fig. 17) of all solids, after they are trimmed. Then the sidewards facing face of the resulting volume form the walls of the structure.

The geometry of the roof could also be obtained by performing a Boolean union of the outer sub-solids of all solids. Taking all the upward facing faces of the resulting volume would yield the roof geometry. But double-covered areas make the geometry extraction for the roof more complicated. This method would lead to geometry errors (as seen in Fig. 15(d)).

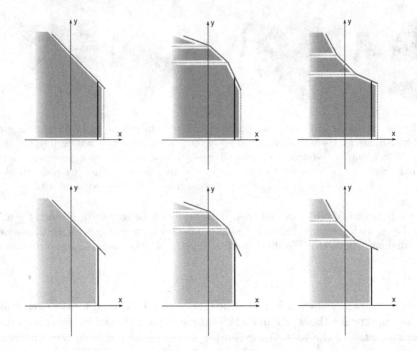

Fig. 16. Side geometry. For the geometry generation each side is represented via convex polyhedra (shaded areas). Top: *inner side-geometry*. Bottom: *outer side-geometry*. First column: Simple roof with one roof face per side. Second column: The roof is specified via a convex profile-polygon. Third column: The roof is specified via a concave profile-polygon.

Therefore, for every solid the roof geometry is extracted separately. The algorithm for extraction is shown in Algorithm 1 and the according description is presented in Table 1.

The result of the geometry extraction can be seen in Fig. 18. Note that the roof has the correct geometry, also in the inside of the building (the roofs bottom side).

5.5   Processing

We have built a system with multiple steps where the input data is transformed. The input format is XML but we built our own short notation that is semantically equivalent but better read- and writable than pure XML.

The steps of our current implementation are as follows:

1. The input file in short notation created by the user is converted into XML.
2. The XML file undergoes an enrichment step where sides and parameters are automatically added according to Sect. 3.3.
3. The new XML file is converted into GML (our own in-house programming language for procedural modeling).

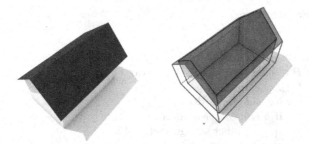

Fig. 17. Each solid consists of two sub-solids, a wall sub-solid (inner black outline) and a roof sub-solid (outer red outline), which are utilized for the trimming process (Color figure online).

4. Our engine in GML creates the geometry according to the principles described in Sect. 5.

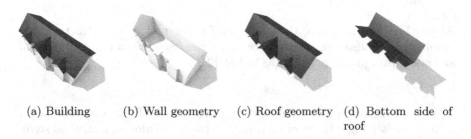

(a) Building   (b) Wall geometry   (c) Roof geometry   (d) Bottom side of roof

Fig. 18. Extracted geometry of a building. Wall and roof geometry are extracted separately. The bottom side of the roof shows that the solids are not simply sticked together, and the geometry is extracted correctly.

6   Results and Applications

We evaluated our prototype implementation by modeling three scenes that exhibit interesting roof structures from aerial images. Our workflow consists of the following steps:

1. Trace important lines via a vector-drawing program.
2. Convert lines into axis.
3. Assign parametrized sides with respect to axis.
4. Assign sides to solids.
5. Specify trimmings between solids.

```
1  S = arbitrary structure
2  for A ∈ solids of S do
3  |   for a ∈ sides of A do
4  |   |   L_solid = empty list
5  |   |   for B ∈ solids of S where A ≠ B do
6  |   |   |   L_side = empty list
7  |   |   |   for b ∈ sides of B do
8  |   |   |   |   if b rises above a then
9  |   |   |   |   |   g = inner side-geometry of b
10 |   |   |   |   else
11 |   |   |   |   |   g = outer side-geometry of b
12 |   |   |   |   end
13 |   |   |   |   append g to L_side
14 |   |   |   end
15 |   |   |   I = ∩ of all in L_side
16 |   |   |   append I to L_solid
17 |   |   end
18 |   |   T = outer sub-solid of A − (∪ of all in L_solid)
19 |   |   render the roof face (according to a) of T
20 |   end
21 end
```

Algorithm 1. Extracting the geometry for the roof of one structure. For simplicity, the algorithm shown here only covers sides with one roof element and not with a profile-polygon (as in Fig. 12).

The result is an abstract building description in an XML file that reflects our specification (see Fig. 14). As of now, the workflow includes some manual steps, for example, the assignment of parametrized sides. We observed that while the models have complex roof cases, the roof shapes follow simple geometric rules when blended together. As it was expected, the decomposition into convex parts turned out to be quite obvious. Evaluation times were measured on the CPU implementation of our prototype system on a 2.6 GHz quad core machine.

The first model is the royal palace of Milan (Fig. 19) where we also placed some dormers on the roof. The model consists of 28 solids (excluding dormers), and its evaluation took 6 s.

The second model is a part of the city of Graz, Austria (Fig. 20). It consist of 7 structures that have 34 solids in total, and its evaluation took 5 s. The roofs have considerable irregularities, which became a challenge in the modeling process.

The third model is the Magdalena palacio in Santander (Figs. 1 and 21), which is assembled from 25 solids, and its evaluation took 8 s without the facade detail and 20 s with the facade detail. The roof of this building exhibits some interesting features, such as the cavities on the middle part of the building, which are hard to model using fully automatic (e.g., straight skeleton based) approaches.

Table 1. Description of Algorithm 1.

Line	Description
1	In our system different structures have independent roofs so we can calculate the roof independently for one structure
2,3	We calculate the roof face for each side of a solid separately
4	The roof of the solid changes when another solid intersects with it. We will trim the solid with all other solids, but because of possible double-covered areas we have to take either the inner or outer side-geometry of another solid, depending on the situation. Therefore we create a new list where we will save the new other solids with inner/outer side-geometry
5	We iterate over all other solids of the house
6–13	For every side of the other solid we decide whether it rises over the side we are currently calculating (and therefore forms a double-covered area). The test for rising over the other side is described in Sect. 5.1. If yes, we take the inner side-geometry. If no, we take the outer side-geometry. We collect the side-geometries in a new list
15–16	We build the Boolean intersection of all the elements in the list and thereby form a custom sub-solid that respects the double-covered areas for each of its sides
18	All the custom sub-solids are now Boolean subtracted from the outer sub-solid of our initial solid. This removes all areas from the roof where another solid intersects
19	The new roof of this side can now be rendered

When doing direct comparison, the third model exhibits a more constrained structure: the ridges follow two principle axes which are perpendicular to each other. So we realigned the traced lines from the aerial view with the operators described in Sect. 4.2. A more irregular layout, like that in the first and second model, can make the modeling harder; at regions where solids adjoin or intersect, artifacts are more likely to arise.

For all models, we did not have any measurements, therefore we estimated values for missing parameters, e.g., the side heights, by using photographs of the buildings as guidelines. While in this case the result is not a fully accurate model, it produces a good approximation and visually satisfying result (e.g., see Fig. 21). Due to the missing parameters, we had to try different parameter sets several times to ensure that the roof has the right topology. Nevertheless, our abstract definition allows for quick reparametrization if real measurements become available.

The geometry can be exported to .obj or other file formats for further usage in other programs. We did our renderings in Blender where materials and lighting were defined.

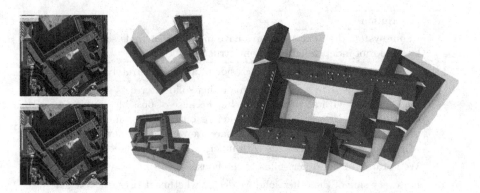

Fig. 19. Model of the royal palace of Milan. For this model, the modeling process was done in four steps: (1) obtaining an aerial image of the building (top left); (2) manual tracing of important lines in a vector-drawing program (bottom left); (3) extraction of the vector coordinates to the XML format; (4) manual augmentation of remaining parameters in the XML format (like height, roof angle, etc.). The resulting model was created by our prototype implementation, and then rendered (top middle, bottom middle, right). Aerial images: Imagery ©2015 Google, Map data ©2015 Google.

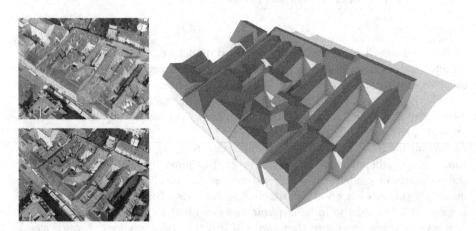

Fig. 20. The inner city of Graz, Austria. The detail is the same as in Fig. 4. Top left: 3D view from Google maps. Bottom left: 3D view from Google earth. Right: Our model. While the models from Google have high detail, they do not ensure constraints like planarity of roof faces or perfectly straight ridges, eaves, or other edges. Our model ensures this by construction. The modeling process was done with aerial images as in Fig. 19. Aerial images: Imagery ©2015 Google, Map data ©2015 Google.

Fig. 21. Model of the Magdalena palacio in Santander, Spain (as in the teaser - Fig. 1). The modeling process was done with aerial images (middle left, middle middle) as in Fig. 19. The detail of the model is increased with existing procedural approaches. Here we used a conventional shape grammar approach for modeling the facades (top). The model has three cases where roof topology changes because of a specified trimming (middle right - marked with yellow circles). (a) is the top row case from Fig. 9, (b) is the middle row case from Fig. 9, and (c) is a complex case where five solids with different trimming specifications are involved. The bottom row shows the 3D model in Google maps on the left. Again the constraints of planarity of roof faces and straightness of edges are not satisfied. Two additional regions with wrong geometry are emphasized in yellow circles. Aerial images: Map data ©2015 Google, basado en BCN IGN España.

7   Conclusion

Modeling the coarse structure of a building by the composition of parts proved to be suitable for buildings of classical architectural style. However, in many cases a building is not a simple union of such parts. In this paper, we proposed automatic trimming of adjacent parts, which facilitates a concise, abstract decomposition of a building into parts and their geometric influence. A coarse 3D model of a building can then be generated from such a description, which can further be fed into a conventional pipeline (e.g. shape grammars) that generates detailed geometry for building parts (e.g. windows and doors), see Fig. 21. Our abstract building description facilitates easy re-parametrization of building parts, as the 3D model just has to be re-evaluated after a parameter has been changed (as seen in Fig. 11).

We see applications for our method in production pipelines of virtual worlds. This includes the digitalization of cultural heritage, since it can reproduce the complex geometry of roof landscapes in historic cities. It is also suitable for the movie and video games industry, where sometimes man years of work have to be spent on modeling the environment. Our approach, which integrates into existing procedural methods, further enhances the expressiveness of those methods and advances the automatic generation of geometry.

8   Future Work

The main focus in future work is directed towards more automation in the modeling process. One direction is the automatic generation of solid and side descriptions by a rule based system (e.g. stochastic grammars). The other direction is headed towards automatic reconstruction by automatic tracing of important roof lines and the incorporation of additional measurement data for automatic parametrization of building sides (e.g., height of solids). Another interesting direction for future research poses the incorporation of more complex geometry (curves) into the cross-sectional profiles of building sides.

References

1. Aichholzer, O., Aurenhammer, F., Alberts, D., Gärtner, B.: A novel type of skeleton for polygons. J. Univ. Comput. Sci. **1**, 752–761 (1996). Springer
2. Ameri, B., Fritsch, D.: Automatic 3d building reconstruction using plane-roof structures. In: ASPRS, Washington, D.C. (2000)
3. Aurenhammer, F.: Weighted skeletons and fixed-share decomposition. Comput. Geom. **40**(2), 93–101 (2008)
4. Dörschlag, D., Gröger, G., Plümer, L.: Semantically enhanced prototypes for building reconstruction. In: Stilla, U., et al. (eds.). Proceedings of 36th Photogrammetric Image Analysis, PIA 2007. International Archives of ISPRS (2007)
5. Finkenzeller, D.: Detailed building facades. IEEE Comput. Graph. Appl. **28**(3), 58–66 (2008)

6. Finkenzeller, D.: Modellierung komplexer Gebäudefassaden in der Computergraphik. KIT Scientific Publishing (2008)
7. Fischer, A., Kolbe, T.H., Lang, F., Cremers, A.B., Förstner, W., Plümer, L., Steinhage, V.: Extracting buildings from aerial images using hierarchical aggregation in 2d and 3d. Comput. Vis. Image Underst. **72**(2), 185–203 (1998)
8. Grün, A.: Semi-automated approaches to site recording and modeling. Int. Arch. Photogram. Remote Sens. **33**(B5/1; PART 5), 309–318 (2000)
9. Huang, H., Brenner, C.: Rule-based roof plane detection and segmentation from laser point clouds. In: Joint Urban Remote Sensing Event (JURSE 2011), pp. 293–296. IEEE (2011)
10. Huang, H., Brenner, C., Sester, M.: 3d building roof reconstruction from point clouds via generative models. In: Proceedings of the 19th ACM SIGSPATIAL International Conference on Advances in Geographic Information Systems, pp. 16–24. ACM (2011)
11. Huang, H., Brenner, C., Sester, M.: A generative statistical approach to automatic 3d building roof reconstruction from laser scanning data. ISPRS J. Photogram. Remote Sens. **79**, 29–43 (2013)
12. Kelly, T., Wonka, P.: Interactive architectural modeling with procedural extrusions. ACM Trans. Graph. (TOG) **30**(2), 14 (2011)
13. Kim, K., Shan, J.: Building roof modeling from airborne laser scanning data based on level set approach. ISPRS J. Photogram. Remote Sens. **66**(4), 484–497 (2011)
14. Krecklau, L., Kobbelt, L.: Procedural modeling of interconnected structures. Comput. Graph. Forum **30**, 335–344 (2011). Wiley Online Library
15. Krecklau, L., Pavic, D., Kobbelt, L.: Generalized use of non-terminal symbols for procedural modeling. Comput. Graph. Forum **29**, 2291–2303 (2010). Wiley Online Library
16. Laycock, R.G., Day, A.: Automatically generating roof models from building footprints (2003). https://otik.zcu.cz/handle/11025/991
17. Liu, Y., Xu, C., Pan, Z., Pan, Y.: Semantic modeling for ancient architecture of digital heritage. Comput. Graph. **30**(5), 800–814 (2006)
18. Merrell, P., Schkufza, E., Koltun, V.: Computer-generated residential building layouts. ACM Trans. Graph. (TOG) **29**(6), 181 (2010)
19. Milde, J., Brenner, C.: Graph-based modeling of building roofs. In: AGILE Conference on GIScience (2009)
20. Milde, J., Zhang, Y., Brenner, C., Plümer, L., Sester, M.: Building reconstruction using a structural description based on a formal grammar. Int. Arch. Photogram. Remote Sens. Spatial Inf. Sci. **37**, 227–232 (2008)
21. Müller, P., Wonka, P., Haegler, S., Ulmer, A., Van Gool, L.: Procedural modeling of buildings. ACM Trans. Graph. **25**, 614–623 (2006). ACM
22. Stiny, G., Gips, J.: Shape grammars and the generative specification of painting and sculpture. In: IFIP Congress, vol. 2, pp. 1460–1465 (1971)
23. Sugihara, K., Hayashi, Y.: Automatic generation of 3d building models from building polygons on GIS. In: ICCCBEXI Proceedings of the 11th ICCCBE, Montreal, Canada, pp. 14–16 (2006)
24. Sugihara, K., Hayashi, Y.: Automatic generation of 3d building models with multiple roofs. Tsinghua Sci. Technol. **13**, 368–374 (2008)
25. Taillandier, F.: Automatic building reconstruction from cadastral maps and aerial images. Int. Arch. Photogram. Remote Sens. **36**(3/W24), 105–110 (2005)
26. Teoh, S.T.: Generalized descriptions for the procedural modeling of ancient east asian buildings (2009). http://dl.acm.org/citation.cfm?id=2381290

27. Thaller, W., Krispel, U., Zmugg, R., Havemann, S., Fellner, D.W.: Shape grammars on convex polyhedra. Comput. Graph. **37**(6), 707–717 (2013)
28. Verma, V., Kumar, R., Hsu, S.: 3d building detection and modeling from aerial lidar data. In: IEEE Computer Society Conference on Computer Vision and Pattern Recognition, vol. 2, pp. 2213–2220. IEEE (2006)
29. Wonka, P., Wimmer, M., Sillion, F., Ribarsky, W.: Instant architecture. ACM Trans. Graph. **22**(3), 669–677 (2003). doi:10.1145/882262.882324. http://doi.acm.org/10.1145/882262.882324

Isometric Shape Correspondence Based on the Geodesic Structure

Taorui Jia[1,2], Kang Wang[1,2], Zhongke Wu[1,2]([✉]), Junli Zhao[1,2,3], Pengfei Xu[1,2], Cuiting Liu[1,2], and Mingquan Zhou[1,2]

[1] Beijing Key Laboratory of Digital Preservation and Virtual Reality for Cultural Heritage, Beijing Normal University, Beijing, People's Republic of China
zwu@bnu.edu.cn

[2] College of Information Science and Technology, Beijing Normal University, Beijing, People's Republic of China
jiataorui@126.com, wangkang@mail.bnu.edu.cn

[3] College of Software and Technology, Qingdao University, Qingdao, China

Abstract. Non-rigid 3D shape correspondence is a fundamental and challenging problem. Isometric correspondence is an important topic because of its wide applications. But it is a NP hard problem if detecting the mapping directly. In this paper, we propose a novel approach to find the correspondence between two (nearly) isometric shapes. Our method is based on the geodesic structure of the shape and minimum cost flow. Firstly, several pre-computed base vertices are initialized for embedding the shapes into Euclidian space, which is constructed by the geodesic distances. Then we select a serials of sample point sets with FPS. After that, we construct some network flows separately with the level point sets of the two shapes and another two virtual points, source point and sink point. The arcs of the network flow are the edges between each point on two shapes. And the L_2 distances in the k dimensional Euclidian embedding space are taken as the arc costs and a capacity value is added on each point in the above network flow. At last we solve the correspondence problem as some minimum cost max flow problems (MCFP) with shortest path faster algorithm (SPFA), and combine the results of these MCFP as the last correspondence result. Experiments show that our method is accurate and efficient for isometric, nearly isometric and partially shapes.

Keywords: Correspondence · MCFP · Geodesic structure · Isometric · FPS

1 Introduction

Finding a meaningful correspondence between two shapes is a fundamental problem for numerous applications in computer graphics and computer vision [1], such as mesh parameterization [2], mesh retrieval, shape registration, deformation, shape morphing, symmetry detection, self-similarity detection, and analysis of

© Springer-Verlag Berlin Heidelberg 2016
M.L. Gavrilova et al. (Eds.): Trans. on Comput. Sci. XXVI, LNCS 9550, pp. 41–56, 2016.
DOI: 10.1007/978-3-662-49247-5_3

sequential meshes. In this paper we propose a novel method to solve this problem between isometric (or nearly isometric) shapes based on the geometric structure of a surface. Isometric shapes can be found everywhere in our world, such as different poses of an articulated object, models of a mesh sequence representing the notion of a human actor, or two shapes representing different but semantically similar objects (e.g., two different humans or animals).

If two shapes are perfectly isometric, there exists a distance-preserving mapping between two shapes such that the geodesic between two points on a shape exactly equals the geodesic of the corresponding points on the other shape. Thus in this paper we propose a novel method to find a meaningful correspondence based on the above idea. However, due to the triangulation process and geometry discretization errors, even if for the same rigid object, we can hardly find perfect isometric. Hence our method aims at finding a mapping subject that minimizes the sum of deviation from isometry. The main contribution of our paper is a novel shape correspondence method that minimizes the isometric deviation in a k dimensional Euclidian space that is built through geodesics from some base vertices, where the two isometric (or nearly isometric) shapes are nearly at a same location and have an approximately same surface. We firstly initialize three or more points from the two isometric shapes respectively, and these points locate on different geodesic paths and they have a correspondence order. Then arbitrary point on the mesh can be represented by these base vertices through geodesic distances. Based on the isometric and the ordered base vertices, we get two new meshes, which have a nearly same outline and same location in a k dimensional Euclidian space. So we can find the correspondence in the new space with the effective MCFP algorithm.

A brief survey of the related work about correspondence is given in Sect. 2. And then some fundamentals of our method is presented in Sect. 3. Section 4 is the core of the paper and mainly investigates how to solve the correspondence problem based on minimum-cost flow problem algorithm. The framework of our method is shown in Sect. 5. Some experiments results are described in Sect. 6. At last, Sect. 7 concludes all the paper.

2   Related Work

Isometric is a very important clue for finding correspondence. Many shape matching techniques between isometric surfaces have been proposed in the past decade. And to find a mapping that minimizes the amount of the deviation from the correspondence is a traditional method. A common strategy to achieve this is to embed shapes into a different domain where Euclidean distances replace the geodesic distances so that the isometric distortion can efficiently be measured and optimized in the embedding space [3–8]. Elad and Kimmel [3] proposed to use a subset of the geodesic matrix to embed the shapes and then take the Multi-Dimensional Scaling (MDS) techniques to flatten the surface into a flat Euclidian space, such that the geodesic distances approximately equal to the Euclidian distances. Reference [6] proposed the generalized MDS (GMDS) to embed source shape into the surface of the target shape. Then Jain and Zhang [4] embedded the shapes in the spectral domain based on geodesic affinities and then deal with stretching via thin-plat splines (TPS) in the spectral domain, and then used non-rigid iterative closest points or other local shape descriptors to find the correspondence. Also, the use of conformal factors has been proposed [7], which apply Möbius transformation to transform a shape into a canonical coordinate frame on the complex plane where the set of non-rigid isometric deformations could be simplified.

After that the diffusion geometry became growingly popular because of its robustness to topological noise. Rustamov [5] suggests constructing the global point signature (GPS), which describes the feature of the point with an L_2 sequence based on the eigenfunctions and the eigenvalues of the discrete Laplace-Beltrami operator. A major limitation of this method is about the symmetry of the shape, which may lead to a sign flips of the eigenfunction. Later the Heat Kernel Signature (HKS) [9], which also took the discrete Laplace-Beltrami operator, was descripted by Sun et al. and this signature was based on the physical fundamental solutions of the heat equation (heat kernels). The limitation of HKS is that it is difficult to control the time t and sensitive to scale. Thus in [10] Michael M. Bronstein et al. presented an extension of the heat kernel signature allowing to deal with global and local scaling transformations. Then [11] proposed another physically inspired descriptor, the wave kernel signature (WKS), which solve the excessive sensitivity of the HKS to low-frequency information. After that Ovsjanikov et al. [12] show that the isometry, which was between a pair of generic shapes, can be recovered from a single correspondence with the feature of the heat kernel. In [13], Sharma et al. recommended using a shape descriptor based on properties of the heat-kernel. This provides an intrinsic scale-space representation, which is robust to some topology.

To obtain the correspondence directly between two sets is an NP hard problem. So the researchers have proposed many methods to simplify it and construct some models based on some descripts and metric structure of shape. H. Zhang et al. [14] took a deformation view of shape correspondence and proposed a deformation-driven method. Yusuf Sahillioğlu et al. [15] proposed a greedy optimization on the isometry cost model, and then took different algorithms in [16–18] to detect the correspondence. Ron Kimmel et al. [19,20] combined pointwise surface properties, and global pairwise relationships between corresponding points to measure the correspondence results. And then they treated this problem as Mix Integer Quadratic Programming problem (MIQP).

3   Fundamentals

3.1   Farthest Points Sampling (FPS)

Farthest Points Sampling [21,22] is a generic sampling method. FPS provides an almost evenly-spaced sampling, the next sample is placed in the center of the largest empty disk on the surface, or circle on the plane for 2D case. In other words, the next sample is placed at a point that is farthest from the previous samples. With this effect each sample point is as far as possible from the other points and at the same time as close as possible. Then we review this algorithm as follows.

We denote X to be a surface. Suppose that we choose an arbitrary point x_1 as the first sample point. And then the second point should be as far as possible from the first one. So it should satisfy the following relationship:

$$x_2 = \arg\max_{x \in X} d_X(x, x_1) \tag{1}$$

thus the two sample points are a $d_X(x_2, x_1)$-separate set and an r-covering of X with $r \leq d_X(x_2, x_1)$. The third point should be selected at the maximum distance from x_1 and x_2, i.e.

$$x_3 = \arg\max_{x \in X} d_X(x, \{x_1, x_2\}) \tag{2}$$

and so on. When repeating N times, there will be N sample points $X' = \{x_1, x_2, \cdots, x_N\}$, including the first random one. And the X is an r-covering and r-separated set in X with

$$r = \max_{i=1,\cdots,N} \min_{k=1,\cdots,N} d_X(x_i, x_k) \tag{3}$$

From the procedure of FPS, the points at the anchors (e.g. the feet and the hands of human or other animals) will be selected prior to other points on the mesh. And the several anchor points of each isometric shape will be correspondence and be selected firstly through FPS. Thus the base vertices of our algorithm could be achieved by an improved FPS, which takes the salient key points of shape as the initial point in [23]. FPS can obtain a well-separated covering net of the shape, so we also use it to sample the subsets of the shapes for our correspondence.

3.2   Minimum-Cost Maximum Flow Problem (MCFP)

The minimum-cost flow problem [24] is an important and typical problem in the field of graph theory, and is the core of network optimization problems.

This problem can be described as follows. Giving a flow network, that is, a directed graph $G = (V, E)$, with source point $s \in V$ and a target point $t \in V$, each $arc\,(i, j) \in E$ has an associated cost a_{ij} that denotes the cost per unit flow on that arc. A flow $f_{ij} \geq 0$ and a capacity $c_{ij} > 0$ are associated with every arc. We can send a flow f from **s** to **t**.

The minimum-cost flow problem is an optimization model formulated as follows:

$$Minimize \sum_{(i,j) \in E} a_{ij} f_{ij} \tag{4}$$

Subject to $f_{ij} \leq c_{ij}, f_{ij} = -f_{ji}, \sum_{j \in V} f_{ij} = 0$ for all $i \neq s$, $i \neq t$ and $\sum_{j \in V} f_{sj} = \sum_{i \in V} f_{it} = d.$

Based on this, if the point set, except the **s** and **t** point, can be separated into two sets with the arcs, we call this graph is a bipartite graph. Then with giving a weight to every arc, we will get the minimum weight graph, which will be used in our method to solve the correspondence problem. Next section we will discuss how to transfer the correspondence problem to the MCFP problem.

4 Problem Formulation

In this section we describe how to solve the correspondence problem with minimum cost flow problem. Firstly a new representation for the shape with the geodesic structure is provided. Then a network flow with that representation is constructed. And our method will be discussed in detail as follows.

4.1 Point Representation in Euclidian Space

There are some facts in Euclidian space. In 1D Euclidian space, a point is traditionally described by a real number. Similar to this, a point in 2D Euclidian space can be described by a pair of real numbers, and 3D space will be triple of real numbers. These description systems have a common characteristic, which is take a point (the Origin) and some directions (like x axis, y axis and so on.) as the reference. With the systems, the move, rotation and bend action will change the coordinate of the points. Here we can take more reference point to replace the reference directions. For example, on the Number of Axis, we can take the point **-1** and point **3** as the reference points, and then take the distances from target point to them as the coordinate to describe the target point on the Axis, like **0** point on the Number of Axis can be described as $(1, 3)$. And another example (see in Fig. 1), in 2D space there are two congruent triangles, but the position and direction of them are different. However, when take the three vertices of the triangles as the reference points respectively to represent the plane, it will be same in the embed space as depicted in the following figure.

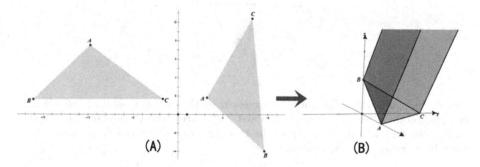

(A)   (B)

Fig. 1. In 2D space, take the three vertices of some congruent triangles respectively as reference points to describe the plane, and the result will be same.

4.2   How to Represent the Surface

To compare the non-rigid shape, firstly the intrinsic geometry is taken into account. Geodesic is a very generic but important intrinsic metric for a surface. For isometric shapes, if two points are the matching points on shapes, then the geodesic distance between the correspondence points are equal.

Considered in 3D space, a surface $S(u, v)$, which is a 2D manifold surface, with a geodesic metric $d_{geo}(\mathbf{x}, \mathbf{y})$, where $\mathbf{x}$, $\mathbf{y}$ are two points on the surface. If three or more points, which is not on a same geodesic path, are selected as the base vertices, arbitrary point p_0 on the surface will have an exact location. And these three points are denoted as p_1, p_2, p_3. The $d_{geo}(\mathbf{p_0}, \mathbf{p_i})$ can be computed, where i = 1, 2, 3. Take these three geodesic distances to be the new coordinates for all the points on the surface, that is $P_0(d_{geo}(p_0, p_1), d_{geo}(p_0, p_2), d_{geo}(p_0, p_3))$ in a three dimensional Euclidian space.

After getting a point $\mathbf{p}$, we compute the geodesic distances from this point, which forms a field on the surface, through the geodesic function $f(\mathbf{q}) = d_{geo}(\mathbf{q}, \mathbf{p})$. Every point only has one value. And all the same value points are on a close curve, similar to the circle contour on the plane in Euclid space.

It is well known that three points, which are not on the same line, can decide one and only one plane in the Euclid geometry theory. And as shown in Fig. 2, this can be described by the intersect point (X_0) of three circles, which takes the base vertices $(X_1, X_2$ and X_3 are the base vertices) as the centers and takes the distances $(d_1, d_2$ and $d_3)$ from the base vertices as the radius respectively. And for each point of the surface, we can find the unique group of circles with the centers as basis vertices.

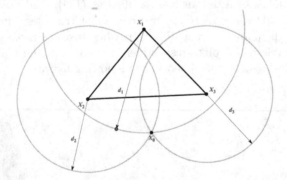

Fig. 2. Any point (like X_0) can be represented by the intersect point of three circles centered by three base vertices $(X_1, X_2$ and $X_3)$. Three base vertices in Euclid space on a plane, then we can see any point on this plane can be use the distances between these base vertices to unique denoted.

Then we extend this to the manifold surface with the geodesic metric. Firstly, we take the geodesic distance to replace the Euclid distance, and take the geodesic contour, which is a closed curve, to replace the circle.

The geodesic contour is some close curves and there is no intersect point between any two geodesic contours because of the unique distance between any point and the source point. If there are two geodesic contours intersect at one point **M**, all the points on the two contours have the same geodesic distance d. Thus if we consider point **P** from the outer contour (see in Fig. 3), the geodesic path from the source point **S** to the point **P** will pass through the area, which is between the two contours. And when the path enters this area, there will be a intersect point **Q** within the inner contour. However the points **P** and **Q** have a same distance d to the source point **S**. So there is no intersecting point between any two geodesic contours.

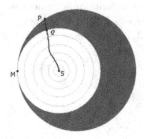

Fig. 3. Two geodesic contours intersect at point **M**. The geodesic distances of **SP** and **SQ** should be equal, then the geodesic distance between **P** and **Q** will be zero.

So when three (or more) base vertices are selected, all the points on the surface can be defined by the geodesic distances to these base vertices. For a given surface, when we select three or more points as the base vertices, then every points on the surface can be represented with a unique sequence of the distances to the base vertices. What's more, after some isometric transformation actions, the surface may be different appearance, but in the new space the surface will no change as shown in Fig. 4.

On the other hand, when considered the correspondence between two (nearly) isometric shapes (2D manifold surface), it is well known that the geodesic distances will be same between the correspondence points on the two isometric shapes. So after representing the two shapes into a k dimensional Euclidian space, they are in the same location and have a same surface. And now the problem has been transformed to another problem.

4.3   Transferring the Problem to MCFP

After embedding the shape into Euclidian space through setting the matched and ordered points of the two original shapes as base vertices, two new shapes are achieved, which have the same location and same surface (see in Fig. 5). So now the problem is transformed to finding the closest pairs of points in two point sets.

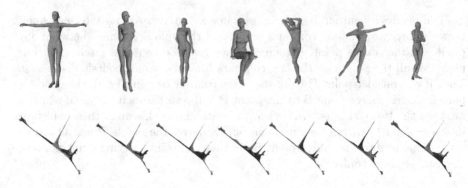

Fig. 4. Original shapes and the corresponding embedded shapes. The upper half part diagram is the original model, in which the red marker are the base vertices. The lower half part is embedded into the 3D space shape (Color figure online).

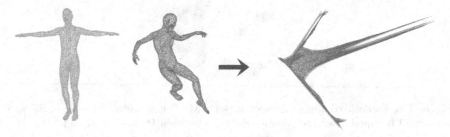

Fig. 5. Put the two new shapes into a same space directly. The two new shapes have the same location and the same surface.

Lets denote the two new shapes as $M_1(V_1, F_1)$ and $M_2(V_2, F_2)$, where V_i $(i = 1, 2)$ is the set of new points, which can be written as $\mathbf{v}$ $(v_1, v_2, v_3, \cdots, v_k)$, k is the number of the base vertices. F_i is the face from the original shape, i.e. the topological properties of the original and the new shape are same. Now we just find the nearest points between the two sets. The greedy strategy can be taken to find the nearest point from M_2 for each point in M_1. However it just meets the locally optima. Our aim is to find a map $\Psi(v_1) : v_1 \in M_1 \rightarrow v_2 \in M_2$, which is given below:

$$\Psi(v) = \underset{v_i \in M_1, \Psi(v_i) \in M_2}{\mathrm{argmin}} \sum_{i=1}^{N} distance\,(v_i, \Psi(v_i)) \tag{5}$$

Here $distance\,(v_i, \Psi(v_i))$ is the L_2 distance and N is the number of the M_1.

A direct graph is constructed to take the MCFP method to solve the optimal problem. Firstly two points are added to the two point sets, the source point $\mathbf{s}$ and the sink point $\mathbf{t}$ (see in the above Fig. 6). Between the source point $\mathbf{s}$ and each point in set M_1 there exists an edge with 0 weight, and between any point in M_1 and any point in M_2 there also exists an edge with an L_2 distance as cost.

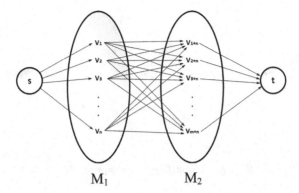

Fig. 6. This graph show that how we change the optimal problem into a MCFP problem. Add a source **s** and a sink **t**, add many arcs between the two points set. M_1 is the first shape, M_2 is the second shape.

From any point in set M_2 to the sink point **t**, there is an edge with the 0 cost. And all of the points in the graph have a weight, called capacity c, which is used to control whether the correspondence is a single map.

5   Proposed Approach

In this section we give the detailed description about our method. The steps in our approach are as follows. Firstly k (3~8) points are initialized as landmarks, and then the geodesic distances for all vertices on the mesh are computed. At last, the shortest path faster algorithm (SPFA) is taken to solve the MCFP to find the correspondence. The following figure show the outline of proposed approach Fig. 7.

5.1   Choose the Base Vertices

In proposed method at least three points are initialized as the base vertices. Here the FPS algorithm is taken to help us initialize the based vertices.

As mentioned in Sect. 3, the FPS method needs an initial point. The global feature point, which has the maximum sum of the geodesics from others, is taken as our initial point, because of the isometric shapes share this point. For a pair of isometric shapes some (about 10) points are sampled respectively. Then we use the enumeration algorithm to get the correspondence between the two point sets. The correspondence result satisfy Eq. (5). Because the number of the sample points is small, it will be very efficient.

5.2   Hierarchical Sampling Method

Searching the correspondence between the shapes without sample is very slowly when the number of the model is large. So we take the FPS to sample the model

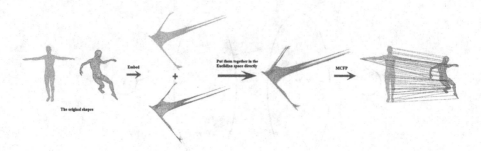

Fig. 7. The outline of our approach.

firstly, and to construct a series of sample points sets. And the small sets are contained by the big one because the next sample point is computed from the selected points. As the next sample point is the farthest point to the points already being selected, all of the sets will be evenly distributed on the model. As shown in Fig. 8, we get a series of sample point sets and from left to right the set becoming bigger and bigger. The left sample set is contained in the right set.

Fig. 8. Hierarchical sampling. From left to right, the number of the sample point becomes bigger (here is 100 to 500).

5.3   Embedding Space

After the above step, the base vertices are selected, and they have been matched to each other. Now the geodesics from these base vertices are computed, and then we take the order of the basis vertices to be the order of new coordinate in the Euclidian embedding space. Here the Fast marching algorithm [25] is used to compute the geodesic distances matrix M_1 and M_2.

The geodesic distances matrix just contained the new sample points, in another words, we only compute the correspondence between new sample point sets in the higher (dense) set. This can speed up the MCFP to solve the correspondence problem.

Algorithm 1. Framework of Proposed Algorithm.

Input: Two isometric shapes **S** and **T** represented by triangle mesh;

Output: One to one mapping $\Psi : \mathbf{S} \to \mathbf{T}$;

    step 1. Read the two shapes **S** and **T**;

    step 2. Select the feature point which has the biggest sum of the geodesic distances for **S** and **T** to initial the FPS method respectively, then sample k ($3 <= k < 10$) points from **S** and **T**.

    step 3. Enumerate all the pairings of the k sample points to find the corresponding results, which minimizes the function (5) in Section 4.3, and make an order for the these base vertices $\mathbf{S_b} = (\mathbf{s_1}, \mathbf{s_2}, \ldots, \mathbf{s_k})$ and $\mathbf{T_b} = (\mathbf{t_1}, \mathbf{t_2}, \ldots, \mathbf{t_k})$.

    step 4. Sample a series of sets from **S** and **T** respectively. $\mathbf{S}_1 \subset \mathbf{S}_2 \subset \ldots \subset \mathbf{S}_{level}$ and $\mathbf{T}_1 \subset \mathbf{T}_2 \subset \ldots \subset \mathbf{T}_{level}$.

    step 5. using the $S_p - S_{p-1}$ and $T_p - T_{p-1}$ ($p <= level$)to construct the two new points set

$$M_1 = \{m_i | m_i = (d_{geo}(v_i, v_1), d_{geo}(v_i, v_2), \ldots, d_{geo}(v_i, v_k))\}, i = 1, 2, \ldots, m.$$

and

$$M_2 = \{m_j | m_j = (d_{geo}(v_j, v_1), d_{geo}(v_j, v_2), \ldots, d_{geo}(v_j, v_k))\}, j = 1, 2, \ldots, n.$$

where $d_{geo}()$ represents the geodesic distance function. m and n represent the number of the set $S_p - S_{p-1}$ and $T_p - T_{p-1}$ respectively.

    step 6. Add a source point **s** and sink point **t** to construct a directed graph **M**, referring to Part 4.3.

    step 7. Apply run the MCFP algorithm on **M** to get the mapping result $\Psi_p : S_p - S_{p-1} \to T_p - T_{p-1}$

    step 8. Repeat **step 5** to **step 7** and combine all the subresult to get the last mapping result $\Psi = \Psi_1 \bigcup \Psi_2 \bigcup \ldots \bigcup \Psi_{level}$

5.4 Correspondence Detecting

After constructing the geodesic matrix, we treat it as a new coordinate in a special space. The new shapes in the embed space have same location and same scale (if in the original space has a same scale with each other). Thus you can find an approximate correspondence by simple greedy algorithm between mutually closest points. It will get local optima, however a global optimal result is needed.

The two new shapes are denoted as points set M_1 and M_2, and the map as $\Psi : \mathbf{M_1} \to \mathbf{M_2}$. Now to find the correspondence can be treated as an optimization problem, which has been described in Sect. 4.3.

The overall of our algorithm has been shown in the following Algorithm 1.

6 Results and Discussion

In this section we provide some correspondence examples based on our method. All the shapes used in our experiments are represented by triangulated mesh with several thousand vertices. We have conducted experiments on the TOSCA dataset [21], the McGill 3D Shape Benchmark dataset [27], the samba dance sequence and jumping man sequence from MIT [26].

Our results are shown in Figs. 9, 10 and 11. In each figure we display the correspondence lines between each pair of shapes. The distances are computed between each correspondence points in the k (in our experiment k = 5) dimensional Euclidian space. And we take average of the sum of these distances as the measure standard to test the quality of the result. Here we show the coarse to dense correspondence for each pair of shapes.

Fig. 9. Correspondence results from coarse to dense for perfect isometric shapes.

Fig. 10. Correspondence results for different objects (i.e. nearly isometric shapes).

In Fig. 9, we show the correspondence result for perfect isometric shapes, and in Fig. 10 the correspondence results for nearly isometric shapes is shown. What's more we try also proposed method to the correspondence of the partial shapes as shown in Fig. 11. In our experiments, when we searching the partial correspondence, less sample points was selected on the small model and some sample points are not used in the result map.

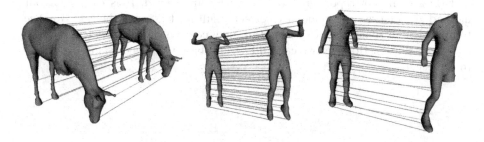

Fig. 11. Correspondence results for partial shape.

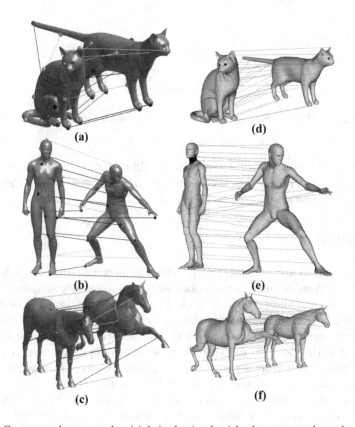

Fig. 12. Correspondence results (right) obtained with the proposed method vs. the results (left) in [20]. We can see the correspondence of the ear of the cat, our method gives the correct match. And our method can give more dense correspondence.

In Fig. 12(a), (b) and (c) are the correspondence results in [20], and (d), (e) and (f) are the correspondence results with our method. It is clear that our method gives more correspondence correct result for the ear of the cat. We have to note that in some cases our algorithm may confuse the symmetrical parts of two given shapes. However we can add several base vertices or sampling points to correct it.

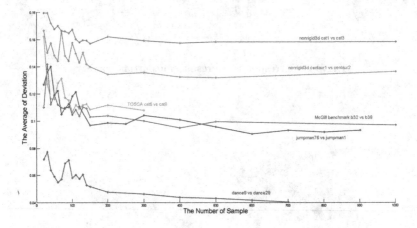

Fig. 13. The average of the deviation in different experiments data

In Fig. 13, the average of the deviation in different pair of shapes are shown. And we can see that the average is becoming smaller and smaller with the number of the sample increasing.

7   Conclusions

We propose a novel and computationally efficient algorithm that can achieve the meaningful correspondences between two isometric (or nearly isometric) shapes represented as manifold triangle meshes. The proposed method is based on the geodesic structure of the shape and minimum cost flow. Starting with initializing k (3~8) base vertices, and then embed the shape into k dimensional Euclidian space through the geodesic distances between the sample points and the base vertices. Then we construct a network flow with the points of the two shapes and another two virtual points, source point and sink point. The arcs of the network flow are the edges between each point on two shapes. So the correspondence problem is transferred to a MCFP with divide-and-conquer method. And we solve the MCFP with SPFA algorithm. The experimental results on different datasets show that proposed method can achieve a good match. And the average of the deviation is smaller and smaller with the increasing of the correspondence density.

In future work, we will find a better initialization method and expand the method to use other metric, which could be more robust and computationally efficient. Another research direction is to detect the symmetry.

Acknowledgement. The research is partially supported by National Natural Science Foundation of China (No.61170170 and 61170203), and the National Key Technology Research and Development Program of China (2012BAH33F04).

References

1. van Kaick, O., Zhang, H., Hamarneh, G., Cohen-Or, D.: A survey on shape correspondence. Comput. Graph. Forum **30**(6), 1681–1707 (2011)
2. Kraevoy, V., Sheffer, A.: Cross-parameterization and compatible remeshing of 3D models. In: ACM Transactions on Graphics (TOG). ACM SIGGRAPH 2004 Papers, vol. 861. ACM, Los Angeles (2004)
3. Elad, A., Kimmel, R.: On bending invariant signatures for surfaces. IEEE Trans. Pattern Anal. Mach. Intell. **25**(10), 1285–1295 (2003)
4. Varun, J., Hao, Z.: Robust 3D shape correspondence in the spectral domain. In: IEEE International Conference on Shape Modeling and Applications, SMI 2006, vol. 19. IEEE, Matsushima (2006)
5. Rustamov, R.M.: Laplace-Beltrami eigenfunctions for deformation invariant shape representation. In: Proceedings of the Fifth Eurographics Symposium on Geometry Processing, vol. 225. Eurographics Association, Barcelona (2007)
6. Bronstein, A.M., Bronstein, M.M., Kimmel, R.: Generalized multidimensional scaling: a framework for isometry-invariant partial surface matching. Proc. Nat. Acad. Sci. U.S.A. **103**(3), 1168–1172 (2006)
7. Lipman, Y., Funkhouser, T.: MöBius voting for surface correspondence. ACM Trans. Graph. **28**(3), 71 (2009)
8. Jain, V., Zhang, H., van Kaick, O.: Non-rigid spectral correspondence of triangle meshes. Int. J. Shape Model. **13**(1), 101–124 (2007)
9. Sun, J., Ovsjanikov, M., Guibas, L.: A concise and provably informative multi-scale signature based on heat diffusion. Comput. Graph. Forum **28**(5), 1383–1392 (2009)
10. Bronstein, M.M., Kokkinos, I.: Scale-invariant heat kernel signatures for non-rigid shape recognition. In: 2010 IEEE Conference on Computer Vision and Pattern Recognition (CVPR), vol. 1704, San Francisco (2010)
11. Aubry, M., Schlickewei, U., Cremers, D.: The wave kernel signature: a quantum mechanical approach to shape analysis. In: 2011 IEEE International Conference on Computer Vision Workshops (ICCV Workshops), vol. 1626, Barcelona (2011)
12. Ovsjanikov, M., Mrigot, Q., Mmoli, F., Guibas, L.: One point isometric matching with the heat kernel. Comput. Graph. Forum **29**(5), 1555–1564 (2010)
13. Sharma, A., Horaud, R., Cech, J., Boyer, E.: Topologically-robust 3D shape matching based on diffusion geometry and seed growing. In: 2011 IEEE Conference on Computer Vision and Pattern Recognition (CVPR), vol. 2481. IEEE, Providence (2011)
14. Zhang, H., Sheffer, A., Cohen-Or, D., Zhou, Q., van Kaick, O., Tagliasacchi, A.: Deformation-driven shape correspondence. Comput. Graph. Forum **27**(5), 1431–1439 (2008)

15. Sahilliog, Y., Yemez, Y.: 3D Shape correspondence by isometry-driven greedy optimization. In: 2010 IEEE Conference on Computer Vision and Pattern Recognition (CVPR), vol. 453. IEEE, San Francisco (2010)
16. Sahillioglu, Y., Yemez, Y.: Coarse-to-fine combinatorial matching for dense isometric shape correspondence. Comput. Graph. Forum **30**(5), 1461–1470 (2011)
17. Sahillioglu, Y., Yemez, Y.: Minimum-distortion isometric shape correspondence using EM algorithm. IEEE Trans. Pattern. Anal. Mach. Intell. **34**(11), 2203–2215 (2012)
18. Sahillioglu, Y., Yemez, Y.: Partial 3D correspondence from shape extremities. Comput. Graph. Forum **33**(6), 63–76 (2014)
19. Dubrovina, A., Kimmel, R.: Matching shapes by eigendecomposition of the Laplace-Beltrami operator. Proc. 3DPVT. **2**(3) (2010)
20. Dubrovina, A., Kimmel, R.: Approximately isometric shape correspondence by matching pointwise spectral features and global geodesic structures. Adv. Adapt. Data Anal. **3**, 203–208 (2011)
21. Bronstein, A.M., Bronstein, M.M., Kimmel, R.: Numerical Geometry of Non-Rigid Shapes. Springer, New York (2009)
22. Eldar, Y., Lindenbaum, M., Porat, M., Zeevi, Y.Y.: The farthest point strategy for progressive image sampling. IEEE Trans. Image Proces. **6**(9), 1305–1315 (1997)
23. Zou, G., Hua, J., Dong, M., Qin, H.: Surface matching with salient keypoints in geodesic scale space. J. Vis. Comput. Animation **19**(3–4), 399–410 (2008)
24. Ahuja, R.K., Magnanti, T.L., Orlin, J.B.: Network Flows: Theory, Algorithms, and Applications, 1st edn. Prentice Hall, Englewood Cliffs (1993)
25. Kimmel, R., Sethian, J.A.: Computing geodesic paths on manifolds. Proc. Nat. Acad. Sci. U.S.A. **95**(15), 8431–8435 (1998)
26. Vlasic, D., Baran, I., Matusik, W., Popovi, J.: Articulated mesh animation from multi-view silhouettes. In: ACM SIGGRAPH 2008 Papers, vol. 1. ACM, Los Angeles (2008)
27. Siddiqi, K., Zhang, J., Macrini, D., Shokoufandeh, A., Bouix, S., Dickinson, S.: Retrieving articulated 3-D models using medial surfaces. Mach. Vis. Appl. **19**(4), 261–275 (2008)

Individual Theta/Beta Based Algorithm for Neurofeedback Games to Improve Cognitive Abilities

Yisi Liu[1(⊠)], Xiyuan Hou[1], Olga Sourina[1], and Olga Bazanova[2]

[1] Fraunhofer IDM@NTU, Nanyang Technological University,
Singapore, Singapore
{LIUYS, HOUX0003, eosourina}@ntu.edu.sg
[2] Scientific Research Institute of Physiology and Basic Medicine,
Russian Academy of Medical Sciences, Moscow, Russia
bazanovaom@physiol.ru

Abstract. NeuroFeedback Training (NFT) can be used to enhance cognitive abilities in healthy adults. In this paper, we propose and implement a neurofeedback system which integrates an individual theta/beta based neurofeedback algorithm in a "Shooting" game. The system includes an algorithm of calculation of an Individual Alpha Peak Frequency (IAPF), Individual Alpha Band Width (IABW) and individual theta/beta ratio. Use of the individual theta/beta ratio makes the neurofeeback training more effective. We study the effectiveness of the proposed neurofeedback system with five subjects taking 6 NFT sessions each. As the neurofeedback protocol based on the power of individual theta/beta ratio training is used, each neurofeedback training session includes an IAPF, IABW and individual theta/beta ratio calculation. Subjects play the "Shooting" game to train cognitive abilities. The feedback on the player's brain state is given by the color of the shooter's target. If the target turns from "blue" to "red", the player is in the "desired" brain state and is able to shoot. IAPF and IABW parameters calculated before and after NFT sessions are used for neurofeedback efficiency analysis. Our hypothesis is that after the neurofeedback training by playing the "Shooting" game, the individual alpha peak frequency increases. The results show that all subjects overall have a higher individual alpha peak frequency values right after the training or the next day.

Keywords: EEG · Neurofeedback training · Neurofeedback game · Individual alpha peak frequency · Individual alpha band width · Theta/beta training

1 Introduction

Neurofeedback uses Electroencephalogram (EEG) to measure the real-time brain activity and teaches the user to do self-regulation. During the training, visual feedback such as color or velocity change of the visualized objects or audio feedback such as beep sound can be used to indicate whether the current brain state is the targeted one or not. Then, the subject can maintain/adjust the current brain state based on the feedback. Traditionally, this technique is used as the treatment for patients with mental illnesses.

M.L. Gavrilova et al. (Eds.): Trans. on Comput. Sci. XXVI, LNCS 9550, pp. 57–73, 2016.
DOI: 10.1007/978-3-662-49247-5_4

For example, the NeuroFeedback Training (NFT) is given to the children with learning disability (LD), and after the training, cognitive performance of these children is enhanced [1]. Recently, it was also used as a training method for healthy people to exercise their brain and to boost their cognitive abilities. For example, healthy adults attended neurofeedback training, and their cognitive performance has been improved significantly after the training [2, 3]. Usually during the neurofeedback training, the target of the training is to increase or suppress some activity in a certain EEG frequency range. For example, the amplitude in the 12−15 Hz band is targeted to be increased [4]. In [5, 6], it is shown that an Individual Alpha Peak Frequency (IAPF) is a positive indicator of the cognitive abilities, which means a better brain performance can be obtained if the individual alpha peak frequency is increased. Different neurofeedback protocols such as increase of upper alpha band power or the beta/theta ratio are applied. The results show that after such training the individual alpha peak frequency is larger, and the Individual Alpha Band Width (IABW) is wider [6].

The theta/beta ratio training is one of the most widely used neurofeedback training protocols to help both children with mental disorders [7, 8] and healthy people [4, 9] to improve their cognitive abilities. In our study [10], it is shown that after NFT based on the individual theta/beta ratio and NFT based on the upper alpha power training the IAPF is increased. Although the training using individual upper alpha is also proved to be effective to improve cognitive abilities, we observe that the individual upper alpha power based training is more likely to be affected by eye artefacts than the ratio training. Moreover, the individual upper alpha power based training usually is recommended to be done with eye-closed [11–14] as upper alpha is suppressed when eyes are open.

In this paper, we propose and implement a neurofeedback system which integrates the individual theta/beta based neurofeedback algorithm in a "Shooting" game. The system includes a neurofeedback algorithm part and a neurofeedback game part implemented in UDK. We did an experiment with five subjects to assess the effectiveness of the neurofeedback training system. Once the individual alpha frequency range is obtained for each subject from open/close eyes 1 min recording, the individual upper alpha, beta, and theta frequency range can be defined. Then, the power of individual beta/theta ratio is calculated and enhanced during the neurofeedback training by playing the game. The NFT efficiency assessment is based on the individual alpha peak frequency and individual alpha band width values before and after NFT sessions.

The paper is organized as follows. In Sect. 2, the related work such as introduction to five frequency bands in EEG, review on neurofeedback training algorithms, and review on EEG-based indexes is given. In Sect. 3, the proposed neurofeedback training system is described. In Sect. 4, a case study with five subjects who used the neurofeedback training system and played the "Shooting" game is given. Section 5 describes the results of the case study. Section 6 concludes the paper.

2 Related Work

2.1 EEG Frequency Ranges

In neurofeedback training systems, different algorithms related to EEG frequency bands are used. Five EEG frequency bands are defined based on their frequency ranges as follows: from low to high frequency, namely delta, theta, alpha, beta, and gamma.

- Delta waves (0.5−4 Hz)

  The delta waves are related to deep sleep [15].

- Theta waves (4−8 Hz)

  The theta waves are related to drowsiness. It is also found to be associated with learning and memorial processes and attention recently. Neurofeedback training to increase theta power can benefit an artist as his/her creativity and performance technique are enhanced [16]. Training to decrease theta power is used to improve the verbal IQ, executive functions and attention for seniors [17] or in the treatment for children with mental disorder such as Attention Deficit Hyperactivity Disorder (ADHD) [7, 8].

- Alpha waves (8−12 Hz)

  Generally, alpha is related to relaxation. Recently, it was also shown that neurofeedback training to increase individual upper alpha power can help improve the ability of memorization [18] and visuospatial skills [2, 3] for healthy people.

- Beta waves (12−30 Hz)

  Beta band is related to emotional arousal. If a subject is in a scared state, the power of beta band may increase [15]. It is also believed to be relevant to motor functions [19]. Training to increase beta power can help ADHD children who have problems with attention [7, 8] and can also help healthy subjects reduce the reaction time in the Test of Variables of Attention [9].

- Gamma waves (above 30 Hz)

  These rhythms are used to confirm certain brain diseases [15].

  Despite the above-mentioned standard frequency ranges, use of individual frequency ranges can improve efficiency of neurofeedback training [3, 6]. The individual alpha peak can be obtained from the EEG recording during eyes closed, and the individual alpha bandwidth can be obtained by comparing the EEG recorded during eyes closed and eyes open [20]. Based on the individual alpha bandwidth, theta and beta ranges can be decided correspondingly. The individual frequency range can make the neurofeedback training strategy more efficient. For example, in [6], an example is given that the individual alpha peak frequency of a subject was 11.7 Hz which was larger than the norms of alpha peak frequency in the similar age group (that is around 9.61 Hz), but the individual alpha bandwidth for this subject was narrower (1.52 Hz) than the standard definition which ranges from 8 to 12 Hz. When the standard frequency range is used in the neurofeedback training, the subject can have a headache and the irritability [6]. This problem can be solved when the individual frequency ranges are used. The effectiveness of neurofeedback training with use of individual frequency ranges is much higher.

2.2 Review on Neurofeedback Training

Neurofeedback training based on individual alpha frequency has been proved to be effective for cognitive performance [2, 3] and working memory performance enhancement [21]. In such neurofeedback training, the individual upper alpha (UA) power is targeted to be increased. For example, in [2], the subjects needed to increase the individual upper alpha power and to decrease theta power; in [3], the training protocol was enhancing the individual upper alpha power. In both works, the cognitive performance of healthy participants was increased significantly after the training. The training based on the suppression of theta/alpha power ratio is another effective method for cognitive performance enhancement. In [1], children with learning disabilities (LD) needed to decrease their theta/alpha power ratio to get a reward during the training. When it comes to ADHD children, the neurofeedback protocol is suppressing theta band power and enhancing beta band power, in other words, the theta/beta ratio should be decreased [7, 8]. The theta/beta training can be used in the training for adults as well. It is proved that after such training, the cognitive performance of the subjects was improved [6]. Another neurofeedback training protocol is based on SensoryMotor Rhythm (SMR, 12–15 Hz) activity. In such neurofeedback training, the subjects need to increase the amplitude in SMR band without concurrent increase in theta and high beta band. After the training, the commission errors in the divided attention task were reduced, and perceptual sensitivity in the continuous performance tasks was improved [4]. In [22], the cognitive performance of healthy subjects was improved after 8 sessions of neurofeedback training based on the enhancement of SMR amplitude.

When the subjects are too anxious or stressed and they need to relax, for example, the performers can be under the stress before the show, the neurofeedback training is designed to relief the anxiety. The training protocol is to raise the power of theta over alpha with auditory feedback and eyes closed. After such training, it shows that music performance is improved [23]. In [24], it is found that by increasing the frontal theta amplitude in the neurofeedback training among healthy elderly people, the executive attention and working memory are improved.

Neurofeedback training can be done in different forms such as games, simple visual feedback such as color changes, or audio feedback such as a beeping sound. These changes can give feedback on whether the current brain activity is the targeted one or not. For example, the speed of a car depends on the attention level of the player [25]. It means if the player has a high level of attention, he/she can drive faster. In [26], the color and the movement speed of the icon in the pacman-type neurofeedback game indicates whether the brain activity of the subject reaches the reward criteria based on the corresponding neurofeedback protocol.

In our work, we propose and implement a neurofeedback system with theta/beta protocol that needs calculation of individual alpha peak frequency and individual alpha bandwidth for better neurpfeedback efficiency. We also develop a neurofeedback game named "Shooting" to make the neurofeedback experience more engaging.

2.3   Review on EEG-Based Indexes

A number of studies show that the difference in cognitive abilities of subjects could be assessed by indexes extracted from EEG. For example, individual parameters of the alpha band can be used for prediction of cognitive abilities of subjects. Different patterns of alpha band activity are proved to be indicators of different cognitive abilities and performances. For example, the alpha rhythm of different subjects was analyzed and compared in frontal and parietal lobes areas in [27]. It is found that people with high cognitive abilities make greater use of the parietal lobe region, while people with low cognitive abilities use more the frontal lobe region. Additionally, people with a high verbal aptitude make a greater use of the left parietal lobe region, while people with high nonverbal aptitude use more the right parietal lobe region. In [28], it shows that the individual alpha peak frequency and mean power of alpha band can reflect the intelligence level of healthy adults. [29] concludes that a decrease in the individual alpha peak frequency is related to a drop of the subject's performance in a modified version of Schneider's test and Shiffrin's memory search paradigm. [30] shows that within the same age group, children with the higher individual alpha peak frequency has higher reading performance than the others. In [5, 6], it is claimed that the individual alpha peak frequency is a positive indicator of cognitive abilities such as attention and the speed of information processing, which means a better performance can be obtained if the individual alpha peak frequency and individual alpha bandwidth are increased by neurofeedback training.

Another EEG-based index is a relative theta (4−6.5 Hz) power (the relative theta power is computed as the ratio of absolute bandpower to the total power across the 1–30 Hz range) which was used in the study of healthy older adults [31]. It shows that the relative theta power has a significant positive correlation with the immediate and delayed verbal recall, and attention in healthy older adults.

From the review above, we can see that EEG parameters/indexes can be used as the indicators to assess cognitive abilities of people. The reliability of EEG to assess the changes in cognitive functions is confirmed in [32].

In this paper, we use IAPF and IABW values to validate the hypotheses that NFT following the individual theta/beta ratio training protocol can enhance the individual alpha peak and alpha bandwidth.

3   Neurofeedback Training System

The procedure of neurofeedback training is illustrated in Fig. 1. The subject's EEG signals are acquired by EEG device in real time and filtered by artifact removal methods such as band-pass filter. Then, the features are extracted from the EEG data and compared with the threshold to judge whether the brain activity of the subject is as targeted or not. Then, the result is sent to the neurofeedback games to give the feedback

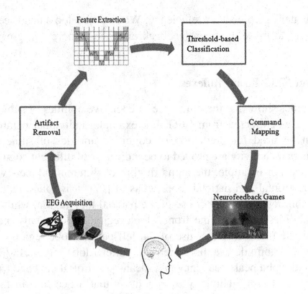

Fig. 1. The procedure of neurofeedback training.

to the user. Our proposed neurofeedback training system consists of two parts. One is the neurofeedback algorithm part and the other is the neurofedback game. Both parts are described in the following sections.

3.1 Theta/Beta Based Algorithm

To get the theta/beta ratio, initial parameters such as individual alpha bandwidth, theta, beta frequency range, and theta/beta ratio threshold need to be calculated. The individual alpha peak frequency is the peak frequency in the eyes-closed EEG. As the EEG spectrum is suppressed when the eyes are opened compared to the eyes-close condition, the individual alpha band width is calculated using both eyes-closed and eyes-open EEG data. It is defined as the suppressed frequency range when the power spectral density of eyes-open and eyes-closed EEG signals is compared [6, 20] as shown in Fig. 2. In Fig. 2, the red curve (upper curve) is the power spectral density plotting of eyes-closed EEG, and the blue curve is the power spectral density plotting of eyes-open EEG. The frequency where the maximum of the power spectral density is located in the eye-closed EEG curve is the alpha peak frequency. The intersection on the left side of these two curves is the lower alpha boundary and the intersection on the right-hand side of these two curies is the upper alpha boundary. According to the definition, the theta band ranges from 3 Hz to the lower alpha boundary, and the beta-1 band ranges from the upper alpha boundary to 18 Hz.

In the implemented theta/beta-1 based algorithm, the power spectral density $\hat{S}_{NX}(\omega)$ is calculated as follows [33].

First, the Fourier Transform is applied to the input signal,

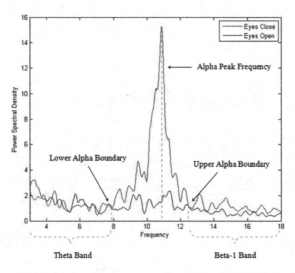

Fig. 2. Power spectral density of eyes-open and eyes-closed EEG (Color figure online).

$$X\left(e^{j\omega}\right) = \sum_{0}^{N-1} x(n)e^{-j\omega n} \tag{1}$$

where $x(n)$ is the input signal, N is the size of the input signal, $\omega = \frac{2\pi}{N}$, and $X(e^{j\omega})$ is the corresponding output after Discrete Fourier Transform.

Then, the output of formula (1) are squared and divided by the length of the original signal.

$$\hat{S}_{NX}(\omega) = \frac{1}{N}\left|X\left(e^{j\omega}\right)\right|^2 \tag{2}$$

where $\hat{S}_{NX}(\omega)$ is the Power Spectral Density.

The theta/beta-1 ratio-based neurofeedback system flow chart is shown in Fig. 3. Channel P8 is selected in the neurofeedback training system to calculate the features according to the research in [6] where parietal lobe channel was used in the neuro-feedback training. EEG data is recorded and transmitted to computer via Bluetooth. In the real-time brain state recognition during neurofeedback training, the ratio values are calculated according to the most recent 128 samples and compared with the threshold. If the beta/theta ratio exceeds the pre-defined threshold, the subject gets the reward in the "Shooting" game: the robots in the game turn "red", and disappear after the subject shoots them; otherwise the robots are blue and run around.

The implemented system includes an EEG recorder and Neurofeedback training software. The EEG recorder (shown in Fig. 4) records a pre-training one-minute eyes-closed and eyes-open EEG. The eyes-closed and eyes-opened EEG recording is used to calculate the individual alpha peak frequency, individual alpha band, the corresponding theta, beta-1 band, and the pre-defined threshold for the ratio-based

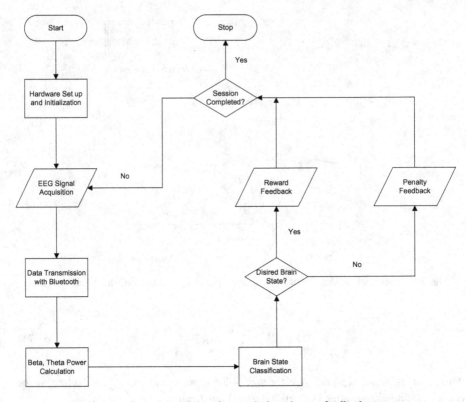

Fig. 3. The flow chart of theta/beta ratio-based neurofeedback system.

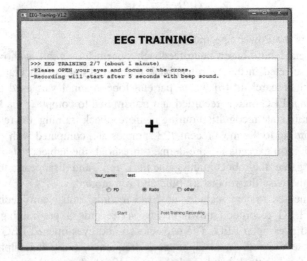

Fig. 4. Screenshot of EEG recorder of NFT.

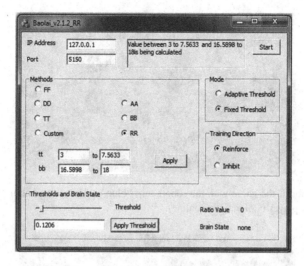

Fig. 5. Screenshot of neurofeedback training software.

neurofeedback training as mentioned above. The screenshot of neurofeedback training software is shown in Fig. 5. During the neurofeedback training, the features in the selected methods such as theta/beta-1 ratio are extracted and compared with the threshold calculated from 1 min eyes-closed and 1 min eyes-opened EEG recording before NFT session. Then, the result is sent to the game module via a TCP port to trigger certain command in the neurofeedback game. In the rest of the paper, we follow notion "beta" for "beta-1" band range.

3.2 Neurofeedback Game

Different neurofeedback games can be used with the neurofeedback algorithm part. A "Shooting" game is designed and implemented in our work.

The user has to shoot the enemies (robots). When the subject's brain activity is recognized as undesired one, the robots are blue and run around (Fig. 6). The robots change the color to "red" and stay still if the brain activity is the desired one. Then, the user can shoot the robots and they will be destroyed (Fig. 7).

4   Methods

A study was done to assess the effectiveness of the proposed neurofeedback training system.

4.1   Subjects

Five subjects (four male and one female) with age ranging from 24−30 years old participated in the study. None of them had mental illness.

Fig. 6. Screenshot of the game with the robots turn "blue" color corresponding to "undesired" brain state of the player (Color figure online).

Fig. 7. Screenshot of the game with the robots turn "red" color corresponding to "desired" brain state of the player (Color figure online).

4.2 Procedure

For all subjects, the procedure of each neurofeedback session consists of three parts. In the first part, EEG data of one minute close eyes and one minute open eyes is recorded. These data are used to calculate the IAPF, IABW, and theta beta ratio for each subject. Then, the subjects need to play the neurofeedback game for entire 40 min (3 times game playing, 10 min each time with 5 min of resting in between). For all 5 subjects, the neurofeedback protocol is to increase the individual beta/theta power ratio. After that, EEG data of one minute Eyes Closed (EC) and one minute Eye Opened (EO) are recorded again. The data from EO/EC recordings before and after NFT are used to analyze the training effects.

Four subjects had 6 neurofeedback sessions and one subject attended 5 neurofeedback sessions. One session was performed each day at the same time slot.

4.3 EEG Device

The 14 electrodes Emotiv device [34] is used to obtain EEG signals. This device is wireless and easy to set up. The locations of the electrodes are standardized by the

American Electroencephalographic Society [35] which include AF3, F7, F3, FC5, T7, P7, O1, O2, P8, T8, FC6, F4, F8, AF4. The technical parameters of the device are as follows: bandwidth - 0.2−45 Hz, digital notch filters at 50 Hz and 60 Hz; A/D converter with 16 bits resolution and sampling rate of 128 Hz.

5 Data Processing and Analysis Results

Before each neurofeedback training, one minute eyes-closed and eyes-open EEG data are recorded for all five subjects. IAPF/IABW values before and after NFT are calculated. Some subjects increase IAPF/IABW values immediately after the training. Other subjects have a decrease in IAPF/IABW immediately after the training but before the next NFT session their IAPF/IABW value can be higher (enhanced by the previous NFT). In our analysis, if we study overall change in IAPF and IABW to calculate IAPF/IABW enhancement (if any) we compare the first and last "before" values.

The initial individual alpha peak frequency of Subject 1 is calculated as 8.94 Hz; the lower alpha boundary frequency is 8.64 Hz; the upper alpha boundary frequency is 10.44 Hz (individual alpha band width 1.80 Hz). The alpha peak frequency, lower and upper alpha frequency boundary, and the alpha bandwidth of Subject 1 before and after each neurofeedback training session are given in Table 1. In Table 1, we can see that when we compare the alpha peak of Subject 1 before the first training and before the last training session, it is increased from 8.94 Hz to 9.55 Hz. The individual alpha peak increases after each training session in most of the cases. We can see that the individual alpha bandwidth of Subject 1 increases immediately after the NFT session in most of the cases, and when we have a look at the changes across different days, the alpha bandwidth is increased from 1.8 Hz to 2.55 Hz.

Table 1. The changes across 6 neurofeedback training sessions of subject 1

Training		Alpha peak frequency	Lower alpha frequency boundary	Upper alpha frequency boundary	Alpha bandwidth
1	Before training	8.94	8.64	10.44	1.80
	After training	9.14	8.50	10.64	2.14
2	Before training	9.17	8.92	10.46	1.54
	After training	9.27	8.78	11.22	2.44
3	Before training	9.13	8.99	10.77	1.78
	After training	9.33	8.72	10.88	2.16
4	Before training	9.33	8.94	10.92	1.98
	After training	9.49	8.57	10.3	1.73
5	Before training	9.52	9.21	10.03	0.82
	After training	9.46	8.77	10.03	1.26
6	Before training	9.55	8.05	10.6	2.55
	After training	9.46	8.85	10.32	1.47

The initial individual alpha peak frequency of Subject 2 is calculated as 9.24 Hz; the lower alpha boundary frequency is 8.72 Hz; the upper alpha boundary frequency is

9.67 Hz (individual alpha band width 0.95 Hz). In total, the subject attended 6 neurofeedback training sessions based on theta/beta ratio. The detailed alpha peak frequency, lower and upper alpha frequency boundary, and the alpha bandwidth of Subject 2 before and after each neurofeedback training session are given in Table 2. The table shows that when we compare the alpha peak frequency of Subject 2 before the first training and before the last training, the alpha peak is increased from 9.24 Hz to 9.66 Hz. The individual alpha bandwidth is boosted after the 4th session, from 0.95 Hz to 1.63 Hz. However, there is no increase of individual alpha bandwidth between the first training and the last training.

Table 2. The changes across 6 neurofeedback training sessions of subject 2

Training		Alpha peak frequency	Lower alpha frequency boundary	Upper alpha frequency boundary	Alpha bandwidth
1	Before training	9.24	8.72	9.67	0.95
	After training	8.83	8.46	9.44	0.98
2	Before training	9.25	8.86	9.86	1.00
	After training	9.55	9.1	9.94	0.84
3	Before training	10.03	9.03	10.33	1.30
	After training	9.27	8.3	9.58	1.28
4	Before training	9.53	8.74	9.97	1.23
	After training	9.25	8.78	10.41	1.63
5	Before training	9.35	8.8	9.85	1.05
	After training	8.99	8.8	9.8	1.00
6	Before training	9.66	8.91	9.81	0.90
	After training	9.02	8.88	9.55	0.67

The initial individual alpha peak frequency of Subject 3 is calculated as 7.06 Hz; the lower alpha boundary frequency is 6.52 Hz; the upper alpha boundary frequency is 7.25 Hz (individual alpha band width 0.73 Hz). Subject 3 attended 6 neurofeedback training sessions. The alpha peak frequency, upper alpha frequency boundary and lower alpha frequency boundary, and the alpha bandwidth are given in Table 3. From the table, we can observe that: (1) the individual alpha peak of Subject 3 increases immediately after neurofeedback training in most of the cases. If we compare the alpha peak before the first training session and before the last training session (after last training 1 min EO/EC recording of Subject 3 is not available), it is increased from 7.06 Hz to 10.89 Hz; (2) the individual alpha bandwidth is increased immediately after the neurofeedback training in most of the cases, and if the changes across different days are compared, there is an improvement from 0.73 to 1.59 between the first training and the last training.

The initial individual alpha peak frequency of Subject 4 is calculated as 12.27 Hz that is considered as very high; the lower alpha boundary frequency is 8.61 Hz; the upper alpha boundary frequency is 17.24 Hz (individual alpha band width 8.63 Hz). Subject 4 attended 5 neurofeedback training sessions in total. The IAPF, upper alpha

Table 3. The changes across 6 neurofeedback training sessions of Subject 3.

Training		Alpha peak frequency	Lower alpha frequency boundary	Upper alpha frequency boundary	Alpha bandwidth
1	Before training	7.06	6.52	7.25	0.73
	After training	8.30	7.96	8.42	0.46
2	Before training	9.89	9.67	10.07	0.40
	After training	10.80	9.97	11.50	1.53
3	Before training	10.46	9.21	11.67	2.46
	After training	9.21	8.56	10.16	1.60
4	Before training	10.82	10.66	11.50	0.84
	After training	10.24	9.05	11.28	2.23
5	Before training	10.39	9.38	10.77	1.39
	After training	10.52	9.60	11.19	1.59
6	Before training	10.89	10.02	11.61	1.59
	After training	–	–	–	–

frequency boundary and lower alpha frequency boundary, and the alpha bandwidth are given in Table 4. From the table, we can observe that: (1) the initial alpha peak frequency of Subject 4 as high as 12.27 Hz, however, if we compare the alpha peak before the first training session and before the last training session, it doesn't have any improvement; (2) the individual alpha bandwidth is increased immediately after the neurofeedback training in most of the cases and if the changes across the different days are compared, there is an increase from 8.63 to 10.1 between the first training and the last training sessions.

Table 4. The changes across 6 neurofeedback training sessions of Subject 4.

Training		Alpha peak frequency	Lower alpha frequency boundary	Upper alpha frequency boundary	Alpha bandwidth
1	Before training	12.27	8.61	17.24	8.63
	After training	11.97	8.11	17.35	9.24
2	Before training	11.85	8.89	15.89	7.10
	After training	11.57	6.75	17.57	10.82
3	Before training	11.91	7.33	15.96	8.63
	After training	12.28	3.02	14.21	11.19
4	Before training	12.57	11.58	13.18	1.60
	After training	11.78	11.14	16.29	5.15
5	Before training	11.61	7.31	17.41	10.10
	After training	11.57	9.89	16.29	6.40

The initial individual alpha peak frequency of Subject 5 is calculated as 9.60 Hz; the lower alpha boundary frequency is 7.47 Hz; the upper alpha boundary frequency is 11.32 Hz (individual alpha band width 3.85 Hz). Subject 5 attended 6 neurofeedback training sessions. The alpha peak frequency, upper alpha frequency boundary and lower alpha frequency boundary, and the alpha bandwidth are given in Table 5. From the table, we can observe that: (1) the individual alpha peak of Subject 5 increases immediately after neurofeedback training in most of the cases, and if we compare the alpha peak before the first training session and before the last training session, it is increased from 9.60 Hz to 10.07 Hz; (2) the individual alpha bandwidth is not always increased immediately after the neurofeedback training, however, if the changes across different days are compared, there is an increase from 3.85 to 4.45 between the first training and the last training.

Table 5. The changes across 6 neurofeedback training sessions of Subject 5.

Training		Alpha peak frequency	Lower alpha frequency boundary	Upper alpha frequency boundary	Alpha bandwidth
1	Before training	9.60	7.47	11.32	3.85
	After training	10.25	8.47	10.53	2.06
2	Before training	9. 60	8.96	11.03	2.07
	After training	9.71	7.97	11.03	3.06
3	Before training	6.05	5.14	11.05	5.91
	After training	9.67	9.03	11.42	2.39
4	Before training	8.78	8.55	10.36	1.81
	After training	9.47	8.56	10.00	1.44
5	Before training	9.50	7.89	10.20	2.31
	After training	9.13	8.64	10.55	1.91
6	Before training	10.07	6.83	11.28	4.45
	After training	9.33	8.10	10.64	2.54

In summary, except Subject 4 (who has high individual alpha peak frequency) all other subjects have an increase in alpha peak frequency after NFT. Subject 4 still has an increase in individual alpha band width. Except Subject 2, all subjects have an increase in alpha band width after the training. Subject 2 still has an increase in individual alpha peak frequency.

6   Conclusion

In this work, we proposed and implemented a neurofeedback training system with theta/beta based training protocol. First, we calculate IAPF, IABW and individual theta/beta ratio. Then, the individual theta/beta ratio is applied in the "Shooting" game. The user has to put his brain into the "desired" state to be able to shoot the target. We designed and implemented the experiment with 5 subjects taking 6 neurofeedback training sessions each to assess the effectiveness of the proposed neurofeedback system. Subject has to increase theta/beta ratio. The results show that four out of five subjects had a higher individual alpha peak frequency after the training that indicates an enhancement of the subjects' cognitive abilities related to attention, memory, etc. We validated the hypotheses that NFT following the individual theta/beta ratio training protocol can enhance the individual alpha peak and alpha bandwidth.

Acknowledgments. This research was done for Fraunhofer IDM@NTU, which is funded by the National Research Foundation (NRF) and managed through the multi-agency Interactive & Digital Media Programme Office (IDMPO) hosted by the Media Development Authority of Singapore (MDA). The "Shooting" game is original and designed by NTU final year student Qiuyu Xiang using UDK game engine.

References

1. Fernández, T., Harmony, T., Fernández-Bouzas, A., Díaz-Comas, L., Prado-Alcalá, R., Valdés-Sosa, P., Otero, G., Bosch, J., Galán, L., Santiago-Rodríguez, E., Aubert, E., García-Martínez, F.: Changes in EEG current sources induced by neurofeedback in learning disabled children. an exploratory study. Appl Psychophysiol Biofeedback 32(3–4), 169–183 (2007)
2. Zoefel, B., Huster, R.J., Herrmann, C.S.: Neurofeedback training of the upper alpha frequency band in EEG improves cognitive performance. NeuroImage 54(2), 1427–1431 (2011)
3. Hanslmayr, S., Sauseng, P., Doppelmayr, M., Schabus, M., Klimesch, W.: Increasing individual upper alpha power by neurofeedback improves cognitive performance in human subjects. Appl. Psychophysiol. Biofeedback 30(1), 1–10 (2005)
4. Egner, T., Gruzelier, J.H.: Learned self-regulation of EEG frequency components affects attention and event-related brain potentials in humans. NeuroReport 12(18), 4155–4159 (2001)
5. Klimesch, W., Doppelmayr, M., Schimke, H., Pachinger, T.: Alpha frequency, reaction time, and the speed of processing information. J. Clin. Neurophysiol. 13(6), 511–518 (1996)
6. Bazanova, O., Aftanas, L.: Individual EEG alpha activity analysis for enhancement neurofeedback efficiency: two case studies. J. Neurother. 14(3), 244–253 (2010)
7. Lubar, J.F.: Neurofeedback for the management of attention-deficit/hyperactivity disorders. In: Schwartz, M.S. (ed.) Biofeedback: A Practitioner's Guide, 2nd edn, pp. 493–522. Guilford Press, New York (1995)
8. Clarke, A.R., Barry, R.J., McCarthy, R., Selikowitz, M.: Electroencephalogram differences in two subtypes of attention-deficit/hyperactivity disorder. Psychophysiology 38(2), 212–221 (2001)
9. Egner, T., Gruzelier, J.H.: EEG biofeedback of low beta band components: frequency-specific effects on variables of attention and event-related brain potentials. Clin. Neurophysiol. Official J. Int. Fed. Clin. Neurophysiol. 115(1), 131–139 (2004)
10. Liu, Y., Sourina, O., Hou, X.: Neurofeedback games to improve cognitive abilities. In: 2014 International Conference on Cyberworlds (CW), 6–8 Oct 2014, pp. 161–168 (2014)
11. Vernon, D., Dempster, T., Bazanova, O., Rutterford, N., Pasqualini, M., Andersen, S.: Alpha neurofeedback training for performance enhancement: reviewing the methodology. J. Neurother. 13(4), 214–227 (2009)
12. Cho, M.K., Jang, H.S., Jeong, S.-H., Jang, I.-S., Choi, B.-J., Lee, M.-G.T.: Alpha neurofeedback improves the maintaining ability of alpha activity. NeuroReport 19(3), 315–317 (2008)

13. Fell, J., Elfadil, H., Klaver, P., Röschke, J., Elger, C.E., Fernandez, G.: Covariation of spectral and nonlinear EEG measures with alpha biofeedback. Int. J. Neurosci. **112**(9), 1047–1057 (2002)

14. Yamaguchi, H.: Characteristics of alpha-enhancement biofeedback training with eyes closed. Tohoku Psychologica Folia (1980)

15. Sanei, S., Chambers, J.: EEG Signal Processing. Wiley, Chichester (2007)

16. Gruzelier, J.H.: EEG-neurofeedback for optimising performance, I: A review of cognitive and affective outcome in healthy participants, Neuroscience & Biobehavioral Reviews (2013)

17. Becerra, J., Fernandez, T., Roca-Stappung, M., Diaz-Comas, L., Galán, L., Bosch, J., Espino, M., Moreno, A.J., Harmony, T.: Neurofeedback in healthy elderly human subjects with electroencephalographic risk for cognitive disorder. J. Alzheimers Dis. **28**(2), 357–367 (2012)

18. Escolano, C., Aguilar, M., Minguez, J.: EEG-based upper alpha neurofeedback training improves working memory performance. In: 2011 Annual International Conference of the IEEE Engineering in Medicine and Biology Society, EMBC, pp. 2327–2330 (2011)

19. Sammler, D., Grigutsch, M., Fritz, T., Koelsch, S.: Music and emotion: Electrophysiological correlates of the processing of pleasant and unpleasant music. Psychophysiology **44**(2), 293–304 (2007)

20. Bazanova, O., Aftanas, L.: Individual measures of electroencephalogram alpha activity and non-verbal creativity. Neurosci. Behav. Physiol. **38**(3), 227–235 (2008)

21. Escolano, C., Aguilar, M., Minguez, J.: EEG-based upper alpha neurofeedback training improves working memory performance. In: Annual International Conference of the IEEE Engineering in Medicine and Biology Society, EMBC, pp. 2327−2330 (2011)

22. Vernon, D., Egner, T., Cooper, N., Compton, T., Neilands, C., Sheri, A., Gruzelier, J.: The effect of training distinct neurofeedback protocols on aspects of cognitive performance. Int. J. Psychophysiol. **47**(1), 75–85 (2003)

23. Egner, T., Gruzelier, J.H.: Ecological validity of neurofeedback: modulation of slow wave EEG enhances musical performance. NeuroReport **14**(9), 1221–1224 (2003)

24. Wang, J.-R., Hsieh, S.: Neurofeedback training improves attention and working memory performance. Clin. Neurophysiol. Official J. Int. Fed. Clin. Neurophysiol. **124**(12), 2406–2420 (2013)

25. Pope, A.T., Bogart, E.H.: Extended attention span training system: video game neurotherapy for attention deficit disorder. Child Study J. **26**(1), 39–50 (1996)

26. Fuchs, T., Birbaumer, N., Lutzenberger, W., Gruzelier, J.H., Kaiser, J.: Neurofeedback treatment for attention-deficit/hyperactivity disorder in children a comparison with methylphenidate. Appl. Psychophysiol. Biofeedback **28**(1), 1–12 (2003)

27. Gevins, A., Smith, M.E.: Neurophysiological measures of working memory and individual differences in cognitive ability and cognitive style. Cereb. Cortex **10**(9), 829–839 (2000)

28. Anokhin, A., Vogel, F.: EEG alpha rhythm frequency and intelligence in normal adults. Intelligence **23**(1), 1–14 (1996)

29. Klimesch, W., Schimke, H., Pfurtscheller, G.: Alpha frequency, cognitive load and memory performance. Brain Topogr. **5**(3), 241–251 (1993)

30. Suldo, S.M., Olson, L.A., Evans, J.R.: Quantitative EEG evidence of increased alpha peak frequency in children with precocious reading ability. J. Neurother. **5**(3), 39–50 (2002)

31. Finnigan, S., Robertson, I.H.: Resting EEG theta power correlates with cognitive performance in healthy older adults. Psychophysiology **48**(8), 1083–1087 (2011). doi:10.1111/j.1469-8986.2010.01173.x

32. McEvoy, L., Smith, M., Gevins, A.: Test–retest reliability of cognitive EEG. Clin. Neurophysiol. **111**(3), 457–463 (2000)

33. Oppenheim, A.V., Schafer, R.W.: Digital Signal Processing. Prentice-Hall, Englewood Cliffs (1975)
34. Emotiv. http://www.emotiv.com
35. American Electroencephalographic Society: American electroencephalographic society guidelines for standard electrode position nomenclature. J. Clin. Neurophysiol. **8**(2), 200–202 (1991)

Scale-Invariant Heat Kernel Mapping for Shape Analysis

Kang Wang[1,2], Zhongke Wu[1,2(✉)], Sajid Ali[1,2], Junli Zhao[1,2,3], Taorui Jia[1,2], Wuyang Shui[1,2], and Mingquan Zhou[1,2]

[1] Beijing Key Laboratory of Digital Preservation and Virtual Reality for Cultural Heritage, Beijing Normal University, Beijing, People's Republic of China
[2] College of Information Science and Technology, Beijing Normal University, Beijing, People's Republic of China
wangkang@mail.bnu.edu.cn, zwu@bnu.edu.cn
[3] College of Software and Technology, Qingdao University, Qingdao, China

Abstract. In shape analysis, scaling factors have a great influence on the results of non-rigid shape retrieval and correspondence. In order to eliminate the effects of scale ambiguity, a method with scale-invariant property is required for shape analysis. Previous mapping method only focus on the isometric conditions. In this paper, a Scale-invariant Heat Kernel Mapping (SIHKM) method is introduced, which bases on the heat diffusion process on shapes. It is capable of handling various types of 3D shapes with different kinds of scaling transformations. SIHKM is the extension of the Heat Kernel and related to the heat diffusion behavior on shapes. With SIHKM, we will obtain the intrinsic information from the scaled shapes while without regard to the impact of their scaling. SIHKM method maintains the heat kernel between two corresponding points on the shape with scaling deformations. These deformations include scaling transformation only, isometric deformation and scaling, and local scaling on shapes. The proof of the theory and experiments are given in this work. All experiments are performed on the TOSCA dataset and the results show that our proposed method achieves good robustness and effectiveness for scaled shape analysis.

Keywords: Shape analysis · Heat kernel · Eigenmaps · Heat Kernel Map · Scale invariance

1 Introduction

With the development of 3D data acquisition technology, the repositories of 3D geometric data is growing. But the obtained 3D shapes manifest a vast variability due to the different categories of data acquisition equipment and the acquisition environment. Even for the same object, since the scanning circumstances are distinct, its scanned 3D shapes are not always with the same measurement, especially the scaling factors. So the arbitrary scale of shapes is an important

M.L. Gavrilova et al. (Eds.): Trans. on Comput. Sci. XXVI, LNCS 9550, pp. 74–90, 2016.
DOI: 10.1007/978-3-662-49247-5_5

challenge to shape processing. To remove the affection of the scale to these acquisition systems, a scale-invariant shape analysis method is in urgent need.

Maps or correspondence are particularly useful in shape analysis. Most of the maps and correspondence method require the deformations of shape to be intrinsic isometry. When the deformations are isometric, the geodesic distances between points on each shape are preserved. Fortunately most of deformations in the real world are approximately isometric, such as the articulated motions, inelastic deformations and so on. In most situations, we are looking for the maps that are consistent under approximately isometric deformations. In contrast to the isometric deformations, scaleing transformation is also ubiquitous in geometry processing. But it does not conflict with the isometric deformation, because most of the scaling transformations on shapes are combined with the isometric deformations. However, we usually require the shapes come in consistent scales and most applications such as shape correspondence, shape maps, shape retrieval, need these shapes in same scale.

Diffusion Geometry is an umbrella term about the intrinsic geometry. Coifman and Lafon [1,2] introduced the diffusion distances as an average length of paths connecting two points on a shape. The diffusion distance is a useful metric for data representation and dimensionality reduction. It is related to the probability of a random walk on the surface from one point to another in a fixed number of random steps. For its dependence on the Laplace-Beltrami operator, diffusion distance is easier for us to compute from the eigenvalues and eigenvectors of discrete Laplace-Beltrami operator, just like the Heat Kernel Signature (HKS) [3]. Based on the merits of heat diffusion procedure on shapes, HKS captures the intrinsic information of one point with its neighborhood by recording the dissipation of heat between them over time. As a signature HKS inherits many nice properties from the heat kernel, especially the multi-scale performance.

This paper proposes a new shape analysis method called Scale-invariant Heat Kernel Mapping (SIHKM) through extension of the scale-invariant heat kernel theory [4]. With this theory we could analyze the shapes regardless the scaling factors, such as the shapes with only scaling transformations, isometric deformation and scaling, or local scaling deformations.

The rest of this paper is organized as follows. Related works are presented in Sect. 2. Section 3 introduces the mathematical background about the Heat Kernels and gives definition of Scale-invariant Heat Kernel and Heat Kernel Map. Scale-Invariant Heat Kernel Map is presented in Sect. 4. Experimental results and analyses are provided in Sect. 5. Finally, conclusions are provided in Sect. 6.

2   Related Work

There are many methods to deal with the scale ambiguity problem in the shape processing algorithms such as shape correspondence, shape parameterization, and shape segmentation. Scaling effect could be removed with respect to some global intrinsic property, such as maximum geodesic distance [5], maximum node-centricity [6], or by the spectral graph theory of commute time distance [7]. But all of these methods suffer from the shapes global similarity. In [8] Y. Sahillioǧlu used the ratios between geodesic distances on a surface as the base to define scale-invariant isometric distortion function. But it is still needed a pretreatment to find the shape extremities. Y. Aflalo et al. in [9] presented a scale-invariant intrinsic distance measurement by normalizing the induced Euclidean metric according to the Gaussian curvature. But this method is not robust in the case of local scaling. Therefore a scale-invariant method appropriate for arbitrary scaled shapes is needed.

The Laplace-Beltrami operator is a generalization of the Laplacian from flat spaces to Riemannian manifolds [10]. In particular, harmonic functions and Eigen functions of the Laplace Beltrami operator have been studied a great deal [11–15]. Spectral methods [16], especially based on Eigen decomposition of the Laplace Beltrami operator have intrinsic properties induced by this operator. Reuter and Peinecke [17] proved Laplace-Beltrami eigenvalues as isometry-invariant shape descriptors could be used to recognize the isospectral models dubbed as Shape-DNA. By the decomposition of the Laplace-Beltrami operator, Reuter got the isometry-invariant signature of a manifold from the Eigen function corresponding to the first few smallest non-zero eigenvalues. Jiaxi Hu [18] transformed different shapes of poses from the 3D spatial domain to the spectral space to do pose analysis. Many schemes have been proposed to estimate it [19, 20].

Heat diffusion is a concept in physics. The heat diffusion equation is a partial differential equation which describes the distribution of heat (or the variation in temperature) in a given location and over time [21]. The heat diffusion on a manifold is the diffusion process whose infinitesimal generator is the Laplace-Beltrami operator [1]. Coifman and Lafon [1,2] have introduced the diffusion processes on manifold which formed a basis for the diffusion geometry in shape analysis. Sun and Ovsjanikovs [3] proposed an intrinsic, multi-scale and robust shape descriptor HKS. This signature is based on the physical processes of heat propagation on a shape and also related to the diffusion geometry proposed by Lafon. This novel shape signature was obtained by taking the heat kernel of different time interval, so it provides a multi-scale way to capture information about neighborhoods of a given point [3]. When time is short, the HKS takes more information from the close neighbors and catches the local features. And this situation is opposite when time is long.

However, HKS is not scale-invariant due to its dependence of eigen-decomposition of Laplace-Beltrami operator. So M. Bronstein [4] developed a Scale-invariant HKS (SIHKS) by means of sampling logarithmically in time and derivation to eliminate the scaling factor. Then the discrete-time Fourier Transform is taken to remove the shift of time. SIHKS is a kind of shape descriptor, but lack of ability to perform automatic scale adaptation in shape analysis. So we propose a scale-invariant mapping method for the automatic self-adapting scale selecting problem.

In the following section, we will present some theoretical underpinnings of Laplace-Beltrami Operator and Heat Kernel. For the invariance of heat kernel under isometry follows from the intrinsic natures of the Laplace-Beltrami operator. And we also review the theory of the Heat Kernel Map presented in the Ovsjanikovs work [22].

3 Mathematical Background

The basic concept of our method is the heat diffusion theory on a compact manifold. In this section we will review the heat diffusion theory and propose the SIHKM.

3.1 Laplace-Beltrami Operator and Shape Representation

Then we need to represent the shape information in a multi-scale way, such as the Euclidean space spanned by Eigen functions of Laplace–Beltrami. The Laplace–Beltrami operator is the generalization of the Laplace operator from flat domain to compact Riemannian manifolds. Given a differentiable manifold M with Riemannian metric, its Laplace–Beltrami operator is given by the following equation:

$$\Delta_M f = -div_M(\nabla_M f), f : M \to \Re \qquad (1)$$

where the and are the divergence and gradient on the manifold M [23]. The Laplace–Beltrami operator Eigen decomposition is stated as follows:

$$\Delta_M \phi_i = \lambda_i \phi_i \qquad (2)$$

$\{\lambda_i\}$ and $\{\phi_i\}$ are the eigenvalues and their corresponding eigen functions of Δ_M. Since the Laplace–Beltrami operator is semi positive definite, the spectrum of the Laplace–Beltrami operator consists of positive eigenvalues $\{\lambda_i\}$ and their corresponding eigen functions $\{\phi_i\}$ form an orthonormal basis [24]. While M is a connected manifold without boundary, then Δ_M has an eigenvalue equal to zero. And its corresponding eigen function is constant. These eigenvalues are sorted by their magnitudes so as to establish a correspondence for computing the similarity distance between two shapes. Thus the sequence of the eigenvalues from small to big is as follows:

$$0 = \lambda_0 \leq \lambda_1 \leq \cdots \leq \lambda_i \leq \lambda_{i+1} \leq \cdots + \infty \qquad (3)$$

We take the first K largest eigenvalues and its corresponding eigenvectors to build the spectral embedding domain. And the eigenvectors corresponding to the K smallest eigenvalues are called K leading eigenvectors (unnormalized). The reason for choosing the K leading eigenvectors is that they are high frequency eigenvectors and catch more local information.

In practical application, 3D shapes are represented by meshes which are discretization of closed Riemannian manifolds (compact and without boundaries). In this work we treat these meshes as undirected graphs with vertex set V, edge set E, and face set F. There exist various approximations for the Laplace–Beltrami operator. Here we use the convergent discretization scheme [19].

3.2 Heat Kernel and Heat Kernel Signature

Let M be a compact Riemannian manifold without boundary, the amount of heat at a point $p \in M$ at time t is defined by $u(p,t) : M \times \Re^+ \to \Re^+$. So at time 0, the heat at every point could be represented as the function $f : M \to \Re^+$. And the diffusion of heat on M is governed by the heat equation as follows:

$$(\Delta_M + \frac{\partial}{\partial t})u(p,t) = 0 \qquad (4)$$

Here the Δ_M is a Laplace–Beltrami operator of M. If the heat distribution f at time t is given by the heat operator H_t, then the following equations are satisfied: $\lim_{t \to 0} H_t f = f$, and $u(p,t) = H_t f(p)$. And these two operators have the relation $H_t = e^{-t\Delta_M}$. The heat kernel is a function as the fundamental solution to the above heat equation:

$$k_t(p,q) : \Re^+ \times M \times M \to \Re^+ \qquad (5)$$

which satisfies $H_t f(p) = \int_M k_t(p,q)f(q)dq$ for all $p \in M$ and measures the amount of heat transferred from point p to point q in time t. According to the eigen-decomposition of Laplace–Beltrami operator and the relation of Δ_M and H_t, the heat diffusion maps embed a given shape into the Euclidean space spanned by the eigenfunctions of the shapes Laplace–Beltrami operator. So the spectral expansion of the heat kernel on any compact manifold M has following form:

$$k_t(p,q) = \sum_{i=0}^{\infty} e^{-t\lambda_i} \varphi_i(p)\varphi_i(q) \qquad (6)$$

Here the λ_i and φ_i are the i-th eigenvalue and its corresponding eigen function of Laplace–Beltrami operator. From above equation, we can see that, the heat kernel is symmetric $k_t(p,q) = k_t(q,p)$. According to [3], the HKS is also isometry-invariant for the shapes with isometric transformations. Inversely if two shapes have the same HKS, then they are isometric. $HKS(p) : \Re^+ \to \Re$, $HKS(p,t) = k_t(p,p)$ is exactly the Heat Kernel Signature defined on the point p of the manifold M. It could be represented as:

$$k_t(p,p) = \sum_{i=0}^{\infty} e^{-t\lambda_i} \varphi_i(p)^2 \qquad (7)$$

As a local shape descriptor HKS has also many properties such as multi-scale property especially sampled at a finite set of time $t_1, \cdots, t_n$:

$$HKS(p) = (k_{t_1}(p,p), k_{t_2}(p,p), \cdots k_{t_n}(p,p)) \qquad (8)$$

With the help of HKS, Maks Ovsjanikov et al. [22] devised an intrinsic point signatures for the shapes with isometric deformations dubbed Heat kernel Map (HKM). But HKM is not exactly the same with HKS. HKM is a theory more suitable for the discretely sampled shapes. But HKM is not scale-invariant.

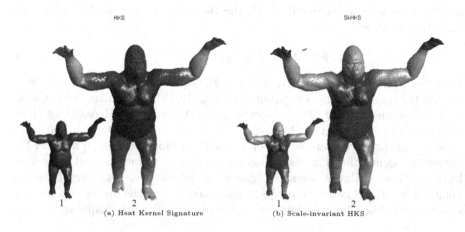

(a) Heat Kernel Signature   (b) Scale-invariant HKS

Fig. 1. The HKS (a) and SIHKS (b) on same shape with different scales.

3.3 Scale-Invariant HKS

Most shapes we obtained are under different conditions, thus the scales of the shapes may be different. To solve the problem of inconsistent scales, we need a scale-invariant signature. Due to the dependence of eigen-decomposition of Laplace–Beltrami operator, HKS is sensitive to the scale. Supposing the shape X is scaled β times, thus we get its scaled version $X' = \beta X$. Its eigenvalues and eigenfunctions of the Laplace–Beltrami operator are scaled by β:

$$\lambda' = \beta^2 \lambda, \varphi' = \beta \varphi \tag{9}$$

And the HKS is also scaled as shown in Eq. (10):

$$k'_t(p,p) = \sum_{i=0}^{\infty} e^{-t\beta^2 \lambda_i} \varphi_i(p)^2 \beta^2 \tag{10}$$

According to the M.M. Bronstein [4], these scaling factors could be removed by the logarithmically sampling, discrete derivative and discrete-time Fourier transforms. This approach created scale-invariant feature descriptors, and the SIHKS extend the heat kernel signature to deal with global and local scaling transformations. Figures 1 and 12 shows the results of the HKS and SIHKS on the same shape with different scales and local scaling respectively. Same color on the points means the signatures are the identical at a fixed time. From these Figures we can see that, HKS on the scaled shapes is not consistent.

3.4 Heat Kernel Map

The Heat Kernel Map was proposed in the [22] by M. Ovsjanikov et al. In that paper Heat Kernel Map constructed an isometric global map as follows. For a point p on a compact manifold M, the Heat Kernel Map is defined by the following equations:

$$\Phi_p^M : M \to F, \Phi_p^M(x) = k_t^M(p, x) \tag{11}$$

Here the F is a space of functions from $\Re^+$ to $\Re^+$. Thus the $k_t^M(p, x)$ is a real-valued function with two parameters x and t. M. Ovsjanikov also proved that it is a unique map that preserves the heat kernel to a fixed point. But the HKM mainly focused on the shape with non-rigid deformations in the same scale. In this paper we concentrate on the scaled shapes. And in [4] Michael M. Bronstein mainly aimed at the definition of signature from the scale-invariant local descriptors. But it seems to ignore the relations of heat kernel among points. The SIHKS could be properly used, not just as the descriptors for the shape retrieval benchmarks, but also as the tool for isometric mapping.

4   Scale-Invariant Heat Kernel Map

In this section we give the definition of Scale-invariant Heat Kernel and Scale-invariant Heat Kernel Map.

4.1   Scale-Invariant Heat Kernel

Inspired by the Heat Kernel Map and the Scale-invariant HKS, we propose the Scale-invariant Heat Kernel Map (SIHKM). For the heat kernel on any compact manifold M, its form is as follows:

$$k_t(p, q) = \sum_{i=0}^{\infty} e^{-t\lambda_i} \phi_i(p)\phi_i(q) \tag{12}$$

If the manifold is scaled by β, its scaled version is $M' = \beta M$. Thus we could get its scaled eigenvalues and eigen functions of the Laplace–Beltrami operator, and its scaled heat kernel is:

$$k_t'(p, q) = \sum_{i=0}^{\infty} e^{-t\beta^2 \lambda_i} \phi_i(p)\phi_i(q)\beta^2 \tag{13}$$

We simply denote the Eq. (13) as $k_t'(p, q) = \beta^2 k_{\beta^2 t}(p, q)$. We take the differences of logarithms to remove the scaling constant β in Eq. (13). Then the Fourier transform is taken to convert the scale shift into a complex phase. A detailed process is shown in the following: Firstly, the heat kernel is sampled logarithmically in time ($t = \alpha^\tau$) and converted into the discrete function:

$$k_\tau = k(x, \alpha^\tau) \tag{14}$$

According to the Eq. (13), the scaled shape will result in a time shift $s = 2\log_\alpha \beta$ and amplitude-scaling by β^2:

$$k_\tau' = \beta^2 k_{\tau+s} \tag{15}$$

Secondly, the multiplicative constant β^2 will be removed by the logarithm of k'_τ and discrete derivative of τ. Then the scaled heat kernel is turned to:

$$\dot{k}'_\tau = k_{\tau+s}, \dot{k}'_\tau = \log k'_{\tau+1} - \log k'_\tau \tag{16}$$

Finally, the discrete-time Fourier transforms of $\dot{k}'_\tau$ is taken to turn the time shift into a complex phase:

$$K'_\omega = K_\omega e^{2\pi\omega s}, \omega \in [0, 2\pi] \tag{17}$$

Here K and K' are the Fourier Transform of $\dot{k}$ and $\dot{k}'$ respectively. And the phase is eliminated by taking the Fourier transform modulus:

$$|K'_\omega| = |K_\omega| \tag{18}$$

The result of this process could be seen from the Fig. 2.

4.2   Scale-Invariant Heat Kernel Map

For the above point p fixed on M, the Scale-invariant Heat Kernel Map is defined by the following equations:

$$\Psi_p^M : M \to F, \Psi_p^M(x) = K_\omega^M(p, x) \tag{19}$$

Thus the $K_\omega^M(p, x)$ is also a function with two parameters x and ω. From the SIHKM Eq. (19), we can see that, the value of SIHKM depends on the selected source point p and the frequencies. In [22], Maks Ovsjanikov gave a mild genericity condition that HKM is injective. From the derivations of Scale-invariant Heat Kernel and the relations between HKS and SIHKS, we can see that this condition is also adopted by SIHKM. This means that it satisfies the following equation:

$$\Psi_p^M(x) = \Psi_p^M(y) \iff x = y \tag{20}$$

With these foundations, it is possible to find the point correspondence between two shapes with scaling deformations, if their SIHKM coincides with each other. Then we could get the unique SIHKM on scaled shapes by defining their source point.

5   Experimental Validation

In this section, tests of HKM and SIHKM on shapes with different deformations and scaling transformations are shown. These shapes are from the TOSCA (Tools for Surface Comparison and Analysis) dataset [25]. TOSCA dataset contains hi-resolution three-dimensional non-rigid shapes in a variety of poses for non-rigid shape similarity and correspondence experiments. All these shapes we used in TOSCA were represented by triangulated meshes with several thousand vertices. Objects within the same class in this dataset have the same triangulation and an equal number of vertices numbered in a compatible way. In the following tests, we choose pairs of corresponding points respectively between shape and its scaled version. Then we calculate the HKS, SIHKS, HKM, and SIHKM respectively. In practice, the computation of the HKS depends only on the computing the first smallest eigenvalues and eigenvectors of the Laplace–Beltrami operator. When $t \approx 0$ the computation of HKS is numerically unstable [26]. So in the following experiments, we take the value of t avoid starting from the 0.

5.1   The Results of SIHKS Mapping on the Shapes with Scaling Deformation Only

We take one shape from the TOSCA dataset and apply the scaling transformation to it. Just like the Fig. 2(a) shows, the shape of Monkey is scaled two times comparing to its original shape.

In the following results, the signatures from different shapes are shown in Fig. 2(b) and (c). In these figures, signatures from two pairs of corresponding points are marked with the same color but different line styles. The same line style represents signatures from the points on the same shape. The HKS at different time intervals and Scale-invariant HKS at a small number of low frequencies are shown in Fig. 2(b) and (c) respectively. From the results we can see that, the signatures of HKS are not consistent on the two shapes with scaling transformation, but the signatures of SIHKS are completely similar.

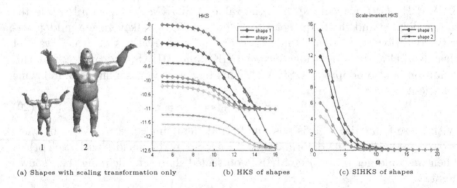

(a) Shapes with scaling transformation only   (b) HKS of shapes   (c) SIHKS of shapes

Fig. 2. (a) Four pairs of corresponding points colored respectively on shapes with scaling; (b) (c) Comparisons among numerical values of HKS and SIHKS. The same line style denotes the signatures from the same shape and the same color corresponds to the point on the shape in (a) (Color figure online).

In this test, heat kernels were approximated using the first 8 eigen pairs of the discrete Laplace–Beltrami operator. And the time scales for the HKS and SIHKS are $t \in [1, 16]$. The log scales space basis for SIHKS is 2, and we sample the frequencies in $\omega \in [2, 20]$.

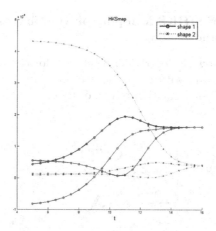

Fig. 3. The HKM of corresponding points on shapes with only scaling deformation.

For the four points from same shape in Fig. 2, we choose one as the source s and calculate the mapping $\Psi_s^M(P_i)$ from other three points $P_{i=1,2,3}$. Figure 3 shows the results of HKM on the points from Fig. 2. The curves represent the values of HKM over time t and these curves with different styles come from different shapes. From Fig. 3, we can see why HKM is not inappropriate for scaled shapes analysis. It is not consistent even for shapes with scaling deformation only.

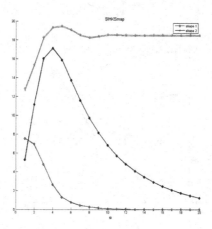

Fig. 4. The SIHKM of corresponding points on shapes with only scaling deformation.

For the SIHKM we also set its frequencies in [2,20]. From the Fig. 4, we can see that the values of SIHKM are almost consistent. These data lines with different style are from corresponding points between shape and its scaled version. As this data chart shows, they are almost coincide. This means SIHKM is more robust than the HKM when applied to the shapes with scaling deformations.

5.2 The Results of SIHKS Mapping on the Shapes with Isometric Deformation and Scaling

We choose two shapes with non-rigid isometric deformation from the TOSCA dataset. So the shapes are with isometric deformations in the same scale, then we apply the scaling transformation to one of them.

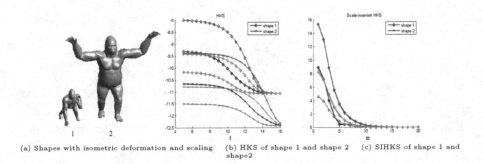

(a) Shapes with isometric deformation and scaling   (b) HKS of shape 1 and shape 2   (c) SIHKS of shape 1 and shape2

Fig. 5. (a) Four pairs of corresponding points colored respectively on shapes with deformation and scaling; (b) (c) Comparisons among numerical values of HKS and SIHKS. The same line style denotes the same shape and the same color corresponds to the point on the shape in (a) (Color figure online).

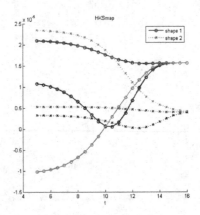

Fig. 6. HKM of corresponding points on shapes with isometric deformation and scaling.

The results of scaling transformation to these shapes are shown in Fig. 5(a) above. Their HKS and Scale-invariant HKS are also shown there Fig. 5(b) and (c). The setting for HKM and SIHKM is the same as experiment Sect. 5.1. The results from Figs. 6 and 7 show that, SIHKM is also robust to these scaled shapes with non-rigid isometric deformations and scaling.

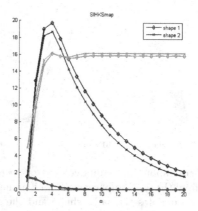

Fig. 7. SIHKM of corresponding points on shapes with isometric deformation and scaling.

5.3 The Results of SIHKS Mapping on the Partial Shapes with Isometric Deformation and Scaling

Partial shapes are parts of shapes, such as the broken shapes. One partial shape in Fig. 8 is from the TOSCA dataset. We choose the other complete shape from this datasets as a reference shape. Then we do the same operations as above and the results are shown in the Figs. 9, 10 and 11.

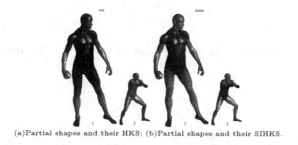

(a)Partial shapes and their HKS; (b)Partial shapes and their SIHKS.

Fig. 8. The same color means same value of the signatures. And red color vale means value is bigger than the blue ones (Color figure online).

5.4 The Results of SIHKS Mapping on the Shapes with Local Scaling

These shapes are from the TOSCA dataset without our deformations. They are scaled locally, just like the shape 1 and shape 2 in Fig. 13. Shape 2's rear legs are not in the same scale with shape1, but the other parts are the with shape 1. From the Fig. 13 we could get that, the local scaling is more influential than

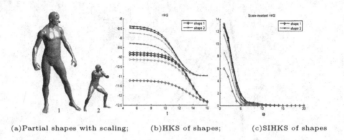

(a)Partial shapes with scaling;   (b)HKS of shapes;   (c)SIHKS of shapes

Fig. 9. (a) Four pairs of corresponding points colored respectively on partial shapes with deformation and scaling; (b) (c) Comparisons among numerical values of HKS and SIHKS. The same line style denotes the same shape and the same color corresponds to the point on the shape in (a) (Color figure online).

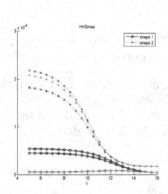

Fig. 10. HKM of corresponding points on partial shapes with isometric deformation and scaling

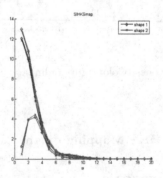

Fig. 11. SIHKM of corresponding points on partial shapes with isometric deformation and scaling

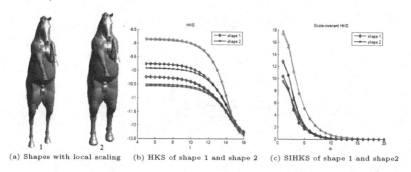

(a) Shapes with local scaling   (b) HKS of shape 1 and shape 2   (c) SIHKS of shape 1 and shape2

Fig. 12. (a) Four pairs of corresponding points colored respectively on shapes with Shapes with local scaling; (b) (c) Comparisons among numerical values of HKS and SIHKS. The same line style denotes the same shape and the same color corresponds to the point on the shape in (a) (Color figure online).

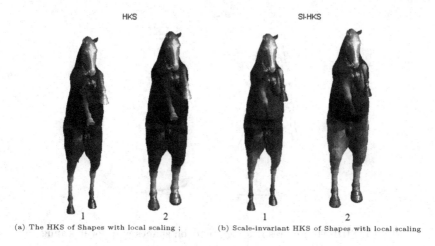

(a) The HKS of Shapes with local scaling ;   (b) Scale-invariant HKS of Shapes with local scaling

Fig. 13. The HKS (a) and SIHKS (b) on the shapes with local scaling.

other scaling situations for its uniformity. The SIHKS value on the rear legs are changed a lot with the local scaling transformation (Figs. 14 and 15).

All these experiments above are done on shapes with different deformations and scaling transformations. The results illustrate the difference between HKM and SIHKM in different scaled shape analysis situations. From these results we show that our method performs better in scaled shape analysis than the HKM. The accuracy of SIHKM is shown only in data graphs. In future work, we will apply it to other shape processing method, such as shape retrieval.

6 Conclusions and Future Works

In this paper, we present a Scale-invariant Heat Kernel Mapping shape analysis method to deal with the global and local scaling transformations on shapes.

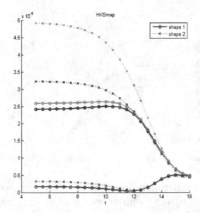

Fig. 14. HKM of corresponding points on shapes with local scaling

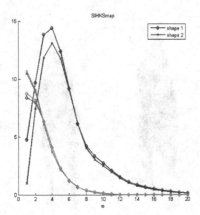

Fig. 15. SIHKM of corresponding points on shapes with local scaling

Base on the theory of Scale-invariant Heat Kernel, we propose the Scale-invariant Heat Kernel Mapping. This mapping procedure is an automatic scale adaptation method. By this method, we could do the shape analysis without being confused by the scaling factors. The results of the above experiments demonstrate that SIHKM is suitable for the situations of scaling transformation only, isometric deformation and scaling, and local scaling on shapes. Even for these partial shapes, SIHKM is still valid. The relation between SIHKM and Diffusion distances is also an interesting field because of their inner relations. We have done some experiments on this orientation. In the future, we will apply this method to more applications, such as shape correspondence, shape retrieval, etc.

Acknowledgement. The research is partially supported by National Natural Science Foundation of China (No. 61170170 and 61170203) and the National Key Technology Research and Development Program of China (2012BAH33F04).

References

1. Coifman, R.R., Lafon, S.: Diffusion maps. Appl. Comput. Harmonic Anal. **21**, 5 (2006)
2. Lafon, S.S.: Diffusion maps and geometric harmonics (2004)
3. Sun, J., Ovsjanikov, M., Guibas, L.: A concise and provably informative multi-scale signature based on heat diffusion. Comput. Graph. Forum **28**, 1383 (2009)
4. Bronstein, M.M., Kokkinos, I.: Scale-invariant heat kernel signatures for non-rigid shape recognition. In: 2010 IEEE Conference on Computer Vision and Pattern Recognition (CVPR), San Francisco, CA, vol. 1704 (2010)
5. Sahillioglu, Y., Yemez, Y.: 3D Shape correspondence by isometry-driven greedy optimization, p. 453. IEEE (2010)
6. Kin-Chung, A.O., Tai, C.L., Cohen-Or, D., Zheng, Y., Fu, H.: Electors voting for fast automatic shape correspondence, p. 645
7. Lipman, Y., Funkhouser, T.: MöBius voting for surface correspondence. ACM Trans. Graph. **28**, 71 (2009)
8. Sahillioglu, Y., Yemez, Y.: Scale normalization for isometric shape matching, p. 2233
9. Aflalo, Y., Kimmel, R., Raviv, D.: Scale Invariant Geometry for Nonrigid Shapes. SIAM J. Imaging Sci. **6**, 1579 (2013)
10. Dierkes, U., Hildebrandt, S., Sauvigny, F.: Minimal Surfaces. Springer, Heidelberg (2010)
11. Ruggeri, M.R., Patané, G., Spagnuolo, M., Saupe, D.: Spectral-driven isometry-invariant matching of 3D shapes. Int. J. Comput. Vis. **89**, 248 (2010)
12. Wetzler, A., Aflalo, Y., Dubrovina, A., Kimmel, R.: The Laplace-Beltrami operator: a ubiquitous tool for image and shape processing. In: Hendriks, C.L.L., Borgefors, G., Strand, R. (eds.) ISMM 2013. LNCS, vol. 7883, pp. 302–316. Springer, Heidelberg (2013)
13. Rustamov, R.M.: Laplace-Beltrami eigenfunctions for deformation invariant shape representation, p. 225 (2007)
14. Jain, V., Zhang, H.: A spectral approach to shape-based retrieval of articulated 3D models. Comput.-Aided Des. **39**, 398 (2007)
15. Zhang, H., van Kaick, O., Dyer, R.: Spectral mesh processing. Comput. Graph. Forum **29**, 1865 (2010)
16. Zhang, H., van Kaick, O., Dyer R.: Spectral methods for mesh processing and analysis, pp. 1–22
17. Reuter, M., Wolter, F., Peinecke, N.: Laplace-Beltrami spectra as shape-DNA of surfaces and solids. Comput.-Aided Des. **38**, 342 (2006)
18. Hu, J., Hua, J.: Pose analysis using spectral geometry. Visual Comput. **29**, 949 (2013)
19. Meyer, M., Desbrun, M., Schröder, P., Barr, A.H.: Discrete differential-geometry operators for triangulated 2-manifolds. In: Hege, H.C., Polthier, K. (eds.) Visualization and Mathematics III, pp. 35–57. Springer, Heidelberg (2003)
20. Belkin, M., Sun, J., Wang, Y.: Constructing Laplace operator from point clouds in Rd, p. 1031. Society for Industrial and Applied Mathematics (2009)
21. Sharma, A., Horaud, R., Cech, J., Boyer, E.: Topologically-robust 3D shape matching based on diffusion geometry and seed growing. In: 2011 IEEE Conference on Computer Vision and Pattern Recognition (CVPR), vol. 2481. IEEE, Providence (2011)

22. Ovsjanikov, M., Mérigot, Q., Mémoli, F., Guibas, L.: One point isometric matching with the heat kernel. Comput. Graph. Forum **29**, 1555 (2010)
23. Chavel, I.: Eigenvalues in Riemannian Geometry. Academic Press, New York (1984)
24. Rosenberg, S.: The Laplacian on a Riemannian Manifold: An Introduction to Analysis on Manifolds. Cambridge University Press, Cambridge (1997)
25. Bronstein, A.M., Bronstein, M.M., Kimmel, R.: Numerical Geometry of Non-rigid Shapes. Springer, New York (2009)
26. Vaxman, A., Ben-Chen, M., Gotsman, C.: A multi-resolution approach to heat kernels on discrete surfaces. ACM Trans. Graph. (TOG) **29**, 121 (2010)

A Community-Built Virtual Heritage Collection

Helen C. Miles[1]([✉]), Andrew T. Wilson[2], Frédéric Labrosse[1],
Bernard Tiddeman[1], and Jonathan C. Roberts[2]

[1] Department of Computer Science, Aberystwyth University, Aberystwyth, UK
{hem23,ffl,bpt}@aber.ac.uk
[2] School of Computer Science, Bangor University, Bangor, UK
{a.wilson,j.c.roberts}@bangor.ac.uk

Abstract. The HeritageTogether project has developed a web platform
through which members of the public can upload their own photographs
of heritage assets to be processed into 3D models using an automated
Structure-from-Motion work flow. The web platform is part of a larger
project which aims to capture, create and archive digital heritage assets
in conjunction with local communities in Wales, UK, with a focus on
megalithic monuments. The 3D models are displayed online using a lightbox style gallery and a virtual museum, while the large amounts of additional data produced are stored in an online archive. Each representation
provides a different perspective and context to the data, allowing users
to explore the data in a multitude of ways. HeritageTogether is a digital
community and community-built archive and museum of heritage data,
developed to inspire local communities to learn more about their heritage
and to help to preserve it.

Keywords: Structure-from-Motion · Co-production · Archaeology

1 Introduction

Archaeologists and heritage organizations are facing many challenges in their
attempts to preserve sites with cultural heritage value. A digital record is becoming a popular method of documenting sites in their current state, as many of
these sites are under threat of erosion and damage from natural changes in the
landscape and climate change. Digital records allow future, off-site analysis and
comparison between different sites.

One technique used for creating a digital record of a site is photogrammetry,
which allows the construction of a 3D model of an object from a series of photographs taken from known positions. An elaboration on the original technique of
photogrammetry, Structure-from-Motion (SfM), can perform the same function
with no prior knowledge of the position at which the photographs were taken, by
estimating the positions based on features and lighting within the photograph
series [1,2].

In modern archaeology, photogrammetry and SfM have become established
technique for recording data for various applications, such as documenting sites

© Springer-Verlag Berlin Heidelberg 2016
M.L. Gavrilova et al. (Eds.): Trans. on Comput. Sci. XXVI, LNCS 9550, pp. 91–110, 2016.
DOI: 10.1007/978-3-662-49247-5_6

[3,4], excavations [5,6], the exterior structure of buildings [7–9], monitoring erosion [10], and recording artefacts [11]. The technique has become popular as it allows the recording of data in a non-destructive manner, and can be accomplished with an off-the-shelf digital camera. Commercial photogrammetry software packages are expensive, often beyond the budget of many archæology projects. Open source solutions exist, but are perceived as requiring a great deal of proficiency with software to use [9]. Despite the expense, commercial packages are often favoured for offering graphical user interfaces which are perceived as more 'user-friendly'. This is stifling progress for the adoption of open source solutions in archaeology.

The HeritageTogether project is focused on using photogrammetry and SfM to create digital records of megalithic monuments such as standing stones, stone circles, cairns and burial chambers in Wales, UK; an example is shown in Fig. 1. While a dedicated survey team could travel to each of these sites to perform a high quality survey, due to the large number of sites it would take many days and thousands of hours to accomplish these surveys. For instance, there are about 330 cairns alone, in the north-west of Wales; a large proportion of these sites are of national importance, and are protected by the Welsh Government as Scheduled Ancient Monuments.

Fig. 1. Photograph and model of Bodowyr Burial Chamber on Anglesey, UK; a Neolithic chambered tomb and Scheduled Ancient Monument in the care of Cadw, the Welsh Government's historic environment service. The 3D model was created using a set of 257 photographs.

To enable us in the documentation of more sites, we have adopted a crowd-sourcing approach – with the involvement of the general public, it will be possible to visit and document many more sites.

Our system incorporates SfM into a broader, community-based work flow: we perform a metric survey through the use of SfM where contributors take photographs of the site, allowing us to create a 3D model of the environment. In recent years, digital cameras have increased in resolution, lowered in cost and become a common household technology; since SfM does not require photographs to be taken using specialist equipment, it is a reasonable task for the general public to perform. A suitable camera resolution (more than 6 megapixels) can even be found in some modern smart phones.

Alongside the development of our system, we engaged the public throughout the year with workshops, exhibitions and demonstration events at sites to support our community-based approach. Through the project we aim to co-produce the largest national photographic archive of megalithic monuments, inspire the local communities to learn more about their heritage and provide alternative views of the monuments by producing the 3D models [12].

This paper presents our system "HeritageTogether.org", which creates 3D models from photographs taken by the public, then displays the models in several ways in virtual space. We focus on aspects of displaying the models to the user once the photographs of sites have been uploaded and the 3D models have been created. Users need to be able to access and investigate the models, and so it is important to consider not only the methods of displaying the models online, but how a user will interact with them. The system has been designed to accommodate many users from different backgrounds, each with different tasks to perform; to meet this challenge we have developed a suite of methods to display the 3D models.

The paper is organised as follows: Sect. 3 describes the front end of the website, followed by a detailed description of the back-end work flow (Sect. 4) and details of three systems employed to make the data publicly available: the lightbox style gallery (Sect. 5.1), a digital archive (Sect. 5.2) and a virtual museum (Sect. 5.3).

2   Background

Structure-from-Motion (SfM) was developed in the 1990s; a technique which allows the interpretation of 3D structure from a series of sequential 2D images that contain some motion information [13]. SfM approaches have been recently popularised through a range of web-based cloud-processing engines; these tools make use of user-uploaded, crowd-sourced photography to generate the necessary photographic coverage of a site of interest and automatically generate sparse point clouds from the photographs [14].

The principles of SfM are based on the automatic identification and matching of features across multiple images. These features are tracked and matched between each image, enabling camera positions and coordinates to be estimated, then refined with each iteration and additional image analysed. Unlike traditional methods of photogrammetry, SfM lacks the scale and uniform orientation provided by surveyed control points. As such, each point cloud is generated in a world coordinate system, and must be aligned before it is used. To utilise a real world coordinate system, physical targets can be deployed, enabling each target location to be surveyed and recorded [14].

Ease of use, speed of recoding and improvements in processing capability over traditional methods have made this a popular technique for producing 3D digital content for virtual heritage projects.

HeritageTogether is a combination of a community photographic collection, a web-based SfM service and a virtual museum of the monuments recorded by the contributors. The concepts of web-based SfM and virtual museums are by no means new ideas, but have not yet been combined for the purpose of creating a community-built archive and museum.

2.1   Web-Based Structure-from-Motion Services

Web-based SfM services such as 123D Catch (http://www.123dapp.com/catch) by Autodesk, Microsoft's Photosynth (http://photosynth.net/), ARC 3D [15,16] and the CMP SfM Web Service (http://ptak.felk.cvut.cz/sfmservice/) accept uploads directly from the user and return a 3D model; however, there is little sense of community with these systems. Users upload their photographs, which can be from any topic, and view their 3D models. While 123D Catch and Photosynth both host galleries featuring users' models, they are created for the sole purpose of viewing 3D models rather than learning about the underlying academic principles behind the objects they present. Other tools such as ARC 3D and CMP SfM Web Service are merely services to process the data, and do not have an online community. The Architectural Photogrammetry Network Tool for Education and Research (ARPENTEUR) [17] also provided a remote data processing service, but was a photogrammetry software package developed in Java that ran as a web applet. Unfortunately it is no longer available; the benefit of this approach was to allow users to access full features of the software, while the data was sent to a server for processing.

The Photo Tourism project [18–20] and Google Map's Photo Tours used photographs uploaded by multiple users to external photography sites – Flickr for Photo Tourism, and Picasa and Panoramio for Photo Tours. Photo Tourism developed into the Building Rome in a Day project [21], in which 150,000 photos uploaded to Flickr with the tag 'Rome' or 'Roma' were processed using the Bundler SfM software package in under 24 h. The intention was to capture the entire city, but the photographs were clustered around popular tourist attractions, such as the Colosseum and the Pantheon.

None of the web-based SfM services mentioned directly offer a community aspect, further than displaying examples of the models created by other users. Photo Tourism and Photo Tours scrape photographs from external photography sites which features social and community aspects, but do not host a digital community themselves.

2.2   Virtual Museums

The term *virtual museum* can be applied to many different aspects of engaging with a museum through the use of technology. While technology-based exhibits have existed in-situ inside museums for many years, a form of virtual museum that is rising in popularity is the virtual online collection. Virtual Museums and virtual online collections are fast becoming popular amongst physical museums as a method of displaying their collections to a wider audience [22]; examples include the Virtual Vermont Archaeology Museum [23], the Virtual Hampson Museum Project [24], the Herbert Virtual Museum [25] and the 3D Petrie Museum of Egyptian Archaeology (http://www.ucl.ac.uk/3dpetriemuseum).

An example of a virtual museum that exists inside a physical museum can be seen in two interactive applications that were developed for the Herbert Museum. For the first application, visitors use a mobile phone application to guide them round the museum and to access additional information about the artefacts. The second application is a serious game that allows the exploration of the priory undercroft of a Benedictine monastery in Coventry, UK. The game allows the user to interact with virtual characters and learn more about the life and daily activities of the monks. The virtual Vermont Archaeology Museum, the Virtual Hampson Museum Project, the 3D Petrie Museum and the Smithsonian X 3D provide examples of virtual online museums, where portions of the museum's collections have been digitised and made accessible online to view.

The Smithsonian Institute claims that a mere 1 % of their collections are on display in the museum galleries, and propose that their virtual museum project, the Smithsonian X 3D (http://3d.si.edu/), will be "the end of "do not touch"" and provide an opportunity to present the remaining unseen 99 % of their collections. The Smithsonian X 3D virtual online collection is powered by the Beta Smithsonian X 3D Explorer, developed by Autodesk. The software allows the virtual visitor to manipulate the model, change the position and colour of the light sources and open a split screen to view multiple models. It also features a virtual tape measure which allows measurement of the physical size of the real model and the creation of cross-sections. Virtual visitors are invited to take a tour of the model, where an information sidebar displays information about the scanned object or place; as the tour progresses, the model is automatically manipulated to accompany the information with relevant views. All of the models have been prepared for 3D printing and can be downloaded directly in Stereolithography (STL) format. The Smithsonian X 3D is also making associated data sets available to download; for example, for the model of a fossilised dolphin skull, a full-resolution model created from Computerised Tomography (CT) scan data and the original CT scan data can be downloaded.

Recent improvements in 3D graphics on the web have resulted in a rise in popularity of the presentation of online collections of heritage assets in virtual museums. The collections in these virtual museums are generally assets in the care of the presenting museum, and the models are built by museum curators and archaeologists; they do not involve the community or crowd-sourcing. Heritage-Together presents a collection of models from outdoor locations across Wales, created in collaboration with members of the public.

2.3   Community and Crowd-Sourced Archaeology

Archaeology has had a long history of both communities and crowd-sourced involvement in projects, though it has largely been through local excavations and community based field surveys. More recently, the popularity of online community archaeology has grown, with many new projects for collecting data from communities or using online volunteers. The popularity of such projects recently prompted the Arts and Humanities Research Council to fund eleven new projects under the call of "Digital Transformations in Community Research Co-Production".

History and a sense of heritage in Wales is often contained within the local communities in which it is born; in an attempt to collect and document some of these personal stories, the People's Collection Wales was created [26]. Through the project, people are invited to tell the stories of their heritage by uploading their own photographs, sound recordings, documents, videos and written stories to the People's Collection Wales website.

Cymru1900Wales (http://www.cymru1900wales.org/) is a project dedicated to digitising an Ordnance Survey map of Wales from 1900. Contributors work on an online map interface by finding any text on the map, creating a marker pin and typing the text they can see.

Focusing on crowd-sourcing work and crowd-funding for projects as opposed to gathering information from volunteers, MicroPasts [27] is a platform created specifically for volunteers and projects in heritage, history and archaeology applications. Volunteers can sign up to the platform to get involved with the projects on offer, while projects can join the platform to find volunteers from a relevant audience.

The Hillforts Atlas project (http://www.arch.ox.ac.uk/hillforts-atlas.html) by the School of Archaeology, Oxford University employs a more traditional method of collecting information by simply asking volunteers to complete a written survey form about the hillforts they visit, and return them via the Hillforts Atlas project website.

3   HeritageTogether.org

The primary challenge facing many of the projects discussed in Sects. 2.2 and 2.3 is the requirement to display models online in a way that allow users to can browse and interact with them. For museums putting their assets online, such as the Smithsonian, and digitising projects, such as MicroPasts, the models must be displayed in a robust and accessible way. This challenge is crucial to the HeritageTogether project, and is further complicated by the different potential needs of the users. Target audiences are both academic researchers and members of the general public – including general interest, education and amateur enthusiasm. This challenge led the HeritageTogether team to investigate several solutions, with several ways to display and provide access to the 3D models.

Familiarity with interfaces is another aspect that enables users to feel at-ease with the system. This led to the creation of a website with a tripartite design. First, there must be an area for users to gain information about the project. Second, an area for contributors to upload their images, to display the models and allow users to search through this visual data. Third, an area to engage

Fig. 2. The HeritageTogether website: the information hub (left), gallery (centre), and forum (right).

with the public and encourage discussions and thoughts; for instance, if one of the standing stones was damaged or difficult to access, this would provide a method to capture that information. To follow this design, the website (http://heritagetogether.org/), shown in Fig. 2, consists of three main areas:

1. The main body of the website – an 'information hub' through which material about the project can be disseminated;
2. A gallery area to manage image uploads and display the models produced; and
3. A forum to allow interaction between users and project team members.

As the project is being led from Wales, UK – the majority of the content for the website has been produced bilingually in English and Welsh. The website is, by default, displayed in the primary language of the user's browser, but can also be specified during the registration phase.

Users who wish to contribute to the project by uploading their photographs, or by participating in forum discussions and following the progress of the project must register as a member of the website. As the information hub, gallery and forum are managed by separate software packages, a bridge is used to ensure users are logged in to all sections of the website. To ensure ease of access to the users, it is possible to sign in using their Facebook credentials.

3.1 Information Hub

The information hub is managed using the WordPress content management system (CMS). The primary benefit of using a well-known CMS is that it provides management facilities that are familiar to both technical and non-technical administrators. This is valuable to the HeritageTogether project as this ease allows the opportunity to train volunteers to operate and manage the site after the completion of the academic project. The primary function of the information hub is to publish news of the project, disseminate guides on how to contribute to the project and advertise workshops and events organised by the community outreach team.

The information hub hosts a numbers of guides and resources, including an interactive map which guides users to the locations of 2,550 sites of interest. Location data for the sites has been provided by the Royal Commission on the Ancient and Historical Monuments of Wales' (RCAHMW) through the National Monuments Record of Wales (NMR). Clicking on location markers on the map provides a link to the site's record in the online interface to the NMR, Coflein (http://coflein.gov.uk/), using their unique identification number (National Public Record Number, or NPRN). Linking to archaeological data that is already available allows us to direct users to the official data record and prevents data being endlessly duplicated.

3.2   Gallery

Images taken by contributors and project team members are uploaded to the gallery section of the website. The gallery is driven by Coppermine Photo Gallery (http://coppermine-gallery.net/), an open source PHP web gallery software package which is managed using MySQL. The gallery is divided into three sections: the images taken by the project's survey team; images taken by community contributors; and the 3D models produced from the images. The images and models uploaded to the gallery can be rated and commented on by members, further enhancing the sense of community in the gallery. Coppermine provides a convenient way to manage the photographs and models online; it is widely used on the web and enables users to search through the photographs stored in it.

There are several methods for displaying 3D graphics through a web browser (for a review, see [28]). X3DOM [30], an open-source JavaScript framework which uses WebGL to integrate X3D and HTML5, has been used on the HeritageTogether gallery. There are several benefits for using X3DOM, most importantly it runs natively in any WebGL-enabled browser. This allows users to display the models on any architecture, without needing to download a browser plug-in or extension.

To enable fast viewing through the browser, the models have been greatly reduced in resolution, but employ high-quality textures to mask the low resolution model [29]; the models can be manipulated through basic zoom and rotation features using a mouse.

3.3   Forum

The forum section of the website allows users and contributors to interact with each other and the team. Users are invited to share their experiences of visiting sites, offer suggestions for the project and website, initiate discussions and ask questions of the archaeologists working on the project. The forum is powered by the Simple Machines Forum (http://www.simplemachines.org/) open source forum software package.

The forum has provided an excellent platform to enable the HeritageTogether team to talk to contributors and interested members of the general public. Feedback via the forum has enabled us to modify our website, produce guides for best practice, and collect information from contributors who have recently visited sites. Some contributors have provided information for others, such as descriptions of sites including location, condition, and accessibility.

4   The HeritageTogether Platform Work Flow

The automated SfM work flow fits into a larger work flow structure encompassing the entire HeritageTogether platform; the complete structure is illustrated in Fig. 3. In Fig. 3, each stage of the work flow is shown in a box, with smaller processes contained within. As data is used or created, it is indicated in a circle and differentiated from the main work flow using dashed lines.

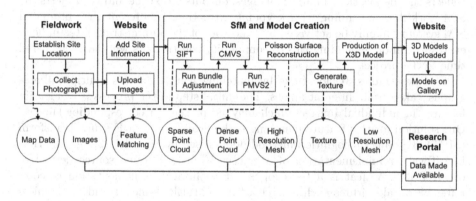

Fig. 3. Work flow for the HeritageTogether platform.

4.1   Fieldwork

The first stage of the work flow directly involves the community members of the project. The map section of the website supplies the locations of all of the sites we are currently trying to survey with the help of the community. Contributors can establish the location of a site either directly via the map data or using the directions link held within the site information. Once a site has been chosen, the contributor must ensure they have permission to access the site in question, and that it is easily accessible. The contributor can then visit the site and take photographs. Contributors, as members of the general public, are not expected to know how to photograph the site for model creation, therefore guidance on how best to take photographs is provided on the project website.

4.2   Uploading Images to the Website

When the location has been established and the site photographed, contributors are able to upload the images directly to the project's server and thus begin the SfM process. Once the image upload is complete, additional site information can be appended to the images, such as site location, condition, national grid reference and the sites unique identification number NPRN (National Public Records Number). This community collected information provides the images with added archaeological value, providing information about the current welfare and status of the heritage assets.

4.3   Structure-from-Motion and Model Creation

After the images have been loaded onto the gallery system and the database entries updated for the site, the automated SfM system is initialised. The system is activated by selecting the album containing the images for the site of interest and clicking the SfM button. This button activates a batch script process which collects the file locations of all the images, outputs a text file and then starts the SfM work flow, beginning with keypoint extraction. At present the automated SfM system can only be activated by a member of the administration team, however, we plan on expanding this to community contributors who have dedicated time to the project.

SfM determines 3D locations by matching features across multiple photographs, taken from different angles. The initial step in the process is to identify features in individual images which may be present in corresponding images. One solution for this feature matching is the Scale Invariant Feature Transform (SIFT) [31] object recognition method popularised by Snavely [19,20]. The HeritageTogether implementation of SfM uses VLfeat, an open source derivative of SIFT [32]. VLfeat is a C++ open source library implementation of computer vision algorithms such as HOG, SIFT, MSER, k-means and hierarchical k-means. This implementation of SIFT identifies features in each image by scaling, rotating, and identifying variations between the images such as changes in illumination conditions and camera viewpoint. Keypoints in the images are automatically identified and feature descriptors created.

Once the keypoint identification and descriptor assignment are complete, a sparse bundle adjustment system [19,20] is used to estimate camera pose and extract a sparse point cloud (an example is shown in Fig. 4).

Features that are in motion within the area of interest and are only present in a small number of images, will be automatically removed from the final 3D reconstruction. Although keypoints for these objects are created, as they are not present in a number of overlapping images and thus not suitable for the scene reconstruction they are automatically filtered from the final 3D scene [33].

To enhance the sparse data, the Clustering View for Multi-View Stereo (CMVS) [33,34] and Patch-based Multi-View Stereo (PMVS2) [33] algorithms are used sequentially to produce a dense point-cloud (see Fig. 4). CMVS decomposes the sparse point cloud into a manageable set of image clusters. PMVS

Fig. 4. The sparse point cloud (left), dense point cloud (centre), and untextured mesh (right) generated for Bodowyr Burial Chamber.

then reconstructs the 3D structure of the object of interest in the images, producing a set of oriented points where both the position and the surface normal are estimated.

Once the dense point-cloud has been created, a 3D mesh is generated. In order to produce a mesh, the areas between each of the dense points need to be triangulated. This can be achieved by running a point-to-mesh surface reconstruction, in this case we utilise Kazhdan et al.'s Poisson Surface Reconstruction for the calculation [35]. Kazhdan et al.'s algorithm considers all the points at once without utilising a bounding interval hierarchy, and is therefore resilient to noise in the data; this makes it ideal for a point-cloud dataset produced using SfM (an example can be seen in Fig. 4).

A texture is produced using a Mutual Information filter [36]. Using the estimated photograph positions from the SfM process, the texture is created through mosaicing or averaging all the digital image based on the camera locations producing a high quality texture.

Once a high resolution mesh has been generated, a low resolution version of the mesh must be created for display on the website. The high resolution mesh is decimated to approximately 8,000 vertices using Quadric Edge Collapse Decimation [37] and saved in the X3D file format. The Quadric Edge Collapse Decimation produces an optimised mesh by determining the most important edges of the mesh and reducing the polygons between them, and tries to keep the shape of the original model intact. The high resolution texture is mapped over the mesh, giving it a more aesthetically pleasing final output (Fig. 1 is an example of this).

The process of creating a model is often successful without any external intervention; Poisson Surface Reconstruction is robust against noise and successfully removes most disconnected blobs. Before the final model is uploaded to the website it is inspected by a project team member to verify any noise has been successfully removed. If this is not the case, then they may perform some manual work to remove the remaining noise. For some site photographs, masking may be required to prevent noisy data becoming part of the model – for example, clouds above a tall monument may be interpreted by SfM as being connected to the top of the monument.

5   Methods to Use and Access the Model Data

Once the model data has been created there are three alternative methods to access the data: a lightbox gallery, a digital archive and a virtual museum. Each of the three methods provide a different approach to the data, benefiting a different task or purpose.

The lightbox gallery offers a quick view of the models, while also allowing the user to explore each individual model thoroughly and view it in more detail. A novice user can quickly load and view the model in a casual analysis, while an expert user can scrutinize the model for a detailed examination.

The digital archive offers long-term storage of the data and access to the data not displayed online. The archive has been implemented with an open source framework, which allows the users and developers to access the project data through permanent links and the framework API. The data archive provides a long-term solution for making the data remotely accessible and available to other digital archives (such as the Archaeology Data Service (ADS, http://archaeologydataservice.ac.uk/), developers and researchers who can add value to the data by using it and producing subsequent data, and the community who co-created the data.

The virtual museum presents the data using the metaphor of a museum containing items of historical interest. The users can wander through the museum and compare models in a familiar setting, and are more likely to explore a number of models here than through the gallery where they are required to select individual models for viewing. Placing the models in view of the visitor encourages them to take more time to look around, where interesting models may get their attention and inspire them to view additional information that they would not have in the lightbox gallery.

The following three sections will describe each of the methods in detail: Sect. 5.1 for the lightbox gallery, Sect. 5.2 for the digital archive and Sect. 5.3 for the virtual museum.

5.1   A Lightbox Gallery

Once the X3D models have been produced, they can be directly uploaded to the website gallery system. Each of the pages within the gallery accesses the X3DOM [30] JavaScript framework directly on the X3DOM website, allowing the interpretation of the X3D files in any WebGL-enabled browser. The use of X3DOM server-side allows the gallery to display the models without requiring the user to download any extra software or plug-ins client-side; an example can be seen in Fig. 5. The low resolution models are small – typically under 1 megabyte in size – making them quickly accessible to most users.

The models each appear on an individual basis, where each model can be examined in detail. The models are shown in a lightbox style, where they are placed at the centre of an otherwise empty X3D scene under even lighting conditions and without shading. The models appear to have shading as a result of the real shade being captured in the photographs, and during the texture creation

Fig. 5. The model of a standing stone displayed using X3DOM in the gallery interface.

process the shade from the original images is baked into the texture. This does result in a loss of colour information in the shaded areas of the site, but is not a viable requirement in a crowd-sourcing project for outdoor subjects.

Manipulating the models by moving, rotating, and zooming with the mouse allows the user to examine the model in detail. Below the model is a table holding information about the site, and includes a link to download the X3D file and a credit to the contributing photographer(s) with a link to the original photographs used to create the model. Crediting the community with their involvement in creating the models maintains a sense of co-production and involvement; community members can see the result of their contributions directly.

5.2   A Digital Archive

The final stage of the HeritageTogether platform work flow is the Research Portal. The Research Portal (http://heritagetogether.org/research, see Fig. 6) is an archive containing the data produced throughout the project; it is part of the main HeritageTogether website and is openly accessible to everyone.

Archaeology has slowly been going through an information revolution, affecting the ways in which it is researched and published. These changes have come about as a result of an idea: being 'open'. Open source software, open access to archaeological data and open ethics. 'Open' has become an increasingly

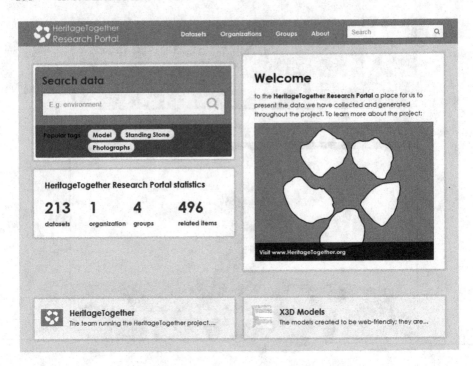

Fig. 6. The front page of the Research Portal, where data from the HeritageTogether project is still being uploaded.

attractive thing to be; from research, to corporations and governments. Openness gives an air of transparency, ideas of public accountability and scientific repeatability, and as such provides a buzzword for perceived public good [38].

The HeritageTogether project is no different, following established open-access concepts throughout every stage of the research process. The research data produced has been made available for the digital community to use, re-analyse and re-interpret. This 'openness' has provided the general public, project contributors and the research community unprecedented access to an ongoing research project.

Data uploaded to the Research Portal includes the original images provided by contributors, the final models created, and data produced during the creation of the models. Each site recorded has three main entries, and may have additional entries if subsequent models have been created:

– *Site photographs*: all the images of a site, zipped per contributor and session.
– *Original model data*: a selection of data produced during the initial model creation, including:
  • the original high resolution model in Wavefront Object (Obj) format with the texture and material (Mtl) file,
  • a low resolution model in Obj format with texture and Mtl, and
  • a dense point cloud in Obj format.

– *X3D model data*: the X3D file and texture uploaded to the gallery.

The Research Portal was built using the Comprehensive Knowledge Archive Network (CKAN, http://ckan.org/), an open source data archiving system. The HeritageTogether project has collected data for over 80 sites so far, and is hosting a new and unique dataset created by the general public. All of the data on the Research Portal is available for any individual to download and use for non-commercial purposes under the Creative Commons Attribution-Non Commercial 4.0 International License (CC BY-NC 4.0), and we encourage the use of the dataset for further research.

5.3   A Virtual Museum

The gallery system already provides a lightbox style approach to viewing the models that have been created – models are placed in an evenly-lit and otherwise empty scene for easy manipulation and investigation. Many of the virtual museums in Sect. 2.2 employ the same approach, where each individual model can be systematically examined. Such systems do not allow for the comparison of the models as they place the model in an isolated environment where the individual site lose their original context, not only in terms of their original location and surrounding environment, but also their physical size and relationship to other monuments in the environment. Additional information can be provided in the form of images, descriptions and systems of conveying the real size of the objects using 'virtual tape measures' where two points can be selected on the model to get an integer describing the equivalent measurement in reality.

The objects displayed in virtual museums are created by professionals working in the equivalent real museum, digitising their collections. The collection of models created by the HeritageTogether project has allowed the creation of a virtual museum where the collection within has been contributed by our digital community (see Fig. 7). The HeritageTogether project is focused on heritage assets which cannot be removed from their original environment, and thus the collection can not be assembled in this way in reality.

The virtual museum system is available through the website (http://heritagetogether.org/?page_id=2913), and was built using the same 3D model presentation system as the other sections of the site: X3D files and the X3DOM plug-in. Again, use of the X3DOM plug-in server-side means that no client-side downloads are required, and the low-resolutions models are used to provide an experience with as little latency as possible to the user.

The museum can be navigated entirely with the mouse using X3D's walking movement; a left click moves the user forward, while a right click moves them backwards, while moving the mouse around will rotate the view. The layout of the virtual museum is designed to replicate a gallery space with objects around the outside wall of the area. Each site is presented on a green plinth to make the sites easily distinguishable, with a standard one metre scaling bar alongside for a quick size comparison and one of the original site images to provide an

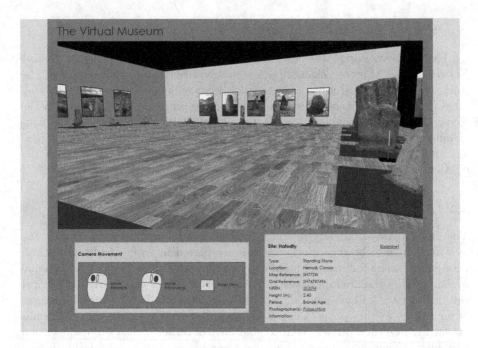

Fig. 7. The virtual museum containing a number of models.

environmental context (see Fig. 8). Clicking on a model moves the user to a pre-defined viewpoint in front of the model, then populates the table below with information about the site. The information table also provides the user with several links to additional related content:

- the model in the gallery, allowing closer and isolated examination in the light-box view;
- the site's entry in the RCAHMW online database; and
- the original images contributed by the community.

Members of the community are credited for their contribution of images to models, maintaining a sense of collaboration and communal ownership over the data. Populating a virtual exhibition hall with community-created content demonstrates the collective achievement of the HeritageTogether community.

An initial version of the virtual museum has been created and populated with a selection of monuments. The selection was based upon those which could be scaled to real measurements made by archaeologists available through the NMR data on Coflein. More models can be introduced to the museum as new sites or more data are added to the dataset. The virtual museum provides an accessible, easy to navigate viewing platform for the models, and partially re-contextualises them through displaying images of their original environment and providing a sense of real-world scale. It also allows the comparison of the different shapes and sizes of the stones chosen to become the megaliths by placing them in a

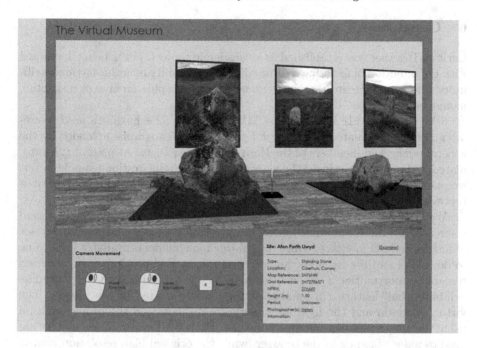

Fig. 8. Examining one of the models up close navigates the user to a pre-defined viewpoint, then provides site information on the table below and an image of the real site in its original environment.

single room; in reality, these sites are spread across Wales, and many of these sites are tens of miles apart if not more.

As more sites are added to the virtual museum, it will be necessary to create a dynamic gallery to display all of the content. The size of the museum may need to grow or shrink in size dynamically depending up the number of models selected. Users may be able to select the models appearing in the gallery by selecting a site type (e.g. standing stone, stone circle), a location of interest (models from a single county or region of Wales), period in history, or even models created by an individual community member.

The pre-determined viewpoints offer a fast way for the user to move across the room to a model of interest and position them in front of the model, but it is a very simplistic method of viewing which does not guide the user around the museum. Offering a guided route around the museum may further increase the user's enjoyment of visiting the virtual museum by allowing them to relax and follow a pre-determined walking path until they found a model which they wished to spend more time examining [39]. The walkthrough mode and video content generation system proposed by Hayashi et al. [39] would afford the users a further-enhanced method of exploring the models.

6 Conclusion

HeritageTogether was established as an academic project, but is being developed with the intention of fostering a future digital community of enthusiastic contributors who can co-create the most extensive photographic archive of megalithic monuments in Wales, UK.

SfM – through SIFT, Bundler, CMVS and PMVS2 – has been used to create an online automated work flow for processing photographs uploaded by the general public and members of the HeritageTogether team. At present the automated SfM system is activated by a member of the administration team, however, we plan on expending this responsibility to community members and contributors who have dedicated time to the project.

We have published an extensive digital archive of the data contributed and co-created by the community during the project. This new and unique dataset of images and 3D models of Welsh megalithic monuments is available for anyone to download and use for non-commercial purposes, and provides many exciting research opportunities. One such example is our virtual museum – an online exhibition hall featuring a number of the models created in the project. The virtual museum and the lightbox gallery are displayed on the project website using the open source JavaScript framework X3DOM; low-resolution models are used to reduce latency in the browser, while the original high resolution models are available through the Research Portal archive.

The web platform has been active for 22 months at the time of writing, in which time it has attracted a number of contributors who have uploaded over 17,000 photographs to the website, allowing the creation of over 90 models of different megalithic monuments, in Wales and beyond.

Acknowledgment. We acknowledge the AHRC (UK) AH/L007916/1 for funding "co-production of alternative views of lost heritage of Gwynedd" (http://heritagetogether.org), and members of our research team and digital community for their continued involvement in this research.

References

1. Linder, W.: Digital Photogrammetry: A Practical Course, 3rd edn. Springer, Heidelberg (2009)
2. McGlone, J.C.: Manual of Photogrammetry, 6th edn. American Society for Photogrammetry and Remote Sensing, Bethesda (2013)
3. Yilmaz, H., Yakar, M., Gulec, S., Dulgerler, O.: Importance of digital close-range photogrammetry in documentation of cultural heritage. J. Cult. Herit. **8**, 428–433 (2007)
4. Kjellman, E.: From 2D to 3D: A Photogrammetric Revolution in Archaeology?. University of Tromsø, Norway (2012)
5. Grussenmeyer, P., Yasmine, J.: Photogrammetry for the preparation of archaeological excavation. a 3D restitution according to modern and archive images of Beaufort Castle landscape (Lebanon). In: International Society Photogrammetry, pp. 809–814 (2004)

6. De Reu, J., De Smedt, P., Herremans, D., Van Meirvenne, M., Laloo, P., De Clercq, W.: On introducing an image-based 3D reconstruction method in archæological excavation practice. J. Archaeol. Sci. **41**, 251–262 (2014)

7. Bitelli, G., Girelli, V.A., Remondino, F., Vittuari, L.: Surface modelling of complex archaelogical structures by digital close-range photogrammetry. Brit. Archaeol. Rep. In. **1568**, 321–327 (2006)

8. Ducke, B., Score, D., Reeves, J.: Multiview 3D reconstruction of the archaeological site at Weymouth from image series. Comput. Graph. **35**, 375–382 (2011)

9. Green, S., Bevan, A., Shapland, M.: A comparative assessment of structure from motion methods for archaeological research. J. Archaeol. Sci. **46**, 173–181 (2014)

10. Fujii, Y., Fodde, E., Watanabe, K., Murakami, K.: Digital photogrammetry for the documentation of structural damage in earthen archaeological sites: the case of Ajina Tepa. Tajikistan. Eng. Geol. **105**, 124–133 (2009)

11. Mudge, M., Schroer, C., Earl, G., Martinez, K., Pagi, H., Toler-Franklin, C., Rusinkiewicz, S., Palma, G., Wachowiak, M., Ashley, M., Matthews, N., Noble, T., Dellepiane, M.: Principles and practices of robust, photography-based digital imaging techniques for museums. In: Artusi, A., Joly, M., Lucet, G., Pitzalis, D., Ribes, A. (eds.) International Symposium on Virtual Reality, Archaeology and Cultural Heritage (VAST), pp. 111–137. The Eurographics Association (2010)

12. Miles, H.C., Wilson, A.T., Labrosse, F., Tiddeman, B., Griffiths, S., Edwards, B., Ritsos, P.D., Mearman, J.W., Möller, K., Karl, R., Roberts, J.C.: Alternative representations of 3D-reconstructed heritage data. ACM J. Comput. Cult. Herit. **9**(1), 1–18 (2015)

13. Koenderink, J.J., van Doorn, A.J.: Affine structure from motion. J. Opt. Soc. Am. **8**, 377–385 (1991)

14. Westoby, M., Brasington, J., Glasser, N., Hambrey, M., Reynolds, J.: 'Structure-from-Motion' photogrammetry: a low-cost, effective tool for geoscience applications. Geomorphology **179**, 300–314 (2012)

15. Vergauwen, M., Van Gool, L.: Web-based 3D reconstruction service. Mach. vision Appl. **17**, 411–426 (2006)

16. Van Gool, L., Tingdahl, D.: A public system for image based 3D model generation. In: Gagalowicz, A., Philips, W. (eds.) MIRAGE 2011. LNCS, vol. 6930, pp. 262–273. Springer, Heidelberg (2011)

17. Grussenmeyer, P., Drap, P., Gaillard, G,: ARPENTEUR 3.0: recent developments in web based photogrammetry. ISPRS Archives, vol. XXXIV, part 6 (2002)

18. Snavely, N., Seitz, S.M., Szeliski, R.: Photo tourism: exploring photo collections in 3D. ACM T. Graphic **25**, 835–846 (2006)

19. Snavely, N., Garg, R., Seitz, S.M., Szeliski, R.: Finding paths through the world's photos. ACM T. Graphic **27**, 11–21 (2008)

20. Snavely, N., Seitz, S.M., Szeliski, R.: Modeling the world from internet photo collections. Int. J. Comput. Vision **80**, 189–210 (2008)

21. Agarwal, S., Furukawa, Y., Snavely, N., Simon, I., Curless, B., Seitz, S.M., Szeliski, R.: Building Rome in a day. Commun. ACM **54**, 105–112 (2011)

22. Carrozzino, M., Bruno, N., Bergamasco, M.: Designing interaction metaphors for web3D cultural dissemination. J. Cult. Herit. **14**, 146–155 (2013)

23. Peebles, G.: Sharing data, swapping knowledge, and building community: moving archaeology from deep storage into the public eye through the internet. In: International Conference on Computer Applications and Quantitative Methods in Archaeology (CAA). CAA (2009)

24. Payne, A., Cole, K.: Designing the next generation virtual museum: making 3D artifacts available for viewing and download. In: International Conference on Computer Applications and Quantitative Methods in Archaeology (CAA). CAA (2009)
25. Petridis, P., Dunwell, I., Liarokapis, F., Constantinou, G., Arnab, S., de Freitas, S., Hendrix, M.: The herbert virtual museum. J. Electr. Comput. Eng. **2013**, 1–8 (2013)
26. Tedd, L.A.: People's collection wales: online access to the heritage of wales from museums, archives and libraries. Program **45**, 333–345 (2011)
27. Bonacchi, C., Bevan, A., Pett, D., Keinan-Schoonbaert, A.: Developing crowd- and community-fuelled archaeological research. Early results from the MicroPasts project. In: International Conference on Computer Applications and Quantitative Methods in Archaeology (CAA). CAA (2014)
28. Evans, A., Romeo, M., Bahrehmand, A., Agenjo, J., Blat, J.: 3D graphics on the web: a survey. Comput. Graph. **41**, 43–61 (2014)
29. Rushmeier, H.E., Rogowitz, B.E., Piatko, C.: Perceptual issues in substituting texture for geometry. In: Rogowitz, B.E., Pappas, T.N. (eds.) Human Vision and Electronic Imaging V, vol. 3959, pp. 372–383. SPIE (2000)
30. Behr, J., Eschler, P., Jung, Y., Zöllner, M.: X3DOM: a DOM-based HTML5/X3D integration model. In: Spencer, S.N. (ed.) ACM International Conference on 3D Web Technology (Web3D), pp. 127–135. ACM Press, New York (2009)
31. Lowe, D.G.: Object recognition from local scale-invariant features. In: IEEE International Conference on Computer Vision (ICCV), pp. 1150–1157. IEEE (1999)
32. Vedaldi, A., Fulkerson, B.: VLFeat: an open and portable library of computer vision algorithms. In: del Bimbo, A., Chang, S. (eds.) ACM International Conference on Multimedia (MM), pp. 1469–1472. ACM Press, New York (2010)
33. Lazebnik, S., Furukawa, Y., Ponce, J.: Projective visual hulls. Int. J. Comput. Vis. **74**, 137–165 (2007)
34. Furukawa, Y., Curless, B., Seitz, S.M., Szeliski, R.: Towards internet-scale multi-view stereo. In: IEEE Conference on Computer Vision and Pattern Recognition (CVPR), pp. 1434–1441. IEEE (2010)
35. Kazhdan, M., Bolitho, M., Hoppe, H.: Poisson surface reconstruction. In: Polthier, K., Sheffer, A. (eds.) Eurographics Symposium on Geometry Processing (SGP), pp. 61–70. Eurographics Association (2006)
36. Corsini, M., Dellepiane, M., Ponchio, F., Scopigno, R.: Image-to-geometry registration: a mutual information method exploiting illumination-related geometric properties. In: Computer Graphics Forum, vol. 28, pp. 1755–1764. Wiley-Blackwell (2009)
37. Garland, M., Heckbert, P.S.: Surface simplification using quadric error metrics. In: Owen, G.S., Whitted, T., Mones-Hattal, B. (eds.) 24th Annual Conference on Computer Graphics and Interactive Techniques (SIGGRAPH), pp. 209–21. ACM Press, New York (1997)
38. Lake, M.: Open archaeology. World Archaeol. **44**, 471–478 (2012)
39. Hayashi, M., Bachelder, S., Nakajima, M., Iguchi, A.: A new virtual museum equipped with automatic video content generator. In: Iglesias, A., Shinya, M., Galvez-Tomida, A. (eds.) International Conference on Cyberworlds (CW), pp. 377–383. IEEE (2014)

Identifying Users from Online Interactions in Twitter

Madeena Sultana$^{(\boxtimes)}$, Padma Polash Paul, and Marina Gavrilova

Department of Computer Science, University of Calgary,
2500 University DR NW, Calgary, Canada
{msdeena, pppaul, mgavrilo}@ucalgary.ca

Abstract. In recent years, the mass growth of online social networks has introduced a completely new platform of analyzing human behavior. Human interactions via online social networks leave big trails of behavioral footprints, which have been investigated by many researchers for the purpose of targeted advertising and business. However, analysis of such online interactions is rarely seen for user identification. The main objective of this paper is to analyze individuals' online interactions as biometric information. In this paper, we investigated how online interactions retain behavioral characteristics of users and how consistent they are over time. For this purpose, we proposed a novel method of identifying users from online interactions in Twitter. Identification performance has been evaluated on a database of 50 Twitter users over five different time periods. We obtained very promising results from experimentation, which demonstrate the potential of online interactions in aiding the authentication process of social network users'.

Keywords: Social behavioral biometrics · Online social networks · Cyber security · Person authentication · Biometric recognition · Knowledge discovery · User profiling

1 Introduction

User identification is the key requirement for secured access of information and service. The traditional user authentication mechanisms are based on PIN, Passwords, or identity cards. However, reports on security of traditional identification systems point out how easy it is nowadays to break majority of "strong" passwords or PINs [5–7]. Moreover, passwords, PINs, or identity cards can easily be shared, stolen, or forgotten. Biometric-based user identification systems can overcome such drawbacks by using physiological or behavioral characteristics of individuals. Physiological characteristics such as face, fingerprints, iris etc. and behavioral characteristics such as voice, gait, signature etc. cannot be shared, stolen or forgotten as well as quite difficult to change or forge. Although behavioral biometrics are more volatile to changes one undergoes through the life time, they offer advantages of being dynamic, non-intrusive and cost effective over physiological biometrics [3, 4]. Behavioral biometrics are difficult to fake or imitate because of its dynamic nature. For instance, impersonating a person's walking style or gait is way more difficult than creating a fake fingerprint. For such advantages,

© Springer-Verlag Berlin Heidelberg 2016
M.L. Gavrilova et al. (Eds.): Trans. on Comput. Sci. XXVI, LNCS 9550, pp. 111–124, 2016.
DOI: 10.1007/978-3-662-49247-5_7

behavioral biometrics are becoming a popular alternative to well-established physio-logical biometrics in many authentication applications to reduce security threats, espe-cially in the cyberworld [1–3]. In [8], we introduced a novel biometric trait called Social Behavioral Biometrics (SBB), which is based on the hypothesis that a person can be identified from social activities and interactions. At present, with the advent of social online social networks, human behavior has been expanded in virtual world. In [9], we identified online social media as the source of social behavioral biometrics. This paper validates the idea by identifying behavioral patterns in online interaction of users, eval-uate their performance for user identification. In other words, our aim is to investigate the underlying patterns of user interactions in social networking platforms and evaluate their discriminability for being used in identification purpose.

The increasing popularity of social networking websites such as Facebook, Twitter, Myspace, LinkedIn, Flickr, etc. has turned them to massive sources of 'big data", which offer new opportunities of studying human behaviors from different perspectives. In fact, they are considered as one of the most valuable, diversified, and dynamic repository of information which can avail data from health sector to targeted adver-tising [10]. Human behavior and social relationships via social networking websites have been studied by many researchers for many different applications such as targeted marketing, recommendation systems, prediction of stock market, and so on. Twitter is one of the most studied social networking website from diverse fields of research. Twitter is a platform, which enables users to interact with other users through con-nections. According to a statistical report [11], Twitter has around 5.5 billion of active registered users who produces 58 million tweets per day and 9,100 tweets per second. In addition, 135,000 new users are signing up to twitter every day. This statistics demonstrates that billions of users nowadays are communicating to each other through Twitter. In Twitter, users communicate by posting real time micro-blogs called Tweets. Unlike other mediums, tweets are restricted to 140 characters of length. Despite lim-itation of size, tweets are rich sources of information about the user and his commu-nicative behavior. Tweets not only comprise of texts but also contain interactions to other users or websites such as replies, retweets, URLs etc. Therefore, we categorize tweets into two types: textual and interactive. Textual parts are sometimes called original tweets [8] that are produced by the users targeting the general audience. Interactive tweets possess some kind of communicative materials such as replies, retweets, URLs, and hashtags. Replies are tweets intended to another specific user. Replies are directed to a specific user by appending @ symbol at the beginning of the intended user name (e.g. @user_abc). The main difference between reply and original tweets is - replies are intended to a specific user whereas original tweets are more like broadcasting messages to all instead of addressing a particular user. Replies could be very different from original tweets since a person may alter their writing style when addressing another person [12]. Retweets are tweets, originally written by another user but posted or shared by the user in his/her timeline. It is an act of sharing another user's tweets to all of the followers of a user [13]. Another distinctive feature of tweets is the hashtags. Hashtags are shorthand convention adopted by Twitter users for assigning their posts to a wider corpus of messages on the same topic [14]. We have considered hashtags as an interactive feature of a user to a wider corpus. Later in this paper, we would show how personal topics of interest could be explored by analyzing hashtags.

The last interactive features we identified in tweets is shared URLs. Users can direct his followers to a news article, a blog post, related websites, videos, or photographs by sharing the URLs. In this paper, we will investigate whether it is possible to identify some behavioral patterns from such interactive data of Twitter users. Therefore, the main contribution of this paper is to identify some behavioral features from interactive Twitter data of users and formulating a framework for user identification by matching such behavioral patterns. We would extend our study to analyze the impact of feature matching in different time intervals in order to evaluate how consistent such behavioral characteristics are.

2 Literature Review

The security in cyberworld is important as in the real world [4, 15]. In some cases, it is more crucial since breaching the security in cyberspace may jeopardize our life beyond monetary loss. Therefore, person authentication plays an important role in fortifying the security of virtual world. Behavioural biometrics are more popular for person authentication in virtual world rather than in the real world. Many new behavioral biometrics have been proposed within the last few years. Some state-of-the-art works are described below to analyze the current trend of the behavioral biometric research.

In 2011, mouse dynamics have been studied as behavioral biometrics by Jorgensen and Yu [16]. Instead of ordinary static authentication, keystroke dynamics have been utilized for continuous authentication by Bours [17] in 2012. In this work, real time typing pattern of the user is continuously matched with the stored template, which is referred as continuous authentication. Once the matching score or trust level decreases below a certain threshold, there is a possibility of the system of being locked. Frank et al. [18] identified 30 behavioral touch features from raw touchscreen logs of smartphones and named these novel biometric features as Touchalytics. This study demonstrates that different users have distinct pattern of navigation and this behavioral patterns exhibit consistency over time. Guo et al. [19] explored that person can be identified by his/her own style of 'handshaking'. Handshaking is a specific set of human actions, needed to unlock the screen of the smartphone of a user. The authors of [19] observed unique, stable, and distinguishable idiosyncratic patterns in handshaking behaviors of users and used them to authenticate users of their smartphones. In [20], Feng et al. identified biometric characteristics in mobile device picking-up motion. A novel behavioral biometric called hobby driven biometric has been introduced by Jiang et al. [21]. In this work, a comprehensive study on habitual behaviors driven by hobbies is presented. Considering the decorating and tidying style of a room as hobby-driven behavior, the authors conducted a survey on 225 people of different ages and professions. They observed unique and steady characteristics based on style, color, position, and habitual operating order of the object for different persons. This study demonstrates that a person's own choice and habits possess enough discriminability to act as behavioral biometric features. Another study on person's web browsing style has been conducted by Olejnik and Castelluccia [22]. The authors investigated web browsing data of 4,578 users and revealed idiosyncratic patterns of browsing style. The authors claimed that person authentication, anomaly, and fraud detections etc.

would be the potential applications of their browsing style-based behavioral biometric trait. A multimodal behavioral biometric system by combining inputs from keyboard, mouse, writing sample, and web browsing history at decision level has been proposed by Fridman et al. [23]. Another state-of-the-art work by Bailey et al. [24] presents a multimodal behavioral system combining data from keyboard, mouse, and Graphical User Interface (GUI) interactions. Bailey et al. [24] experimented fusion at feature and decision level, where decision level fusion obtained higher recognition performance than feature level fusion.

From the above summary, it is pertinent that idiosyncratic patterns can be found in every aspect of human actions ranging from walking style in real world to browsing style in cyberworld. Therefore, human activities on online social networking platforms should have some patterns for being used as biometric features for person authentication. This has motivated us to study the users' social interactions in Twitter to explore social behavioral biometric features for person identification.

3   Proposed Method

In this paper, we are interested to reveal behavioral characteristics from user interactions via Twitter. Our assumption here is each individual has his own pattern of interactions in social networks such as he has his own set of friends whom he contact regularly, some topics of interests, some preferred websites and so on. Therefore, mining interaction-based data of individuals may reveal the very personal characteristics of a user, which can eventually be used as personal signature. In this paper, we proposed a framework to identify Twitter users based on their dynamic communication behavior rather than analyzing of their static information. Our proposed methodology has the following steps:

(i)   Acquire tweets from selected user profiles.
(ii) Extract interactive data such as replies, retweets, hashtags, and URLs from tweets.
(iii) Analyze acquired social data to explore social behavioral biometric features.
(iv) Apply matching techniques on training and test set for person authentication.

Figure 1 shows a basic block diagram of the proposed method. The following subsections contain detailed description of the aforementioned steps.

3.1   Data Acquisition

We collected tweets of 50 users over a period of more than four months. Initially, 300 active users from Twitter are selected on a random basis who uses English for writing micro-blogs or tweets. Among them, the most prolific 50 users are identified who produces more than 100 tweets per week on average. We have divided our data collection period into five sessions separated by at least 20 days interval to avoid possible overlapping in data. In this paper, we denote session as S_i where $i = 1, 2, 3, 4, 5$. In every session, approximately 200 tweets of each user are collected and stored.

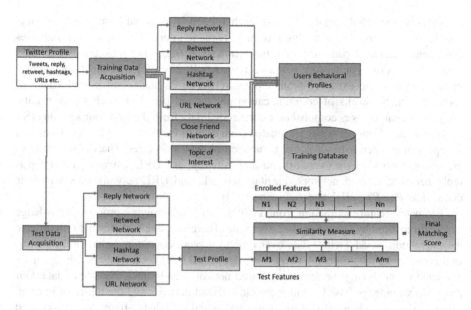

Fig. 1. Block diagram of the proposed framework of Twitter user identification using online behavioral profile.

However, the collected data is unbalanced due to limitation of Twitter API. Our collected dataset includes retweets, replies, hashtags, and URLs along with texts.

Since our goal is to identify behavioral pattern in dynamic communication of users, we considered the interactive or communicative data such as replies, retweets, URLs, and hashtags. In tweets, usually replies are preceded by @, retweets are preceded by RT, and hashtags are preceded by # symbol. Individuals also post URL(s) to share more information with other users that they could not accommodated in timelines. The key challenge for framing person authentication from social interactive data is the selection of feature set that best describes the behavioral pattern of users. For this purpose, retweets, replies, hashtags, and URLs are extracted from the dataset of each user from every session. We also extracted some statistics such as number of tweets, retweets, retweeted persons, replies, replied persons, URLs, distinct URLs, hashtags, and distinct hashtags per week. Unlike other biometric traits, the behavioral characteristics are not readily available in social data. Therefore, social data is needed to be analyzed to extract behavioral features. The feature extraction technique is described in the following subsection.

3.2 Feature Extraction

The communication-based features from Twitter data are analyzed in this paper. Social data of each session is analyzed to discover distinguishable personal characteristics of users. Analysis has been done in two steps.

Initially, extracted social data from each session is analyzed based on frequency. The reason for frequency analysis is that frequent interactions of a user indicates consistent behavioral pattern. For instance, if user A frequently retweets user B, then user A has a strong preference of retweeting user B. Therefore, frequent social communicative data are extracted from replies, retweets, hashtags, and posted URLs of each session. Networks of communication are formed based on such frequent data. Frequency analysis is accomplished on the social data from the first four sessions (S_1, S_2, S_3, and S_4). Four networks are created from each of the data set of S_1, S_2, S_3, and S_4 to represent frequency-based social behavioral biometric features. These four networks are reply network, retweet network, hashtag network, and URL network. In this paper, reply network, retweet network, hashtag network, and URL network of session i is denoted as R_{Si}, RT_{Si}, H_{Si}, and L_{Si}, respectively.

Biometric feature extraction from Twitter data is an evolving process. Knowledge can be discovered by analyzing data over time. Therefore, our next step is to investigate the interaction-based Twitter data over time to explore consistent behavioral patterns. In this paper, we are proposing two knowledge-based behavioral features, which can be extracted by analyzing the frequency-based networks and interactive social data. Our proposed knowledge-based features are close friend network and the topics of interest. Figure 2 shows the hierarchy of frequency-based and knowledge-based features created from social data of four sessions.

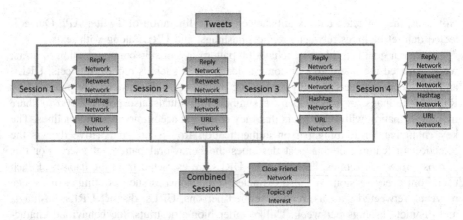

Fig. 2. Hierarchy of frequency-based and knowledge-based features from first four sessions.

The proposed frequency-based and knowledge-based behavioral features are explained hereafter.

- **Reply Network:** Reply network is generated by analyzing the replies of a specific user in Twitter. In this network, nodes are the user him/herself and the other users he/she replies. The process includes three major steps: listing all persons that the user replied to, counting the replies to each person, and finally applying a threshold. A threshold is applied on the counts of the replies for each individual the user replied to, since we are interested to include persons in the network whom the user replies frequently. A person is added to the reply network if and only if the count of reply is greater than a certain threshold. This network explores a short list of friends/persons whom the user communicates the most frequently.

- **Retweet Network:** A retweet network is created similarly to the reply network to find the most frequent retweeted persons in the user's timeline. However, person's retweeting behavior is more likely to be changed over time. For our study, we categorized retweets based on the direction: retweeting and retweeted. Retweeting refers that a person is posting tweets of other users in his/her timeline. On the other hand, retweeted means the person's tweet is retweeted by some other users or acquaintances. Both are related to the proposed retweet network with the differences of direction only. Based on the direction of the retweets two separate networks are constructed. We investigated both ways retweets to explore some consistency of the users retweeting behavior. For this purpose, we listed all the persons who are present in both retweeted and retweeting network for each session. The idea is, if user A retweets B then we also investigated whether B retweets A. This relation strengthens the retweeting relationship among A and B that is less likely of being random. Finally, retweet network is constructed using frequent items of retweeting network and common items of retweeted and retweeting networks.
- **Hashtag Network:** A hashtag network is created similarly to reply network. In this network, all hashtags that qualify over a certain threshold are added as nodes in the network. However, hashtag network should never be used as a static feature. It should be updated after a certain amount of time to cope with the changes of interest of the person over time.
- **URL Network:** URLs are often shared by users in micro-blogs. Building a URL network may reveal personal interests and URL sharing pattern of users. The creation of URL network is similar to reply network.
- **Close Friend Network:** Reply and retweeting activities of users are likely to be changed over time due to various events of life. For example, job switching of a person may initiate active communication to a group of new friends (i.e. colleagues of new job) and communication to some of the early acquaintances (i.e. colleagues of previous job) may disappear. However, some of the acquaintances consistently remain in user's timeline over longer period or may appear after some irregular intervals. We have considered such acquaintances as the close friends of individuals in social media. Creating a network of such close friends and later using it as a social biometric feature would enhance the reliability of the authentication process. Therefore, we analyzed retweet and reply networks to identify close friends of each of our 50 subjects. At first, we listed all the persons who are present in either retweet or reply network for at least two sessions. Here the fact is that if an acquaintance appears regularly in the user's timeline in form of reply or retweets, that acquaintance should have strong relationship with the user. Further strong communicative relationships are explored by combining people who exist in both reply and retweeted network of each session. Finally, a close friend network is created by using all the above listed distinct persons as nodes. It is worth mentioning that these networks would be more consistent if the aforementioned analysis could be conducted over a longer period with more sessions.

- **Topics of Interest:** Hashtag sharing of a Twitter user is an event driven activity and the most likely feature to be changed over time. However, analyzing hashtags over longer period may reveal consistent information about the user such as personal interest. For example, if some hashtags appear regularly in the tweets of a user over long period, then the user is consistently interested about that issue. Such pattern is an important feature to identify the user in virtual domain. The problem of topic analysis in hashtags is that many different hashtags might represent a single topic. Therefore, relevant hashtags have to be clustered to explore a more general topic of interest. Some examples of similar hashtags and their general topic of interest are presented in Table 1. We accumulated all hashtags shared by each user from four sessions. Then, all hashtags are clustered according to the similarity of words. For example, all hashtags presented in the second row of the Table 1 contain a common word "climet". Therefore, we assigned "climet" as one of the topics of interest for that person. Any hashtag shared by that particular user containing "climet" would fall under this topic of interest. Any cluster containing a single element is removed from the list. Finally, we explored consistent topics of interest from the list by discarding topics present in only a one session since such topics are more likely to be random and event driven. In this way, we assigned some general topics of interest for each person by clustering similar hashtags. It is also worth mentioning that clustering is accomplished based on string similarity not semantic similarity of hashtags. Further analysis could be done by finding any correlation between hashtags and shared URLs or replied users.

Table 1. Example of assigning topic of interest for similar hashtags

Similar hashtags	Topic of interest
#Climet, #ClimetLeaders, #ClimetReality, #ClimetChange	climet
#Immigration, #Immigrationreform, #Immigration&hellip, #iamimmigration &amp	immigration
#Sydneyhalfmarathon, #Sydney, #Sydneyweather, #Sydneywinter, #SydneyFires	sydney

3.3 Similarity Matching

For each user in our data set, we created reply network, retweeted network, retweeting network, hashtag network, URL network for each of the first four sessions. Then the close friend network and topics of interest are extracted by combining data from more than one sessions. Feature sets from the first four sessions are considered as training sets. The fifth session is considered as test data set. Reply, retweeted, retweeting, hashtag, and URL networks are generated from the fifth session as well to form features of test set. The difference between test and training networks is that no threshold values are applied during the test networks generation. Initially, matching is accomplished on corresponding reply, retweeted, retweeting, URL, and hashtag networks of test and training sets. Then, test hashtag network is matched with the topic of interest of training sample. Also, close friend network of the training sample is matched with the combined reply and retweeted networks of the test sample. The features of training and testing networks are matched to obtain the final similarity score of a person's identity. The matching of hashtag network of the test set and topics of interests of the training set is accomplished using Levenshtein distance [25]. The similarity scores of the other five test and training networks are calculated as the ratio of the number of mutual nodes in test and training networks to the number of nodes in training network. Therefore, the similarity score, S_p is defined as follows:

$$S_p = \frac{|P_T \cap P_R|}{|P_T|} \ where \ P_T \neq \emptyset \tag{1}$$

Where training and test networks are represented by P_T and P_R respectively. The similarity scores are then normalized and fused to obtain the final matching score. The framework of our feature extraction and matching system is implemented in such a way that we can feed more features in future. The performance of the proposed feature sets for person identification is demonstrated in the following section.

4 Experimental Results and Discussion

During experimentation, we aimed to evaluate the performance of the extracted features for person identification. Performance variations of the proposed features over time were another point of interest of our experiments. Therefore, we performed three sets of experiments to evaluate the performance proposed method. In the first set of experiments, we evaluated the performances of each features and their combined forms. In the second set of experiments, we compared performance of all frequency-based features in different sessions. Finally, in the third set of experiments, we compared performance of all features considering more than one training sessions. All experiments were carried out on Windows 7 operating system, 2.7 GHz Quad-Core Intel Core i7 processor with 16 GB RAM. Matlab version R2013a was used for implementation and experimentation of the proposed method. We collected social data of 50 users from five different sessions. The first four sessions were used as training sets and the fifth session was considered and test set. Table 2 shows training and test set separation of collected Twitter data in different sessions.

Table 2. Training and test sets of collected Twitter data in different sessions.

Session	Number of users	Session interval	Training/test
Session 01	50	0 days	Training
Session 02	50	20 days	Training
Session 03	50	20 days	Training
Session 04	50	20 days	Training
Session 05	50	20 days	Test

In the first experiment, we evaluated the performance of each single feature and their combined forms. As discussed in the feature extraction section, we have two types of feature sets: frequency-based and knowledge-based. In this experiment, a particular feature from the test set of each subject is matched with the corresponding feature of all subjects in the training set. Figure 3 plots the performance of the proposed features in terms of Receiver Operating Characteristics (ROC) curves. ROC curve plots False Rejection Rate (FRR) and False Acceptance Rate (FAR) with respect to different threshold values. Equal Error Rate (EER), the optimal point on ROC where FAR is equal to FRR, is often considered as a measure of identification or verification performance [26]. The training set consists of reply, retweet, URL, hashtag, close friend network, and topics of interest. From Fig. 3, one can see that EER is high for single feature. However, knowledge-based features i.e. close friend network and topics of interest have better performance than frequency-based features i.e. reply, retweet, hashtag, and URL networks. The average EER of the four frequency-based features is around 35 %. On the other hand, the average EER of the two knowledge-based features is around 28 %. This finding confirms the consistency of the knowledge-based features over time. Figure 3 also shows that the EER reduced significantly while all frequency-based features are combined. The best identification performance is achieved by combining all six features. In this case, the EER is as low as 20 % approximately. However, the choice of the optimal point may be altered according to security level [26]. For example, a point where the FAR is low and the FRR is high is suitable for high security applications. Alternatively, a point with low FRR and high FAR is good for low security applications where the system may allow a reasonable amount of false alarms.

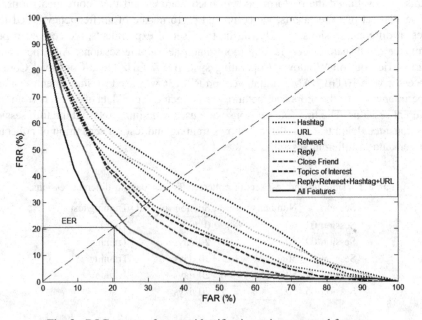

Fig. 3. ROC curves of person identification using proposed features.

As per the discussion in the feature extraction section, frequency-based feature sets, collected within a short span of time, might be subjects of changes over time. Therefore, we are also interested in investigating the effects of changes of the proposed frequency-based features for person identification. We set up the second experiment to evaluate the performance of combined frequency-based features from different sessions. In this case, the test set is consists of reply, retweet, hashtag, and URL networks of 50 users from session 5. The test feature set is then matched with the reply, retweet, hashtag, and URL networks from session 1, 2, 3, and 4, sequentially. The sessions are numbered according to the sequence of data acquisition. Therefore, session 5 contains the most recent social data of the users whereas session 1 comprises of the least recent data. Figure 4 plots the identification results of the four sessions in terms of ROC curves. It has been observed from Fig. 4 that the best identification result (EER = 24 %) is obtained by measuring the similarity between the closest test and training session pairs i.e. session 5 and session 4. A little degradation in performance has been observed when the test data is matched with session 2 and session 3. However, the EER has been increased to around 33 % for the similarity measure between session 5 and session 1. In this case, the training data set (session 1) is more than four months older compared to the test set (session 5). From the second experiment, one can see that frequency-based features need to be updated regularly to cope with the changing social behavior of a person.

In the third set of experiments, we evaluated the performance of the proposed method using more than one training samples. The experiment was conducted using the

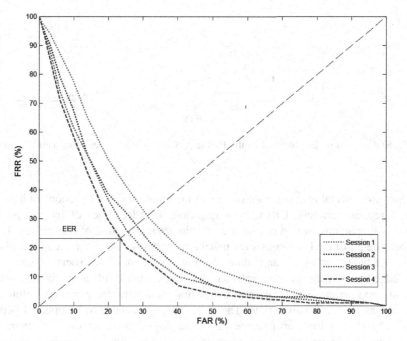

Fig. 4. ROC curves of combined frequency-based features in different sessions.

first two, three, and four sessions as training sets in an incremental order. Therefore, in this experimentation each feature has more than one samples, unlike the first two set of experiments. However, session five is used as the test set, similar to the aforementioned experiments. Figure 5 plots the ROC curves of the combined sessions. From Fig. 5, one can see that consideration of more than one training samples enhanced the performance of the proposed method. Compared to single training session as shown in Figs. 3 and 4, use of combined training features sets as shown in Fig. 5 obtained less EER. The lowest EER = 18 % has been obtained using four training sessions. This experiment demonstrate that all the sessions contain some consistent feature sets. This is why, having more than one sessions in training set reinforces consistent features and increases recognition performance.

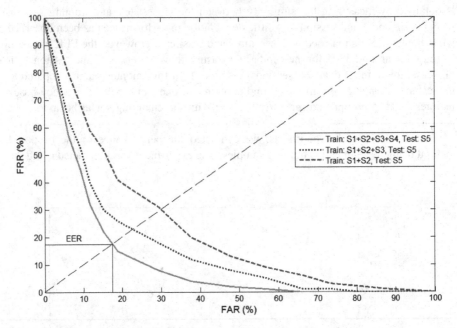

Fig. 5. ROC curves of the proposed method using 2, 3, and 4 training sessions in an incremental order.

Our experimental results demonstrate that the online social interactions of a person such as replies, retweets, URLs, hashtags, close friends, topics of interest possess idiosyncratic patterns, which can be used as biometric signature of that person. It has also been demonstrated that consistent behavioral patterns can be explored by applying knowledge-based analysis and data mining techniques on social data. Such knowledge-based features can enhance the performance of a biometric person authentication system. Similar to other behavioral biometrics, the proposed features are also subjects to changes over time. Therefore, they are needed to be updated period- ically. The recognition performance might be degraded otherwise. However, this requirement should not pose any problem, since social behavioral biometrics can easily be extracted and updated periodically without interfering the users at all. One limitation of our experimentation is that the investigation has been conducted on the data of relatively small number of subjects. We believe that more data would help to further support our findings.

5 Conclusions

In this paper, social interactions via Twitter has been analyzed to discover behavioral signature of users. We introduced frequency-based and knowledge-based behavioral biometric features, which can be extracted from any online social networking platforms. Our experimentation includes performance and consistency evaluation of the proposed behavioral biometric features for closed set person identification. There are three important findings from this research. Firstly, online communication or interactions of users retain behavioral footprints of individuals. Secondly, analyzing social data over a period of time can explore underlying behavioral pattern, which exhibits strong idiosyncratic characteristics. Finally, such behavioral patterns of users maintain stability over time to some extent and do not change overnight. Experimental results demonstrate encouraging performance of using online interaction-based features for user identification. The applications of the proposed social behavioral biometrics features could be as diverse as person authentication, access control, anomaly detection, customer profiling, behavior analysis, situation awareness, risk analysis, friend recommendation systems, and so on. Our future research includes expanding the concept to include broad range of on-line social communications and environments.

Acknowledgement. The authors would like to thank NSERC DISCOVERY program grant RT731064, URGC, NSERC ENGAGE, NSERC Vanier CGS, and Alberta Ingenuity for partial support of this project.

References

1. Moskovitch, R., Feher, C., Messerman, A., Kirschnick, N., Mustafic, T., Camtepe, A., Lohlein, B., Heister, U., Möller, S., Rokach, L., Elovici, Y.: Identity theft, computers and behavioral biometrics. In: Proceedings of IEEE International Conference on in Intelligence and Security Informatics (ISI 2009), pp. 155–160. IEEE (2009)
2. Gavrilova, M.L., Monwar, M.: Multimodal biometrics and intelligent image processing for security systems. IGI Global (2013)
3. Yampolskiy, R.V., Govindaraju, V.: Behavioral biometrics: a survey and classification. Int. J. Biometrics 1(1), 81–113 (2008)
4. Yampolskiy, R.V., Gavrilova, M.L.: Artimetrics: biometrics for artificial entities. IEEE Robot. Autom. Mag. 19(4), 48–58 (2012)
5. Monwar, M., Gavrilova, M.L.: Multimodal biometric system using rank-level fusion approach. IEEE Trans. Syst. Man Cybern. B Cybern. 39(4), 867–878 (2009)
6. Zhang, H., Li, M.: Security vulnerabilities of a remote password authentication scheme with smart card. In: Consumer Electronics, Communications, and Networks, pp. 698–701 (2011)

7. Paul, P.P., Gavrilova, M., Klimenko, S.: Situation awareness of cancelable biometric system. Vis. Comput. **30**, 1–9 (2013)
8. Sultana, M., Paul, P.P., Gavrilova, M.: A concept of social behavioral biometrics: motivation, current developments, and future trends. In: CW Biometric Workshop (2013)
9. Sultana, M., Paul, P.P., Gavrilova, M.: On-line user interaction traits in web-based social biometrics. IGI Chapter, pp. 177–190 (2014)
10. Bringmann, B., Berlingerio, M., Bonchi, F., Gionis, A.: Learning and predicting the evolution of social networks. Intell. Syst. **25**(4), 26–35 (2010)
11. http://www.statisticbrain.com/twitter-statistics/. Accessed 25 March 2015
12. Grant, T., Laboreiro, G., Maia, B., Oliveira, E., Sousa Silva, R., Sarmento, L.: 'twazn me!!!; (' automatic authorship analysis of micro-blogging messages. In: Muñoz, R., Montoyo, A., Métais, E. (eds.) NLDB 2011. LNCS, vol. 6716, pp. 161–168. Springer, Heidelberg (2011)
13. https://support.twitter.com/articles/166337-the-twitter-glossary. Accessed 25 March 2015
14. Carter, S., Tsagkias, M., Weerkamp, W.: Twitter hashtags: Joint Translation and Clustering, pp. 1–3 (2011)
15. Sourin, A.: Computer Graphics: From a Small Formula to Cyberworlds. Prentice-Hall Inc., Singapore (2006)
16. Jorgensen, Z., Yu, T.: On mouse dynamics as a behavioral biometric for authentication. In: Proceedings of 6th ACM Symposium on Information, Computer and Communications Security, pp. 476–482 (2011)
17. Bours, P.: Continuous keystroke dynamics: A different perspective towards biometric evaluation. Inf. Secur. Tech. Rep. **17**(1), 36–43 (2012)
18. Frank, M., Biedert, R., Ma, E., Martinovic, I., Song, D.: Touchalytics: on the applicability of touchscreen input as a behavioral biometric for continuous authentication. IEEE Trans. Inf. Forensics Secur. **8**(1), 136–148 (2013)
19. Guo, Y., Yang, L., Ding, X., Han, J., Liu, Y.: OpenSesame: unlocking smart phone through handshaking biometrics. In: Proceedings of IEEE INFOCOM, pp. 365–369. IEEE, April 2013
20. Feng, T., Zhao, X., Shi, W.: Investigating mobile device picking-up motion as a novel biometric modality. In: Proceedings of IEEE Sixth International Conference on Biometrics: Theory, Applications and Systems (BTAS), pp. 1–6 (2013)
21. Jiang, W., Xiang, J., Liu, L., Zha, D., Wang, L.: From mini house game to hobby-driven behavioral biometrics-based password. In: Proceedings of 12th IEEE International Conference on Trust, Security and Privacy in Computing and Communications (TrustCom), pp. 712–719. IEEE, July 2013
22. Olejnik, L., Castelluccia, C.: Towards web-based biometric systems using personal browsing interests. In: Proceedings of Eighth International Conference on Availability, Reliability and Security (ARES), pp. 274–280. IEEE, September 2013
23. Fridman, A., Stolerman, A., Acharya, S., Brennan, P., Juola, P., Greenstadt, R., Kam, M.: Decision fusion for multi-modal active authentication. IT Prof. **15**(4), 29–33 (2013)
24. Bailey, K.O., Okolica, J.S., Peterson, G.L.: User identification and authentication using multi-modal behavioral biometrics. Comput. Secur. **43**, 77–89 (2014)
25. Cohen, W., Ravikumar, P., Fienberg, S.: A comparison of string metrics for matching names and records. In: Proceedings of KDD Workshop on Data Cleaning and Object Consolidation, vol. 3, pp. 73–78, August 2003
26. Ross, A., Jain, A.: Information fusion in biometrics. Pattern Recogn. Lett. **24**(13), 2115–2125 (2003)

Applying Geometric Function on Sensors 3D Gait Data for Human Identification

Sajid Ali[1]([✉]), Zhongke Wu[1], Xulong Li[2,3], Nighat Saeed[1],
Dong Wang[4], and Mingquan Zhou[1]

[1] College of Information Science and Technology,
Engineering Research Center of Institute Virtual Reality
and Visualization Technology,
Beijing Normal University, Beijing, China
{saa.cs,zwu,ns.cs,mqzhou}@bnu.edu.cn
[2] MOE Key Laboratory of Space Robotics,
Beijing University of Posts and Telecommunications, Beijing, China
[3] Robotics Institute, Carnegie Mellon University, Pittsburgh, USA
xulongli@andrew.cmu.edu
[4] School of Information Science and Technology,
Northwest University, Xian, China
wdong@nwu.edu.cn

Abstract. In surveillance system, the video data has received a great deal of attention, instead of Mocap data, there has enough no work on recognizing of human through this data. Most Surveillance system monitors the behavior, activities, or other changing information in surrounding real life; usually it is used to recognize people to the purpose of security issues in society. This paper aims to propose a novel approach of human identification, which based on sensor data acquired by an optical system. Three joints of the human body, such as the hip, knee, and ankle joint have been selected by the amount of gait movement in this algorithm. By extracting suitable 3D static and dynamic joints feature from data. The Parametric Bezier Curve(PBC) technique applies on the extracted features in order to derive the strong correlation between joint movements. The curve control points are used to construct the triangles of each walking pose. After that centroid of triangle method apply on constructed triangle to compute a 3D center value. Selecting a triangle which has minimum distance between original pose triangle and recursive triangle center value. We then employed the geometric function to compute the area of each walking pose triangle(gait signature). Furthermore, we optimized the gait signature by using statistical moment on computed areas. After an accurate analysis the signature and found that is has a unique relationship among the 3D human gaits, and use this signature as to classify the human identification. The experiments demonstrated on IGS-90 and Vicon motion capture system data that is proved that proposed method is more accurate and reliable results.

Keywords: Geometric gait · Sensor walk · Sensor pose · Gait area

© Springer-Verlag Berlin Heidelberg 2016
M.L. Gavrilova et al. (Eds.): Trans. on Comput. Sci. XXVI, LNCS 9550, pp. 125–141, 2016.
DOI: 10.1007/978-3-662-49247-5_8

1   Introduction

Human identification is one of the important domain of computer vision research today. The aim of human recognizing is to automatically detect from the information acquired from motion capture system 3D data. In human walking manner, termed gait has been well known to have the ability to be used for identification [26]. The biometric system or technology has become famous because of many application needs for human recognition in surveillance system. The significant advancement in the field of computer processing, there are many types of biometric technologies introduced in a number of fields, some of them have been used in monitoring system, and some used to materialize in human identifying and verifying individuals by evaluating face, palm print, fingerprint, iris or a recipe of these traits [19,39,42].

For human identification perspective, classification and gender identification is the first step; and therefore these can improve a wide range of applications [32,37]. They had used for automatic surveillance systems. The number of methods [16,24,27,31,44] used for gender recognition by using gait appearance of human. Whereas, Dong Xu et al. [40] reported the techniques of gait recognition based on a matrix representation, which are applied to further improve classification strategy. Weimin et al. [38] invented a novel method to recognize the human by employing a nearest neighbor algorithm on human silhouettes. In [18], the energy of gait features are computed to combine the statistical gait and synthetic templates and used them to recognize the individual of human. The statistical movement also used to recognized human gait. Shutler et al. [33] also have used the statistical techniques to compute the gaits velocity moments and used it for gait recognition. Changhong et al. [12] used a method on silhouette frame difference energy image for gaits recognition. They used frieze and wavelet features and hidden Markov model is to employ for recognition. In [42], computed a spatio-temporal volume and used it to find the bounding contours of the walker, and then fit a simplified stick model for it; and they have computed the gaits pattern from the model parameters for recognition. Many researchers had focused to human recognition through gait features [11,25,36].

The motion capture system technology has developed since the 1970. Three-dimensional motion capture data is a digital sign picture of the complex spatiotemporal structure of human motion. We use it as an alternate approach of video dataset aims to use the joint markers to capture data for human identification, and this data is used as a new biometrics aims to recognize people via the walking style. The computational human motion study has drawn much warranted attention; and it is a part of the development of motion capture techniques, which in turn have resulted in a growth in many applications. Recently, most work on Mocap data such as animation [5,43], film [46], human interactive game [29], and virtual world [10,35] etc. In terms of animation, motion capture can be used for different aspects [15], authors have been used in character animation and motion retarget; and have the lot of interest in the methods of using and re-using of MoCap data [23,28,41,47]. Some examples of MoCap data applications can be seen in Fig. 1). In [14] describes the optical or magnetic

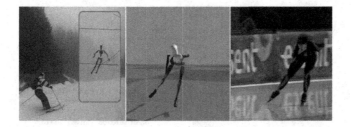

Fig. 1. MoCap data applications.

sensors are attached to the human body joints to record their activities, which can be used to recognize the daily home activities such as eating meals, using bathroom, teeth cleaning, and washing face in a smart home. Zhang et al. [45], introduce an algorithm that applies on the 3D human motion capture data to analyze and classify the human activities feature. The sensor data is recorded from a motion capture system with many types of file format [4,30]; one of them is a BVH file format (see Fig. 2 is a example of BVH format data). This kind of file contains ASCII text, the first part of which provides the specifications for the initial phase of a human skeleton, and the rest, a time-framed sequence of different specifications for subsequent poses information about the human body joints and its movements during the human activities. The topology of the human skeleton and its joint hierarchy are as shown in Fig. 3. In this paper, we propose an approach for human recognition by using sensors 3D data, which is acquired by a motion capture system because of existing information available in the data of polynomial curve and geometric function. We inspired about our work from Ludovic et al. [22], Ali Etemad, and Ali Arya [13]. In [22] authors used 3D motion data, and investigated the issues of human gait activities such as walking, jogging, and dancing. In [13], Ali Etemad and Ali applied the cubic spline curves technique on captured data of different walking styles (Neutral walk, Neutral run, Tire run, and Drunk walk) to analyze them for recognition.

Despite many research works on locomotion databases from the aforementioned discussion, there is not enough study of gaits recognition on 3D sensor data; and to the best of our knowledge, the conclusion that can reach is that not more focused on motion capture data to the purpose of human identification. Our intention is also to use it for more general purpose such as human identification; and has a desire to use 3D sensor data (BVH file) to identify the human by a new approach. In our method, we firstly extract the feature of joints (hip, knee, and ankle) from each frame. Then, the features used as data points to generate the quadratic Bezier curve passing through each joint. The control points of the curve form a triangle and then we compute center of that triangle by using Centroid of triangle method. Furthermore we compute the area by using geometric function (Heros formula). Finally, the triangle areas are used to compute the average area and stored in a proposed database. The results of our proposed method are achieved by matching average area to recognize the human.

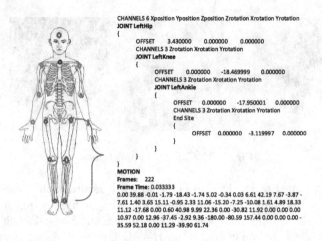

```
CHANNELS 6 Xposition Yposition Zposition Zrotation Xrotation Yrotation
JOINT LeftHip
{
    OFFSET      3.430000      0.000000      0.000000
    CHANNELS 3 Zrotation Xrotation Yrotation
    JOINT LeftKnee
    {
        OFFSET      0.000000     -18.469999      0.000000
        CHANNELS 3 Zrotation Xrotation Yrotation
        JOINT LeftAnkle
        {
            OFFSET      0.000000     -17.950001      0.000000
            CHANNELS 3 Zrotation Xrotation Yrotation
            End Site
            {
                OFFSET      0.000000     -3.119997      0.000000
            }
        }
    }
}
MOTION
Frames:  222
Frame Time: 0.033333
0.00 39.88 -0.01 -1.79 -18.43 -1.74 5.02 -0.34 0.03 6.61 42.19 7.67 -3.87 -
7.61 1.40 3.65 15.11 -0.95 2.33 11.06 -15.20 -7.25 -10.08 1.61 4.89 18.33
11.12 -17.68 0.00 0.60 40.98 9.99 22.36 0.00 -30.82 11.92 0.00 0.00 0.00
10.97 0.00 12.96 -37.45 -2.92 9.36 -180.00 -80.59 157.44 0.00 0.00 0.00 -
35.59 52.18 0.00 11.29 -39.90 61.74
```

Fig. 2. An example of BVH file having with specific human body joints motion.

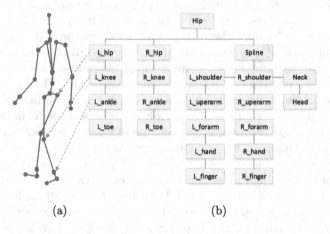

(a)   (b)

Fig. 3. The left figure (a) is a human model, (b) is an example of its skeleton joints hierarchy of a BVH file.

The reminder of this work is organized as follows. In Sect. 2, we give a brief system overview. In Sect. 3, we describe the proposed database and present the proposed flowchart. Then, Sect. 4 focuses on the mathematical and statistical calculations for our algorithm. The experimental results will be demonstrated in Sect. 5. Finally, the conclusion of the study will be described in the last section with future suggestions.

2   System Overview

The objective of this study is to rapidly process three dimensional motion data of gait joints for human identification through the straight walking view. Instead

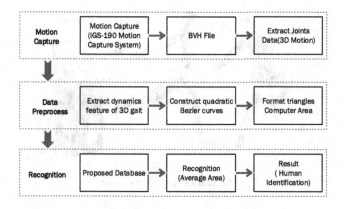

Fig. 4. The workflow of our framework

of using the all joints of the human body, we consider the three important joints such as hip, knee, and ankle in this study. We compute the static and dynamic features set of the lower limb joints of the human body from proposed database. The features set contain the positional information of the joints during walk and use as data point to draw the curves by using a parametric polynomial curve technique. The control points of the curve are used to build the triangles between them. Then, employ the general and geometry functions on triangles to compute the area with transfer features from 3D to 1D space of each pose. After that, by applying the powerful statistical method on extracted 1-dimensional point feature to compute the consolidation across value (average value) that define the core knowledge of information unit between walking poses; and used as threshold value to identify the subject(human). The graphical representation of the system overview is shown in Fig. 4.

3   Proposed Database

3.1   Existing Sensor Dataset Selecting

The existing motion captured sensors dataset [34] was recorded by the IGS-190-M system. This system based on miniature inertial sensors, biomechanical models, and sensor fusion algorithms. The record data of this system was transfer wirelessly to a computer during recording, where it records or views (see Fig. 5). The dataset contains 40 recorded motion subjects, each walking with different speed, and performing several direction changes.

3.2   Preprocessing and Design Database

The proposed database is summarized in Fig. 6; and it contains 41 normal human walking motion examples of different subjects with the BVH file format; that are selected from the above-mentioned dataset (existing motion captured dataset).

Fig. 5. Motion capture system.

Each human skeleton model composed of 26 joints, including end site and 25 bone segments. Each pose of walking contains 3 (joints NUM+1) = 3 (21+1) = 66 dimensional data (digital movements of all skeleton joints) excluding the end site points. This information contains in each frame of the file, which represent, by a number of consecutive multidimensional postures vary with time, ordered in z, x, y-axes. In the channel data, each joint has three rotations Euler angles, which describe the digitally joint movements of the human body. By employing the method [7], especially processing the data part of BVH file by using (3.1), (3.2), (3.3). These equations are used for orientation of each segment of the human body joint movements into x, y, and z homogeneous coordinate axes. After that, using the programming techniques to reconstruct each file, with equal number of frames and walking steps. The motion or channel data stored in matrix of each subject, and an example of motion matrix (channel data) of the BVH file has showed in Fig. 2.

4   Methods

In our recognition scheme, we have to use the straight walking view MoCap data of the lower limb joints of the human body. The important quantities of knowledge of joints positional data will be used to measure the uniqueness of gait characteristics for identifying the human through the Bezier curve and geometric function. The characteristics contain Bezier curve [6], geometric function [2,17] and statistical technique [9].

4.1   Feature Set Extraction

To compute the feature set according to need, first is the extraction motion part of the BVH file from the proposed database. The motion part calls matrix **A** that contains the local position values of the all human body joints and is defined by

$$\mathbf{A} = [p_1, p_2, \ldots, p_N]$$

Where N is the total number of frames (poses), p_i of $\mathbf{A}$ is a walking pose of with containing j joints positional or orientation values of i-th pose defined by

$$p_i = [v_1, v_2, \ldots, v_j], i \in N$$

where j is the total number of joints in i-th pose of the human walk; and $v_j = (x, y, z) \in \mathbb{R}$,$x$,$y$ and z is the local variable orientation of the joint. Now we retrieve three joints (hip, knee, and ankle) motion from matrix $\mathbf{A}$ with m frames defined by

$$M = [x_1, x_2, \ldots, x_m]^T$$

m is the total number of the walking pose of joint positional or orientation values and each pose contain three joints movement information during walk, it can be defined as

$$x_k = (v_1^{(k)}, \ldots, v_L^{(k)}), L \in n = 3, k \in m$$

where n is the total number of gait joints in K-th pose in human walk; and each joint $v_L^j \in (x, y, z)$ are orientation variable of the joints which stored the joint movement during walk. The composite form of the feature matrix of all the poses of gait joint expressed by

$$GM = M[(x)]_{x_m \times v_n^k}^T \tag{1}$$

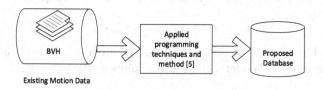

Fig. 6. Proposed database

GM is a motion matrix which contains all poses of lower limb joint (gait joint) during the several steps of human walk.

4.2   Gait Representation Using Bezier Curve

The Bezier curve representation is a approach that is used most frequently in computer graphics and geometric modeling. It has parametric curves, which is widely utilized to model smooth path curves and have the many characteristics [21], because of its solid mathematical equations and intuitive manipulation. There are many types of Bezier curves. The quadratic and cubic curves are the most common types of Bezier curve. It has ability to pass between three points, according to this property; we use here this curve for our solution. Because it has three control points and one minus from control points its degree of the curve. It gives the strong correlation information in-between the tunnel path of the human gait joint (hip, knee, and ankle). Then, a general scheme of a Bezier curve can be expressed as:

$$B(t) = \sum_{i=1}^{n} b_{i,n} P_i, t \in 0, 1 \tag{2}$$

According to our concept to use Eq. (2) and it can be rewritten it as

$$C_k(t) = \sum_{L=1}^{n} X^{KL}(v), c_{L,n}(t), t \in 0, 1 \tag{3}$$

Each $C_k(t)$ represents the pose curve of gait joints in walking of the subject. Here n is the total number of joints of each pose, i.e. $n = 3$, $v \in \mathbb{R} = (x, y, z)$, L indicates the index of the joint; and X^{kL} indicates the human walk pose, which contains the gait joints information such as $x^{k1}(v) = hip, x^{k2}(v) = knee, x^{k3}(v) = ankle$ are considered the control points of the curve; and $c_{L,n}(t)$ for $L = 1, \ldots, n$ is the Bernstein polynomials of degree n, defined as

$$c_{L,n}(t) = [n, L]^T t^L (1 - t)^{n-L}$$

Devoid of uncertainty, the control points can be treated as vectors and the related Bernstein polynomials as scalars. The Eq. (3) has n degree order and is a type of the Bezier curve. Here the quadratic Bezier curve uses to pass three joints in our concept: hip, knee and ankle joints. Thus, the Eq. (3) can represents parametrically as

$$x^{k1}(v) = Q_1, x^{k3}(v) = Q_3$$

Suppose hip location Q_1, knee location Q_2, ankle location Q_3 in each pose data of three joints. Therefore, the control points of the curve are computed as:

$$C_k(t) = (1 - t)^2 x^{k1}(v) - (1 - t)t x^{k2} + t^2 x^{k3}(v) \tag{4}$$

The control point $x^{k2}(t)$ is computed that the curve passes Q_2. Here the parameter t_2 corresponds to Q_2, which computes as

$$t_2 = \frac{|Q_1 Q_2|}{|Q_1 Q_2| + |Q_2 Q_3|} \tag{5}$$

Therefore

$$Q_2 = x^{kL}(v, t2) = (1 - t_2)^2 x^{k1}(v) + 2(1 - t_2)^2 t_2 x^{k2}(v) + t_2^2 x^{k3}(v) \tag{6}$$

$$x^{k2}(v) = \frac{Q_2 - (1 - t_2)^2 Q_1 - t_2^2 Q_3}{2(1 - t_2)t_2} \tag{7}$$

Where $0 < t < 1$. Every $C_k(t)$ represents the motion curve in form of the 3D quadratic Bezier curve, which passes through joints, and elaborates the relationship between the hip, knee and ankle joints of each walking pose. An example

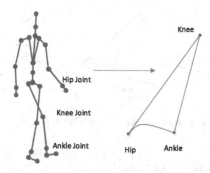

Fig. 7. (a) An example of a particular walking pose; and (b) the corresponding joints motion curve.

of curve (quadratic Bezier curve) of a particular walking pose of a subject is portrayed in Fig. 7.

Let $M = C_k(t) = [w_{c_1(t)}, \ldots, w_{c_k(t)}]$ be the walking poses curves of a subject by using Eq. (2) following by Eq. (4). Each curve has three control points i.e. $w_{c_k(t) \in (cp_{k1}, cp_{k2}, cp_{k3})}$ and $cp_{kj} \in (x, y, z), j = 1, 2, 3$, that shows the joint number such as $j = 1 = Hip, j = 2 = Kee, j = 3 = Ankle$ participating in each pose.

4.3   Computed Triangle Area

Let $w_{c_k(t)} \in \mathbf{R}^3$ be a curve of any particular walking pose of a subject that passing through the corresponding joints position and these positions call the control points of the curve, their names as Cp_{k1}, Cp_{k2} and Cp_{k3}. These points are used to construct the pose triangle; and formed the vertices of triangle. It can be seen in Fig. 8 (see step 1). To compute the center of constructed triangle by applying the very popular formula of computing center. With the help of computing center, we divided the original triangle (see Fig. 8 in step 1) into three sub-triangles (see Fig. 8 in step 2) and calculate the center of each one by employing the same method as step 1. These three centers are used to construct a 3D triangle. After that we compute difference value between original triangle center and constructed triangle (with help of three centers). If difference value is closed to original triangle center then stop this process to repeat the step 3 three until difference value close to original center. At the end of this subsection we have selected those triangle which have closed center values to original one for further processing. For computing the triangle center we follow the following steps and Algorithm 1.

Step 1: Initialize: Given a triangle with vertex as $P_1 = Cp_{k1}, P_2 = Cp_{k2}, P_3 = Cp_{k3}$, calculate the center c as

$$c_0 = \frac{1}{3}(P_1 + P_2 + P_3) \tag{8}$$

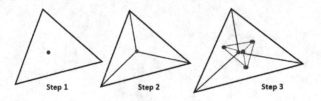

Fig. 8. Process of recursive triangle.

Step 2: set r-th iterate vertex of triangle as

$$P_1^r := \frac{1}{3}(P_1^{r-1} + P_2^{r-1} + c_{r-1})$$

$$P_2^r := \frac{1}{3}(c_{r-1} + P_2^{r-1} + P_3^{r-1}) \tag{9}$$

$$P_3^r := \frac{1}{3}(P_1^{r-1} + c_{r-1} + P_3^{r-1})$$

Step 3: Calculate the new center c_r of r-th iterate

$$c_r = \frac{1}{3}(P_1^r + P_2^r + P_3^r) \tag{10}$$

Step 4: Calculate the r-th iterate error e_r:

$$e_r = (dist(c_r, c_0)) \tag{11}$$

So the algorithm should be,

Data: P_1^0, P_2^0, P_3^0
Result: center point c and triangle P_1^r, P_2^r, P_3^r
initialization: calculate c_0 with Eq. (8);
while $e_r < tol$ *or* $r < r_{Max}$ **do**
 generate new triangle vertex P_1^r, P_2^r, P_3^r with Eq. (9);
 calculate center c_r with Eq. (10);
 calculate center distance with Eq. (11);
end

Algorithm 1. Constructed Recursive Triangle

Figure 9(b) is constructed after applying Algorithm 1 that shows the triangle with having edges length τ_1, τ_2, τ_3. The length of $Cp_{k1}Cp_{k2}$ is τ_1, the length of $Cp_{k2}Cp_{k3}$ is τ_2, the length of $Cp_{k3}Cp_{k1}$ is τ_3. These lengths determine by applying the standard Euclidean distance method [2]. In this case, the lengths of triangle sides can be defined under the functions becomes as

$$\tau_j(Cp_{k,j+1}, Cp_{kj}) = \sqrt{\sum_{\theta=x}^{z} Cp_{k,j+1,\theta} - Cp_{k,j,\theta}}, \quad for \quad j < 3 \tag{12}$$

and

$$\tau_j(Cp_{k,j}, Cp_{kj-2}) = \sqrt{\sum_{\theta=x}^{z} Cp_{k,j,\theta} - Cp_{k,j-2,\theta}}, \quad for \quad j = 3 \qquad (13)$$

where $\theta = x, y, z$.

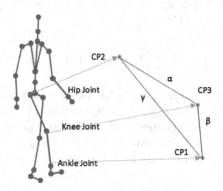

Fig. 9. (a) Specific human model walking pose; (b) a triangle to the corresponding control points of the curve by applying Algorithm 1.

After that, we use the powerful geometric formula (Heros formula) to perform the computation by the function (10), and used to compute the triangle area of K walking pose during walk. This function has ability to compute the features of each pose from $\mathbf{R}^3$ to $\mathbf{R}^1$ feature space. This feature space will utilize to compute the gait signature from each pose of walking. After that, this signature is useful to recognize the human. The area of a triangle can be expressed by the following objective function as

$$\mathfrak{r}_k() = Cp_{k1}Cp_{k2}Cp_{k3} = \sqrt{\Delta\Psi(\Delta\Psi - \tau_1)(\Delta\Psi - \tau_2)(\Delta\Psi - \tau_3)} \qquad (14)$$

Here $\Delta\Psi$ is a semi perimeter of a triangle, and its function can be expressed as

$$\Delta\Psi = \frac{\tau_1 + \tau_2 + \tau_3}{2}$$

Where $\mathfrak{r}_k$ is the area value that identifies the compound relation between the gait joints area of each triangle. This has the advantage of giving bounded area under the gait joints, gives the constant correlation among joints, and conveys the temporal information of joints.

4.4 Typical Value for Gait Signature

Central tendency method is a statistical approach that can be used to identify the typical value of a huge dataset. The average (typical value), median, geometric mean, and harmonic mean are valid measures of location methods. Mean is a popular and well-known measure of location that can be used with both discrete and continuous data. For this purpose, we integrate information in the gait joints are to measure the central location value attempting to describe the relation between bonded triangle area by identifying the typical value or measure of location value within the gait joints area of each pose. Let $\mathfrak{x} = \mathfrak{x}_1, \ldots, \mathfrak{x}_m$ be the robust pose, triangle area of each pose can be computed by (14), $\mathfrak{x}_k \in \mathbf{R}^1$. The objective function of computing the average (mean) can be performed from the K poses appeared in gait walk using (14).

$$\mu_{gait} = \sum_{k=1}^{m} \mathfrak{x}_k / m, k = 1, 2, \ldots, m \tag{15}$$

Where, m is the total number of poses of walking; and $\mathfrak{x}_k$ set of areas that is computed from each pose triangle. μ_{gait} represents the average location (typical value) among poses of triangles in the walk; and defines the unique direct relationship between gait joints, and we call it as a gait signature. It uses to match the stored value of the area in a database for identification, and attain the reliable results.

5   Results and Discussion

In our experiment scenario, we used 41 examples of walking motion (BVH file) of different subjects [3]. In each motion example, the subject walked 8 steps in a straight walking view within 291 frames and 66 dimensional data excluding the end site dimensions, and the frame rate is 0.016667 second or 60 frames per second tending to be the norm. Each subject has 21 joints excluding the end site joint position, the joints are Hip, Left-upleg, left-leg, Left-foot, Left-foot-heel, Right-upleg, Right_leg, Right foot, Rightfootheel, Spine, Spine1, Left-shoulder, Left-arm, left-forearm, left-hand, Right-shoulder, Right-arm, Right-forearm, right-hand, Neck, Head. Among of these joints, we have selected the three joints (hip, knee and ankle mentioned in Fig. 2) with 9 dimensional data or 9 degrees of freedom, that perform the important role during straight walking views. The complex computation relation determine between these joints by the curve (see Figs. 7 and 9).

The curve defines the contribution of each joint with attributes in the form of control points. These points covered area by connecting each other in a triangle shape, this area computed by hero formula (hero algorithm). Because it has the ability to compute the characteristics of area of any type of triangles, such as a right triangle, isosceles triangle, scalene triangle, obtuse triangle etc. Figure 10 shows invariant characteristics among the joints typical value of subjects. The x-axis represents the number of input tested subjects, and the y-axis represents the typical values. These values regard as a characteristic of covered area between joints during the human walk. We have used this typical value to identify the subject and attained the 100 % accuracy result of identification by using proposed dataset. We have used 3D sensor data, and picked up the joints

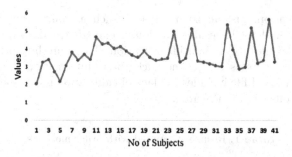

Fig. 10. Shows the result of our proposed method.

information directly during walk, which close to real information of human joints, and no need to convert the original image data into a gray or binary form such as [11,13,20,36]. These authors had been used small video dataset from different databases. In [8], authors had used a simple geometric function and statistical moment techniques on sensors 3D data and attained the 94 % accuracy rate of human identification. Therefore, we compared our proposed method results with others methods, which are mentioned in Table 1, and found that our proposed method is more reliable, and has one of the important improvements in the human identification. For further evidence, we also have to test Carnegie Mellon University (CMU) [1] Mocap walking data sequences (subject no: 7, 8, 16, 35 and 39) and achieved the reliable results (see Fig. 11).

This paper presents the advantages over the others method that is mentioned in Table 1 such as, deal with direct intrinsic motion of the human body, and does not require converting image into grayscale, binary form, and segments of body part such as video dataset for human identification. Finally, our recipe gives the new tunnel of direction to use the sensors 3D data (MoCap data)for

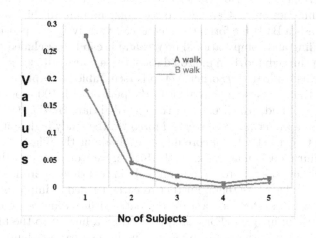

Fig. 11. Shows the result by using CMU Mocap dataset.

human identification, instead to use before such as animation, retarget, and reconstruction. And we have also not found enough trends from literature to use mocap (BVH file) for human identification. There are limitation using this data format, where are as 1-It has no background information when the motion recorded. 2- The BVH file includes the lack of calibration units, such as the scale that the joints offsets are measured.

Table 1. Results compared with other methods.

S.No	Name of methods	Databases	Result
1	Our method	41 subject 3D, motion data (BVH file) (IGS-190 capture system)	100%
2	Geometric & statistical functions [8]	35 subject 3-D, motion data (BVH file) (IGS-190 capture system)	94.28
3	Statistical moments [33]	4 subjects (SOTON database)	93.75
4	Symmetry analysis [20]	6 subjects (SOTON database)	83
5	Positioning human body joint [36]	10 subjects 40, sequences	78
6	Dynamic features [11]	6 subjects 42 sequences	76

6   Conclusion and Future Work

In this study, we proposed a new technique for human identification based on 3D sensor data, gait data, which acquired by an optical system. We have applied mathematical and statistical (Bezier curve, Geometric function and Statistical moment) techniques on MoCap data to recognize human. In this technique, the captured data is a BVH file format, which is comparatively inexpensive in terms of understanding and computational power; and it can be concluded that human identification through biovison motion data of three joints (hip, knee and ankle)is more reliable as compared to other methods (see Table 1). Experimental results demonstrate that the system can identify the person with 100% accuracy using our proposed method, which base on the recorded data by the IGS-190-M and Vicon Optical motion capture systems. Moreover, the study highlighted that it is now possible to extract a lot of core information about the relationship between three joints during a human walk. In the future, we would extend this study to extract the direct skeleton from a human body in real time environment, identify the activities, and analyze them. Further research needed to improve the sensory quality of IGS-190 system to capture the data with a wide range of distance. Then it will useful in space. For example, sending a human to the moon or sun with this system suite through the moon shuttle then capture human activities in the space and analysis them. Some other motion parameters can measure such as velocity, acceleration, energy from this data and it will give new layer of research direction of motion capture data in the space technology field.

Acknowledgments. The data used in this paper were obtained at [3]. We thank them for sharing with us. This work has supported by the National Natural Science Foundation of China under Grant No.61170203, 61170170, The National Key Technology Research and Development Program of China under Grant No.2012BAH33F04, Beijing Key Laboratory Program of China under Grant No.Z111101055281056.

References

1. Cmu graphics lab motion capture database. http://mocap.cs.cmu.edu. Accessed 10 February 2015
2. Hero formula. http://en.wikipedia.org/wiki/Heron's_formula. Accessed 14 February 2015
3. Mocapdata. http://www.tcts.fpms.ac. Accessed 14 February 2013
4. Optical motion. http://en.wikipedia.org/wiki/List_of_motion_and_gesture_file_formats. Accessed 10 February 2015
5. Abson, K., Palmer, I.: Motion capture: capturing interaction between human and animal. Vis. Comput. **31**(3), 1–13 (2014)
6. Ahn, Y.J., Kim, H.O., Lee, K.Y.: G 1 arc spline approximation of quadratic bézier curves. Comput.-Aided Des. **30**(8), 615–620 (1998)
7. Ali, S., Mingquan, Z., Zhongke, W., Razzaq, A., Hamada, M., Ahmed, H.: Comprehensive use of hip joint in gender identification using 3-dimension data. TELKOMNIKA Indonesian J. Electr. Eng. **11**(6), 2933–2941 (2013)
8. Ali, S., Wu, Z., Zhou, M., Razzaq, A., Ahamd, H.: Human identification based on gait joints area through straight walking view. In: International Proceedings of Chemical, Biological & Environmental Engineering, vol. 56 (2013)
9. Anthony, D.: Statistics for Health, Life and Social Sciences. BookBoon, London (2011)
10. Bennett, J., Carter, C.P.: Adopting virtual production for animated filmaking (2014)
11. Chai, Y., Ren, J., Zhao, R., Jia, J.: Automatic gait recognition using dynamic variance features. In: 7th International Conference on Automatic Face and Gesture Recognition, FGR 2006, pp. 475–480. IEEE (2006)
12. Chen, C., Liang, J., Zhao, H., Hu, H., Tian, J.: Frame difference energy image for gait recognition with incomplete silhouettes. Pattern Recogn. Lett. **30**(11), 977–984 (2009)
13. Etemad, S.A., Arya, A.: Extracting movement, posture, and temporal style features from human motion. Biologically Inspired Cogn. Architectures **7**, 15–25 (2014)
14. Fatima, I., Fahim, M., Lee, Y.K., Lee, S.: A unified framework for activity recognition-based behavior analysis and action prediction in smart homes. Sensors **13**(2), 2682–2699 (2013)
15. Feng, X., Qu, S., Wu, L.: Foot trajectory kept motion retargeting. In: 2011 International Conference on Virtual Reality and Visualization (ICVRV), pp. 247–250. IEEE (2011)
16. Golomb, B.A., Lawrence, D.T., Sejnowski, T.J.: Sexnet: a neural network identifies sex from human faces. In: NIPS, pp. 572–579 (1990)

17. Grewal, B.S., Grewal, J.: Higher Engineering Mathematics, vol. 8. Khanna Publishers, Delhi (2005)

18. Han, J., Bhanu, B.: Individual recognition using gait energy image. IEEE Trans. Pattern Anal. Mach. Intell. **28**(2), 316–322 (2006)

19. Hanmandlu, M., Gupta, R.B., Sayeed, F., Ansari, A.: An experimental study of different features for face recognition. In: 2011 International Conference on Communication Systems and Network Technologies (CSNT), pp. 567–571. IEEE (2011)

20. Hayfron-Acquah, J.B., Nixon, M.S., Carter, J.N.: Automatic gait recognition by symmetry analysis. Pattern Recogn. Lett. **24**(13), 2175–2183 (2003)

21. Hill, F., Kelley, S.: Computer Graphics Using OpenGL, 3/E. Pearson, Upper Saddle River (2007)

22. Hoyet, L., Ryall, K., Zibrek, K., Park, H., Lee, J., Hodgins, J., O'Sullivan, C.: Evaluating the distinctiveness and attractiveness of human motions on realistic virtual bodies. ACM Trans. Graph. (TOG) **32**(6), 204 (2013)

23. Hsieh, M.K., Chen, B.Y., Ouhyoung, M.: Motion retargeting and transition in different articulated figures. In: Ninth International Conference on Computer Aided Design and Computer Graphics, p. 6. IEEE (2005)

24. Hu, M., Wang, Y.: A new approach for gender classification based on gait analysis. In: Fifth International Conference on Image and Graphics, ICIG 2009, pp. 869–874. IEEE (2009)

25. Huang, X., Boulgouris, N.V.: Gait recognition using multiple views. In: IEEE International Conference on Acoustics, Speech and Signal Processing, ICASSP 2008, pp. 1705–1708. IEEE (2008)

26. Huang, X., Boulgouris, N.V.: Gait recognition for randomwalking patterns and variable body postures. In: 2010 IEEE International Conference on Acoustics Speech and Signal Processing (ICASSP), pp. 1726–1729. IEEE (2010)

27. Jain, A., Huang, J.: Integrating independent components and linear discriminant analysis for gender classification. In: Proceedings of the Sixth IEEE International Conference on Automatic Face and Gesture Recognition, pp. 159–163. IEEE (2004)

28. Lu, W., Liu, Y., Sun, J., Sun, L.: A motion retargeting method for topologically different characters. In: Sixth International Conference on Computer Graphics, Imaging and Visualization, CGIV 2009, pp. 96–100. IEEE (2009)

29. McCormick, J., Nash, A., Hutchison, S., Vincs, K., Nahavandi, S., Creighton, D.: Recognition: combining human interaction and a digital performing agent. In: Proceedings of the 2014 Virtual Reality International Conference, p. 19. ACM (2014)

30. Meredith, M., Maddock, S.: Motion capture file formats explained. Dept. Comput. Sci. Univ. Sheffield **211**, 241–244 (2001)

31. Moghaddam, B., Yang, M.H.: Learning gender with support faces. IEEE Trans. Pattern Anal. Mach. Intell. **24**(5), 707–711 (2002)

32. Nixon, M.S., Carter, J.N.: Automatic recognition by gait. Proc. IEEE **94**(11), 2013–2024 (2006)

33. Shutler, J.D., Nixon, M.S., Harris, C.J.: Statistical gait description via temporal moments. In: Proceedings of the 4th IEEE Southwest Symposium Image Analysis and Interpretation, pp. 291–295. IEEE (2000)

34. Tilmanne, J., Sebbe, R., Dutoit, T.: A database for stylistic human gait modeling and synthesis. In: Proceedings of the eNTERFACE 2008 Workshop on Multimodal Interfaces, pp. 91–94. Citeseer, Paris (2008)

35. Wallraven, C., Schultze, M., Mohler, B., Volkova, E., Alexandrova, I., Vatakis, A., Pastra, K., Spence, C., Navarra, J., Vatakis, A., et al.: Understanding objects and actions-a vr experiment. Perception **38**, 113 (2014)

36. Wang, A.H., Liu, J.W.: A gait recognition method based on positioning human body joints. In: International Conference on Wavelet Analysis and Pattern Recognition, ICWAPR 2007, vol. 3, pp. 1067–1071. IEEE (2007)
37. Wang, J., She, M., Nahavandi, S., Kouzani, A.: A review of vision-based gait recognition methods for human identification. In: 2010 International Conference on Digital Image Computing: Techniques and Applications (DICTA), pp. 320–327. IEEE (2010)
38. Weimin, X., Ying, L., Hongzhe, H., Lun, X., ZhiLiang, W., et al.: New approach of gait recognition for human id. In: Proceedings of the 2004 7th International Conference on Signal Processing, ICSP 2004, vol. 1, pp. 199–202. IEEE (2004)
39. Xiao, Q.: Technology review-biometrics-technology, application, challenge, and computational intelligence solutions. IEEE Comput. Intell. Mag. 2(2), 5–25 (2007)
40. Xu, D., Yan, S., Tao, D., Zhang, L., Li, X., Zhang, H.J.: Human gait recognition with matrix representation. IEEE Trans. Circuits and Syst. Video Technol. 16(7), 896–903 (2006)
41. Xu, X., Leng, C., Wu, Z.: Rapid 3d human modeling and animation based on sketch and motion database. In: 2011 Workshop on Digital Media and Digital Content Management (DMDCM), pp. 121–124. IEEE (2011)
42. Yih, E.W.K., Sainarayanan, G., Chekima, A.: Palmprint based biometric system: a comparative study on discrete cosine transform energy, wavelet transform energy and sobelcode methods. Biomed. Soft Comput. Hum. Sci. 14(1), 11–19 (2009)
43. Yoo, I., Vanek, J., Nizovtseva, M., Adamo-Villani, N., Benes, B.: Sketching human character animations by composing sequences from large motion database. Visual Comput. 30(2), 213–227 (2014)
44. Yu, S., Tan, T., Huang, K., Jia, K., Wu, X.: A study on gait-based gender classification. IEEE Trans. Image Process. 18(8), 1905–1910 (2009)
45. Zhang, B., Wei, D., Yan, K., Jiang, S.: Human Walking Analysis Evaluation and Classification Based on Motion Capture System. INTECH Open Access Publisher, Winchester (2011)
46. Zhang, M.Y.: Application of performance motion capture technology in film and television performance animation. Appl. Mechan. Mater. 347, 2781–2784 (2013)
47. Zordan, V.B., Van Der Horst, N.C.: Mapping optical motion capture data to skeletal motion using a physical model. In: Proceedings of the 2003 ACM SIGGRAPH/Eurographics Symposium on Computer Animation, pp. 245–250. Eurographics Association (2003)

The Influences of Online Gaming
on Leadership Development

Tinnawat Nuangjumnong[(✉)]

Graduate School of Asia-Pacific Studies, Waseda University, Tokyo, Japan
film.waseda@gmail.com

Abstract. This study seeks to identify the effects gameplay has on leadership
behaviors and establish how video games can be use as a didactic tool for
leadership development. The leadership behaviors, present in both multiplayer
online battle arena games (MOBA) and the real world, are identified. A self-
report questionnaire that categorizes respondents' game roles (carry, support,
ganker) and real-world leadership styles (autocratic, democratic, laissez-faire)
was conducted. Through contingency leadership theory, this study found that
the continuous practice of specific game roles in MOBAs facilitates development of real-world leadership styles. Effects of gameplay on leadership
behaviors were estimated using propensity score matching and doubly robust
estimation. The empirical analyzes revealed that game players who predominantly play a specific role in games exhibit stronger real-world behaviors of the
corresponding leadership style. This study concludes that playing video games
helps improve leadership skills and leadership style development.

Keywords: Leadership style · Game role · Behavior · Online game · Multiplayer online battle arena · MOBA

1 Introduction

Online game industry has gradually extended influence beyond its immediate environment. It has foster technological advancement [1], economic growth [2] and even
social revolutions [3, 4]. Young adults today play online games for more hours than
ever before [5]. Although some studies claim that online games are a negative influence
on game players (e.g., [6–8]), there is a growing movement that argues the contrary.
Many notable real-world leaders claimed that they honed their leadership qualities and
become a better leader by practicing leadership skills in online games [9]. Thus, the
subject of online games as a component of leadership development has become
relevant.

Online games are complex platforms that expose players to various in-game
environments that resemble real-world circumstances [10]. Game players may be able
to connect their in-game characteristics to the real world through online gameplay,
particularly to leadership qualities. This study aims to analyze online gaming's multifaceted influence on leadership behaviors. In non-experimental settings, game players' characteristics in multiplayer online battle arena games (MOBA) and their
real-world leadership behaviors were examined using a self-report questionnaire.

© Springer-Verlag Berlin Heidelberg 2016
M.L. Gavrilova et al. (Eds.): Trans. on Comput. Sci. XXVI, LNCS 9550, pp. 142–160, 2016.
DOI: 10.1007/978-3-662-49247-5_9

The theoretical framework of this study was drawn upon the contingency model of leadership effectiveness [11, 12]. The relationship between roles in games and leadership styles is empirically established using multinomial logistic regression (mlogit). Then the observational data is further investigated using propensity score matching (PSM) together with doubly robust estimation of gameplay effects. The findings will highlight video games' potential as a didactic tool and provide answers to how gameplay can contribute to the development of leadership behaviors.

2 Leadership in Online Games

Online games provide a sophisticated platform that enable virtual human interaction and mimic reality [10, 13]. A variety of studies conducted on the virtual world has been multifaceted, but the most rewarding aspect is perhaps how video games can be a didactic tool. In 2006, Yee conducted a survey that explore demographics, motivations and experiences players derived from massively multiplayer online role-playing games (MMORPGs). It was a pioneering study that explored leadership aspects in online games. Yee highlighted that younger game players claimed to have learned real-world leadership skills from gameplay [14]. In 2007, Reeves et al. linked the Sloan School leadership model to MMORPG environments to examine leadership features in online games. They found that the sensemaking, inventing, relating and visioning dimensions from the Sloan model are embodied in MMORPGs. Reeves et al. pointed out that game environments encourage risk-taking and promote leadership responsibility [15]. However, these findings may be prone to bias because the samples used in that study was limited to one commercial community.

Jang and Ryu also found that leadership factors in MMORPGs — such as value- and motivation-oriented, trust- and respect-oriented and intellectual stimulation-oriented factors — are positively correlated with real-life leadership [16]. Both Reeves et al., Jang and Ryu concluded that being part of a team in online games increases opportunities to experience leadership, which consequently foster the emergence of leadership. However, there remains a gap to be filled in the body of literature that explores specific leadership traits in relation to specific gameplay behaviors.

There are also several social studies that this study used to theorize how behaviors in the virtual environment can interact and impact real-world behaviors. Bandura's notable social learning theory argues that learning process occurs through direct experience or observation of an action and its consequences [17]. This allows game players to learn successful behaviors from games and discard behaviors with bad consequences. The theory can be linked to experiments on the effects of situational primes. Nelson and Norton found that individuals primed with superhero roles are more likely to display helping behaviors and commit to future volunteering activities [18]. A more recent experiment by Yoon and Vargas also found that individuals who played the hero role in games tended to display good behaviors. In contrast, those who played the villain role were likely to exhibit bad actions. The researchers describe this phenomenon as virtual-self representation [19]. Similarly, Greitemeyer and Osswald assigned individuals to video games with prosocial, neutral and aggressive contents and discovered that prosocial game content promotes helping behaviors in individuals [20].

These aforementioned studies hint at how video games influence the way players behave in reality and, perhaps, even shape their characteristics.

3 Theoretical Framework for the Leadership Environment in MOBA Games

This study builds upon the established link between the real world and online games by exploring how games can shape leadership development. The theoretical framework supporting this causality proposal derives from the concept that MOBAs and the real-world environment share similar situational control scenarios as described in the contingency leadership theory, as well as the commonality in traits and behaviors shared between game roles and real-world leadership styles.

The contingency leadership model proposed by Fiedler argues that leadership effectiveness varies based on the compatibility of two factors — personality of a leader, otherwise known as leadership style, and situational control of the scenario at hand [11, 12]. Fiedler's situational control scenarios comprise three fundamental factors — leader-member relations, task structure and position power [21, 22]. Similarly, MOBA environments also present the situational control scenarios in forms of player-to-player interactions, game missions and game character abilities. Real-world leaders have certain personality types that are restricted by social limitations and specific rules that govern each problem-solving scenario. Likewise, game players adapt to their roles during gameplay and they are also restricted by the characteristics of their roles, the game rules and missions. These factors define the levels of control exercised by players over in-game situations. The effectiveness of each game role and the team's performance thus depend on appropriate adaptation to the given situations.

Leadership style is another essential factor in the contingency leadership model. Whereas 'leadership' entails exercising authority and making decisions [23], 'leadership style' refers to the means by which such authority is exercised and the processes through which decisions are made. Leadership styles are the manners and approaches used in directing teams, implementing plans and motivating people. From the perspective of the contingency leadership model, one must recognize his/her leadership style and exercise the style with appropriate situational control to achieve leadership effectiveness. Fiedler defined two leadership styles in his contingency leadership theory — task-oriented and relations-oriented leadership styles [11, 12]. However, Fiedler's leadership styles are focused on work environment rather than aimed at addressing adolescents, who made up the majority of this study's respondents. Hence, this study uses three leadership styles known as the autocratic, democratic and laissez-faire leadership styles. The three leadership styles were defined by Lewin based on leadership behavior experiments conducted on young children [24, 25]. The autocratic and democratic leadership styles are interchangeable with Fiedler's task- and relations-oriented leadership styles respectively [12, 26]. An examination of various leadership theories in the academic literature led to the conclusion that the autocratic, democratic and laissez-faire leadership styles are the least specific to work environment and the most applicable to MOBA game roles. The three leadership styles are described using core behaviors, such as decision-making, task fulfillment, responsibility and trust.

3.1   How Gameplay Influences Leadership Development

As each leader possess a specific leadership style, each game player also plays a specific game role. Leaders are restricted by the given circumstances and problems to be solved. Game players are also restricted by their goals and game environments. Both leaders and game players therefore share similar situational control scenarios. Within these scenarios, leaders and game players practice traits and behaviors that coexist both in the real world and in games and that ultimately define their leadership styles and game roles.

According to social learning theory, game players will be able to acquire new behaviors by direct experience or observation of others' actions and consequences of the actions [17, 27, 28]. MOBA games offer players the same opportunities to adapt leadership behaviors through game roles utilization and to experience situational control scenarios through in-game environments. Trial and error can be achieved in gameplay without irreversible consequences like those in reality [29, 30]. Thus, game players may experiment with their actions in games and discover both the rewarding and punishment consequences from those actions. In-game behaviors that led to rewarding consequences such as kills, gold, experience points, powerful characters, and victory [30] will reinforce players to perform or imitate such actions again. In contrast, in-game behaviors that resulted in punishment consequences which may include death, increase in respawn delay, loss of gold and experience, character weakening, and defeat [30] will reinforce players to avoid and never to repeat such mistakes. As described in the social learning framework, these processes of differential reinforcement guide game players to adopt effective in-game actions — that also correspond to real-world leadership behaviors — or to discard ineffective actions. As mentioned previously, these in-game social learning processes are not restricted only to direct experience but are also possible through observation. Game players can observe other players, team members or enemies who play the same game role or roles of interest and learn from the successes and failures of their actions.

Moreover, by playing a specific game role and learning effective in-game actions, players are simultaneously primed with the game role's characteristics and the prosocial aspects of gameplay [19, 20]. Situational priming through the successful adoption of game roles can make players think of themselves as more decisive, productive, supportive, responsible and trustworthy individuals [18]. As a result, the combination of situational priming by in-game leadership behaviors and exposure to prosocial gameplay can influence individuals to behave correspondingly, thereby allowing game players to acquire the behaviors shared between games and leadership.

Figure 1 depicts a theoretical framework indicating that as a game player exercises a particular game role, he/she simultaneously practices the leadership behaviors that characterize his/her role under simulated situational control scenarios. Accordingly, it is feasible that leadership behaviors are developed through continual exposure to prosocial games. Under the contingent environment, the player is primed with the game role; thus, learns its fundamental characteristics and adapt to its traits over time.

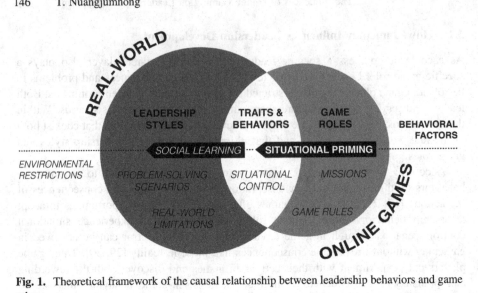

Fig. 1. Theoretical framework of the causal relationship between leadership behaviors and game roles.

3.2 Multiplayer Online Battle Arena (MOBA)

Previous studies on online games and leadership have emphasized the MMORPG genre. This study explores a less frequently studied genre known as MOBA, with a focus on the games Defense of the Ancients (DotA) and Heroes of Newerth (HoN). Two games are used because both are almost identical in game content and mechanics; thus, studying both games provide a larger sample pool.

In MOBAs, an effective team strategy consists not only of gameplay skills but also of the strategic delegation of tasks that deem suitable with the skills [31–33]. MOBAs incorporate straightforward goals and missions that is equivalent to task structure under the situational control scenarios [22]. MOBAs are highly teamwork focused; thus, prosocial [19, 20] and offer meaningful exposure to leadership environments. In comparison with MMORPGs, MOBAs have a much more defined leadership environment and higher level of situational control that exposes players to leadership skill learning opportunities. Each MOBAs match resets to its original settings after the match is over. Players' levels and in-game achievements are not cumulative or transferable to subsequent matches. Therefore, all players are provided with fair and equal opportunities in each competition.

MOBA games are theoretically less addictive because the features that cause addiction, such as curiosity, role-playing, belonging, obligation and collective rewards, are not the highlights of these games [34, 35]. Furthermore, the game players themselves largely determine the games' circumstances because team cooperation and decision-making are limited within the team's five members. Accordingly, cheating is highly discouraged, if not already made impossible by the administration of other game players, thereby reduce the risk of players adopting cheating habits from gameplay [36–38]. Other negative aspects of gameplay such as cyberbullying [39] or aggression [6] are serious concerns that prevent video games from being fully beneficial. Under the theories of social learning and situational prime, game players adopting the bully behaviors by tormenting other players, or aggression from gameplay are not impossible. In this regards, recent studies have pointed out that cyberbullying are unlikely in online games [40] and in-game aggression are caused by players' frustration from their incapability to conquer the games [41], not by its content. Therefore, game contents are not a direct cause of aggression. These features thus make MOBAs the highest potential as a didactic tool for leadership development.

Game Roles. MOBA game roles are an aspect of gameplay strategy that forms an ideal team and defines each player's functions within a small group. The primary categories of game roles are carry, support and ganker [42–44]. Most of the professional game teams participating in DotA and HoN competitions worldwide typically include these three roles [45–47]. Game players must choose from over one hundred heroes, where specific types of heroes are ideally suited to play only certain game roles. Different roles have distinctive duties and goals that players must undertake and achieve to maximize team effectiveness. Therefore, game roles are not objective selections that are made during games but recognized strategies that game players adopt as a team.

The Carry Role. Carry is the role most associated with, and responsible for, a team's expectations of victory [44]. Players who play the carry role are typically expected to gradually become the strongest members of the team because of the role's advantages in abilities and attributes [48]. However, carry role requires protection and assistance in gaining access to additional resources from other team members [43, 49, 50]. A well-balanced team rarely has more than two carry players because in-game resources are limited [42].

The Support Role. Support heroes typically have abilities that benefit other team members, such as healing or enemy disabling abilities [48]. Although they are not equipped with skills that can inflict great damage, their abilities and attributes give them solid defensive strength. Support role heroes do not rely on items and therefore do not require much gold [51]. Instead, gold earned by the support players are spent on items that confer collective advantages to the team, such as couriers for public use or wards, which enable team members to easily spot enemies [52]. The support role's contribution to the team is therefore crucial in providing necessary assistance for other team members and protection against enemies [33, 53].

The Ganker Role. Ganker possesses a combination of carry and support qualities. Ganker heroes are typically equipped with powerful capacities to inflict great damage and disable enemies [42]. A ganker's main responsibilities are thus to disrupt and eliminate enemies and provide the team with advantages over their opposition [54–56]. Accordingly, the ganker's functions are highly flexible in that the role may act as a strategist, decision-maker or supporter depending on the team's needs.

3.3 The Relationship Between Game Roles and Leadership Styles

Carry Role and Autocratic Leadership Behaviors. Individuals with autocratic leadership style tend to dictate group decision-making. They are inclined to be absolute and task-oriented [24, 25, 57]. The traits and behaviors of the carry role share commonalities with the autocratic leadership style. For instance, it is unnecessary for a game's carry to make strategic decisions together with other team members; instead, carry players make quick decisions that maximize their own benefits because they must grow stronger [48–50]. Moreover, carriers are task-focused, which is also a characteristic of autocratic leaders who rule over team decisions and value productivity.

Support Role and Democratic Leadership Behaviors. Individuals characterized by democratic leadership qualities tend to place a significant amount of trust in others. They value input from others and encourage suggestions for decision-making and strongly emphasize group participation. Democratic leaders are people-oriented and value the fair treatment of members [24, 25, 57]. Just as the support role requires players to make decisions based on the optimum benefit for the team and its members [51–53], democratic leaders also make decisions based on group opinions for the good of the group. Both support role game players and democratic leaders prioritize their teammates over themselves. They believe that group members' well-being increases group effectiveness and leads to success. Moreover, because both supporters and democratic leaders rely on other team members to accomplish tasks, their behaviors reflect the high levels of trust they put in other members.

Ganker Role and Autocratic or Democratic Leadership Behaviors. The ganker role mixes the functions of the carry and support roles, which resonates with a mix of the autocratic and democratic leadership styles. A ganker's responsibilities include both self-strengthening and providing team advantages [54, 55]. Self-strengthening is a carry role quality in that the game players must prioritize themselves over others. In addition, the ganker role requires being task-oriented to deliver the most efficient advantages to the team. However, because the ganker role is inherently risky, gankers typically work with the team to reduce risk and deliver effective ganking strategies [56]. Their emphasis on teamwork leads gankers to prioritize group collaboration and group decision-making. Gankers thus place high trust in their team members because they rely on the members to achieve certain goals as part of their ganking strategies. Emphasizing group collaboration and high levels of trust are consistent with democratic leadership traits. Thus, ganker role game players could relate to autocratic leadership style based on their self-prioritization and task-oriented behaviors, and also link to democratic leadership style through their decision-making and trust.

Laissez-Faire Leadership Behaviors Contrast with Game Roles. Laissez-fare leaders emphasize freedom in decision-making. These leaders prefer to delegate decision-making to other members and tend not to intervene in or supervise others' processes [24, 25, 57]. Many literatures classified laissez-faire leadership style as absence of leadership behaviors (e.g., [58, 59]). As discussed above, none of the game roles share any behavior with the laissez-faire leadership style. Laissez-faire leadership behaviors include being very independent and detached from the group. The carry, support and ganker game roles, by contrast, have specific goals and responsibilities that require attentive interaction with the team. Therefore, these three game roles are dissociated from laissez-faire leadership style.

4 Assumption

The theoretical framework of this study is based on the assumption that game players have routine preferences for specific game roles. It is also assumed that the game players attempt to maximize their roles' effectiveness and work towards the team's collective goal for victory. This study is controlled for respondents with no work experience because it is assumed that exposure to a work environment may influence the respondents' behaviors [16, 60].

5 Research Hypotheses

The overarching hypothesis of this study is that continuously playing a specific game role will influence the development of the corresponding leadership behaviors. The hypotheses to be empirically tested are summarized as follows:

- H_1: Game players who predominantly practice the carry role exhibit stronger autocratic leadership behaviors.
- H_2: Game players who predominantly practice the support role exhibit stronger democratic leadership behaviors.
- H_3: Game players who predominantly practice the ganker role exhibit both stronger autocratic and democratic leadership behaviors.

6 Methodology

This study used an observational approach to infer the causality of gameplay on players' leadership behaviors. The hypotheses were tested using mlogit, PSM, sensitivity analysis and doubly robust estimation. First, mlogit was executed to determine the extent to which game roles can predict leadership styles. PSM was then used to estimate the differences in leadership behaviors among players in various roles. A sensitivity analysis and doubly robust estimation with interaction variables were subsequently employed to confirm the outcomes and implications of the PSM estimations.

6.1 Data Collection

This study employed a closed-ended questionnaire in both online and paper-based formats in Thailand. The questionnaire was distributed in online gaming communities, such as Internet cafés, game discussion forums, official game fan pages and social network communities. The questions aimed to examine game players' MOBA gameplay characteristics and their leadership behaviors in daily life. The respondents were intentionally kept uninformed of the objective and the leadership measuring method to avoid evaluation biases of their own characteristics. Questions order was randomized for each respondent to prevent them from recognizing patterns related to the behaviors being measured. After outliers and inconsistent responses were removed, a total of 3,330 samples qualified for empirical analysis.

Game players with no occupational background are chosen as the target group to avoid any work experience which might be confused with the effects to be gained from playing online games [16, 60]. The respondents are therefore characterized by a younger age distribution between 12 to 27 years of age (M = 17.64, SD = 2.90) with a typical allowance of less than 5,000 Thai Baht (70 %, SD = 0.85, 1 USD ≈ 33 THB). This age group is highly suitable for studies on the influence of gameplay because they are found to be learning leadership values from games the most [14]. Only 2 % of the samples were female (M = 19.19, SD = 3.37, n = 69). The majority of the respondents were in high school (40 %, SD = 1.36), and some were attending middle school (23 %).

Measuring Leadership Behaviors. Eleven closed-ended questions were asked to examine behaviors associated with the three leadership styles — autocratic, democratic and laissez-faire. The respondents were asked to self-report the frequency with which they displayed the real-world behaviors described in the questionnaire on a six-point scale from 'never' to 'always'. As an evidence for the measurement's validity, the questions were based on Lewin's predefined leadership traits and behaviors identified in children [24, 25]. Prior studies adopting Lewin's leadership styles have shown adequate measurement validity (e.g., [61, 62]). The reported frequencies of displaying leadership behaviors were summed into scores that reflect the respondents' autocratic (M = 14.85, SD = 3.59, α = 0.78), democratic (M = 17.89, SD = 3.50, α = 0.83) and laissez-faire leadership behaviors (M = 10.53, SD = 3.50, α = 0.82).

Measuring Gameplay Behaviors. The respondents were asked 16 closed-ended questions regarding the behaviors of the three game roles — carry, support, and ganker. The respondents were instructed to self-report the frequency with which they displayed the gameplay behaviors described in the questionnaire on a six-point scale from 'never' to 'always'. The questions regarding game role behaviors were drafted according to the MOBA game guides that are publicly available in the video game media and in communities such as game discussion forums and competition critiques (e.g., [42–44, 48–56]) as well as consultations with game service providers and professional MOBA games players in Thailand. The reported frequencies of displaying the gameplay behaviors were summed into scores that represent the respondents' carry (M = 18.91, SD = 5.27, α = 0.76), support (M = 24.60, SD = 5.14, α = 0.74), and ganker gameplay behaviors (M = 20.83, SD = 4.27, α = 0.61).

6.2   Multinomial Logistic Regression with Marginal Effects

A multinomial logistic regression (mlogit) and its marginal effects were first executed to affirm the relationship between leadership and gameplay. The leadership styles category was the response variable, and the game roles' behaviors and demographic information were explanatory variables. The demographic information includes gender, age, academic degree, income, total number of years played, number of matches played per week, and gameplay environments. Table 1 reports results of the marginal effects, which calculate the probability of possessing a particular leadership style in correlation with the changes in the frequencies of exercising different game roles.

Table 1. Marginal effects after multinomial logistic regression: game roles as predictors of leadership styles.

	Leadership Style					
	Autocratic	SE	Democratic	SE	Laissez-Faire	SE
Carry	0.0230 *	0.01	0.0284 **	0.01	-0.0514 ***	0.01
	(2.47)		(2.69)		(-8.42)	
Support	-0.0414 ***	0.01	0.1095 ***	0.01	-0.0681 ***	0.01
	(-4.03)		(9.51)		(-11.43)	
Ganker	0.0312 ***	0.01	0.0251 *	0.01	-0.0563 ***	0.01
	(3.34)		(2.50)		(-10.88)	
Male	0.0194	0.04	-0.0692	0.04	0.0498 **	0.02
	(0.46)		(-1.57)		(2.80)	
Age	0.0051	0.00	-0.0014	0.00	-0.0037	0.00
	(1.66)		(-0.39)		(-1.76)	
Education	0.0010	0.01	-0.0011	0.01	0.0001	0.00
	(0.16)		(-0.16)		(0.03)	
Income	0.0046	0.01	-0.0031	0.01	-0.0015	0.01
	(0.56)		(-0.31)		(-0.25)	
Game	0.0384 *	0.02	-0.0254	0.02	-0.0130	0.01
Experience	(2.34)		(-1.40)		(-1.28)	
	N	3,330				

Note. Robust t-statistics shown within parentheses.
* $p < 0.05$, ** $p < 0.01$, *** $p < 0.001$

6.3 Propensity Score Matching

PSM[1] is an approach used to draw causal inferences in observational studies under non-experimental settings. In this study, the propensity scores were calculated using covariates, such as gender, age, education, income, hometown, hours of games exposure and gameplay environments. As a result, the effects of these covariates are omitted from the outcomes by means of the matching algorithm. The covariates chosen for the propensity score estimation were considered not only for their relevance but also for the best balance and lowest bias. Thus, this study adopted single nearest-neighbor

---

[1] For detailed information on implementing PSM methodology, please refer to Some Practical Guidance for the Implementation of Propensity Score Matching [63].

matching with calipers and imposed common support in addition to matching by replacing control group members to achieve the least bias possible [63]. By comparing two individuals with similar propensity scores, PSM determines whether the outcomes of the treated group differ significantly from those of the control group by estimating the average treatment effect on the treated (ATT).

In this analysis, the outcome variables are the continuous values of the three leadership behaviors — autocratic, democratic and laissez-faire. The explanatory variables are separated into multiple treatment and control groups. The treated groups consist of those players who have predominantly played the carry, support or ganker roles. 'Predominance' in game role utilization is measured and divided into five levels based on how frequent the players exercised the behaviors of each role, beginning from the moderate level at the top 50 %. The subsequent levels are the top 40 %, 30 %, 20 %, and top 10 %, the latter of which is the level of expert players. Accordingly, this study assigned players who played one or more game roles with at least an above average frequency into treatment groups that corresponded to the roles. Respondents in the treatment groups will be referred to as predominant carriers, predominant supporters or predominant gankers, as applicable. The control groups are individuals who under-performed in each of the role categories and will be referred to as non-carriers, non-supporters and non-gankers.

6.4   Sensitivity Analysis

A sensitivity analysis was conducted to test for the sensitivity of the estimates against hidden bias and the unconfoundedness assumption at a 95 % confidence level. Table 2 reports a comparison of the ATT and the sensitivity analysis gamma values (Γ) compared with the results of the doubly robust estimation. Although previous literatures have not provided a clear rule of thumb for sensitivity analysis, some observational studies have reported sensitivity levels as low as $\Gamma = 1.30$ [64]. Therefore, this study will consider the sensitivity values of no lower than $\Gamma \geq 1.30$ as adequate.

6.5   Doubly Robust Estimation with Interaction Variables

As an additional step, doubly robust estimate was used to confirm the validity of the PSM outcomes [65] by identifying the relationship between substantial leadership behaviors and experiences for each game role. The outcome variables were frequencies of displaying the behaviors that categorize autocratic, democratic and laissez-faire leadership styles. The explanatory variables are similar to those utilized in PSM. The same five game role measurement levels — top 50 %, 40 %, 30 %, 20 %, and 10 % — but differ as they are interacted with gaming experience as measured by total hours of MOBA gameplay. The interaction variable allows individuals' approximate experiences with a specific role utilization to be considered in the statistical modeling.

Table 2. Propensity score matching, sensitivity analysis and doubly robust estimates: Predominant game role adoption.

Game Role		Autocratic		Democratic		Laissez-Faire		Matched Pairs (n)
		PSM ATT / Γ	*Doubly Robust* Coef. / (t)	*PSM* ATT / Γ	*Doubly Robust* Coef. / (t)	*PSM* ATT / Γ	*Doubly Robust* Coef. / (t)	
Carry	50%	1.0953	0.3022 ***	0.4145	0.1034 ***	-0.5575	-0.1440 ***	1,679
		1.51	(8.20)	1.06	(2.89)	1.14	(-4.01)	
	40%	1.2819	0.3548 ***	0.8360	0.2325 ***	-0.9449	-0.2587 ***	1,433
		1.61	(9.10)	1.31	(5.85)	1.39	(-6.55)	
	30%	1.7085	0.4781 ***	0.7866	0.1995 ***	-0.8231	-0.2095 ***	1,012
		1.88	(9.81)	1.24	(4.16)	1.27	(-4.35)	
	20%	1.8446	0.5344 ***	1.0321	0.2839 ***	-1.1138	-0.3099 ***	624
		2.00	(8.91)	1.35	(4.77)	1.43	(-5.31)	
	10%	2.2604	0.6427 ***	1.4820	0.3935 ***	-1.5900	-0.4296 ***	361
		2.20	(7.69)	1.62	(4.80)	1.78	(-5.24)	
Support	50%	0.7276	0.2211 ***	2.1685	0.6272 ***	-2.1583	-0.6215 ***	1,674
		1.29	(6.25)	2.59	(18.50)	2.53	(-18.55)	
	40%	0.6750	0.2061 ***	2.1573	0.6175 ***	-2.0651	-0.5968 ***	1,443
		1.24	(5.35)	2.55	(16.78)	2.48	(-16.41)	
	30%	0.8125	0.2450 ***	2.5000	0.7101 ***	-2.4416	-0.6933 ***	976
		1.31	(5.27)	3.04	(16.70)	2.97	(-16.33)	
	20%	1.0308	0.3187 ***	3.2688	0.9491 ***	-3.1113	-0.9035 ***	584
		1.37	(5.38)	4.44	(17.60)	4.06	(-16.77)	
	10%	1.0195	0.3137 ***	3.4821	1.0074 ***	-3.3029	-0.9601 ***	307
		1.27	(3.65)	4.38	(13.09)	4.05	(-12.59)	
Ganker	50%	2.0234	0.5785 ***	2.2506	0.6473 ***	-2.4499	-0.7067 ***	1,796
		2.37	(17.20)	2.64	(19.77)	2.97	(-21.77)	
	40%	2.4516	0.7085 ***	2.3903	0.6866 ***	-2.6528	-0.7587 ***	1,158
		2.74	(17.11)	2.94	(17.42)	3.41	(-19.46)	
	30%	2.8383	0.8136 ***	2.8371	0.8120 ***	-3.0888	-0.8819 ***	878
		3.40	(17.34)	3.71	(17.91)	4.43	(-19.78)	
	20%	3.0568	0.8597 ***	2.864	0.8033 ***	-3.2033	-0.9030 ***	669
		3.49	(15.49)	3.58	(15.41)	4.22	(-17.54)	
	10%	3.5695	1.0347 ***	3.4542	0.9543 ***	-3.6712	-1.0289 ***	295
		4.12	(12.27)	4.72	(11.80)	5.63	(-12.82)	
	N	3,330						

Note. Γ reported at the 95% confidence level.

Robust t-statistics shown within parentheses.

* p < 0.05, ** p < 0.01, *** p < 0.001.

7 Results

7.1 Marginal Effects After Multinomial Logistic Regression

Carry Game Role. According to the results of the marginal effects based on players' gameplay and leadership behaviors that are reported in Table 1, the carry role showed positive correlations with autocratic (Coef. = 0.023, $p < 0.05$) and democratic leadership styles (Coef. = 0.028, $p < 0.01$). Game players with higher carry behaviors show a greater tendency to display autocratic and democratic leadership styles. The positive correlation of the carry role with both autocratic and democratic leadership styles can be explained by the likelihood that game players gravitate between game roles. Meanwhile, carry role game players are less likely to possess a laissez-faire leadership style (Coef. = −0.051, $p < 0.001$).

Support Game Role. The support role is positively correlated with a democratic leadership style (Coef. = 0.110, $p < 0.001$) and negatively correlated with autocratic (Coef. = −0.041, $p < 0.001$) and laissez-faire leadership styles (Coef. = −0.068, $p < 0.001$). Accordingly, game players who exercise support behaviors are more likely to possess a democratic leadership style and less likely to display autocratic and laissez-faire leadership behaviors.

Ganker Game Role. Interestingly, the results of the marginal effects analysis (Table 1) showed that the ganker role is highly correlated with the autocratic leadership style (Coef. = 0.031, $p < 0.001$), to a greater extent than the carry role. Game players in the ganker role are more likely to possess an autocratic leadership style. Meanwhile, the ganker role is also positively correlated with the democratic leadership style (Coef. = 0.025, $p < 0.05$), revealing the higher tendency of ganker game players to exhibit democratic leadership style. However, the ganker role is negatively correlated with the laissez-faire leadership style (Coef. = −0.056, $p < 0.001$), and such players are thus unlikely to be characterized by a laissez-faire leadership style.

7.2 Outcomes of Propensity Score Matching and Doubly Robust Estimation

The balance diagnostic of PSM yielded well-balanced results. The level of matching bias was reduced to less than 10 %, and the t-statistics reported no significant imbalance between the treated and control groups ($p > 0.10$). The results are consistent with various studies using an observational methodology [66–68].

Carry Role's Effects on Leadership Behaviors. Table 2 reports the outcomes of the PSM and reveals that game players who demonstrate carry role behaviors at the 50 % level or above — or the predominant carriers — displayed significantly stronger autocratic leadership behaviors (ATT = 1.10 to 2.26, Γ = 1.51 to 2.20). Note that the highest ATT for autocratic leadership behaviors is reported at the 10 % level (ATT = 2.26, Γ = 2.20), which is approximately 17 % stronger than non-carriers' average autocratic leadership behaviors. The doubly robust estimation also confirmed that predominant carriers display stronger autocratic leadership behaviors as gaming experience increases (Coef. = 0.30 to 0.64, p < 0.001). Thus, hypothesis H_1 cannot be rejected.

It remains inconclusive whether playing the carry role influences democratic behaviors (ATT = 0.41 to 1.48, Γ = 1.06 to 1.62) or laissez-faire leadership behaviors (ATT = −0.56 to −1.59, Γ = 1.14 to 1.78). The uncertainty arises because the PSM estimates for both leadership styles are highly sensitive despite the significant doubly robust estimates for the democratic (Coef. = 0.10 to 0.39, p < 0.001) and laissez-faire leadership styles (Coef. = −0.14 to −0.43, p < 0.001).

Support Role's Effects on Leadership Behaviors. PSM and the doubly robust estimation yielded interesting results in relation to the support game role. The PSM outcomes in Table 2 show that game players who play the support role predominantly display significantly stronger democratic leadership behaviors (ATT = 2.16 to 3.48, Γ = 2.55 to 4.44), with the peak ATT reported at the 10 % level (ATT = 3.48, Γ = 4.38), approximately 21 % stronger in democratic leadership behaviors compared with non-supporters. The doubly robust estimation also confirmed that there are significant increases in democratic leadership behaviors as predominant supporters' gaming experience increases (Coef. = 0.62 to 1.01, p < 0.001). Therefore, hypothesis H_2 cannot be rejected.

Playing the support role has a negative relationship with laissez-faire leadership behaviors. The PSM outcomes concluded that predominant supporters display significantly weaker laissez-faire leadership behaviors (ATT = −2.07 to −3.30, Γ = 2.48 to 4.06). The weakest outcome reported at the 10 % level (ATT = 3.30, Γ = 4.06) indicated approximately 28 % weaker laissez-faire leadership behaviors for support role players compared with non-supporters. This result parallels the results from the doubly robust estimation, which revealed that predominant supporters display weaker laissez-faire leadership behavior as their gaming experience increases (Coef. = −0.60 to −0.96, p < 0.001).

However, the PSM yielded inconclusive results for autocratic leadership behaviors. Although the doubly robust estimation reported a significant increase in autocratic leadership behaviors (Coef. = 0.21 to 0.32, p < 0.001), the PSM reported highly sensitive outcomes (ATT = 0.68 to 1.03, Γ = 1.24 to 1.37).

Ganker Role's Effects on Leadership Behaviors. The estimates for the ganker role yielded positive outcomes for both autocratic and democratic leadership behaviors, according to Table 2. The PSM outcomes concluded that game players who predominantly play the ganker role display significantly stronger autocratic (ATT = 2.02 to 3.57, Γ = 2.37 to 4.12) and democratic leadership behaviors (ATT = 2.25 to 3.45, Γ = 2.64 to 4.72). The highest ATT for both leadership behaviors was reported at the 10 % level (ATT = 3.57, Γ = 4.12 and ATT = 3.45, Γ = 4.72, respectively). In comparison with predominant carriers, predominant gankers displayed much stronger autocratic leadership behaviors — an approximately 26 % greater tendency than the non-gankers. Compared with predominant supporters, predominant gankers showed a similar increase in democratic leadership behaviors (approximately 21 % higher than the non-gankers). The doubly robust estimation also confirmed the same results that both autocratic (Coef. = 0.58 to 1.03, p < 0.001) and democratic leadership behaviors

(Coef. = 0.65 to 0.95, p < 0.001) are significantly stronger as predominant gankers' gaming experience increases. Hence, hypothesis H_3 cannot be rejected.

Both the PSM outcomes and doubly robust estimation reported a negative influence of the ganker role on laissez-faire leadership behaviors. According to the PSM results, predominant gankers have weaker laissez-faire leadership behaviors (ATT = −2.45 to −3.67, Γ = 2.97 to 5.63). The result is approximately 31 % weaker than the non-gankers' average laissez-faire leadership behaviors. The doubly robust estimation also confirmed the decrease in laissez-faire leadership behaviors as predominant gankers' gaming experience increases (Coef. = −0.71 to −1.03, p < 0.001).

8 Discussion

The results of the quantitative analyzes have provided an empirical evidence that roles in MOBA games and leadership styles share behavioral characteristics and situational control scenarios. Recognizing the leadership styles that individuals possess is essential in achieving leadership effectiveness. In this sense, gameplay can act as a predictor of the individuals' potential leadership styles.

Leadership development occurs through learning and adapting leadership behaviors from continuous practice of specific game roles in a virtual leadership environment similar to that of the real world. At a minimum, game players should achieve a moderate level of game role skills to benefit from gameplay, whereas the empirical estimates suggested that playing game roles at the expert level (i.e., at approximately the top 10 % level) is most effective for leadership learning.

Although none of the game roles studied promote the development of the laissez-faire leadership style, predominantly playing the support and ganker roles can impede the development of laissez-faire leadership behaviors. The rationale behind this phenomenon is laissez-faire leadership style's unique characteristic of being detached from the group [24, 25, 57, 69] or the absence of leadership [58, 59, 70]. Therefore, game roles that require team interactions and attachment to the team do not promote — and may hinder — the development of laissez-faire leadership behaviors.

The sustainability of one single leadership style has greatly been challenged in the modern world, and some argue that mixed leadership qualities make for better leaders [71]. On that note, a mixed of leadership styles is potentially achievable through gameplay. For instance, prominent autocratic leadership style holders may challenge their usual gameplay habits by playing the support role rather than either the carry or ganker roles. This way, game players can experience the characteristics of different leadership styles through gameplay, and learn to gradually adapt the shared traits and behaviors in reality.

It should also be noted that the positive causal relationship between gameplay and leadership development was derived from game players who were most likely unaware of the in-game leadership environment or its relationship with real-world leadership styles. If game players played games not only for entertainment but also recognized them as a didactic tool, they might enhance their leadership behaviors more effectively. Mindfully practicing leadership through games should yield better results than unmindful gameplay [17, 72].

9   Limitations and Future Research

The current study is limited by the involvement of adolescents and its self-report survey method. These limitations increase the difficulty of obtaining an objective measure of gameplay and leadership behaviors, which affects the precision of the data obtained. Future measurements must be improved to ensure greater reliability against adolescents, as well as maintaining pace with the rapid development of video game content and changes in gameplay. Moreover, the implications of this study for female game players must be considered with caution because of the small number of females in the sample. A potential point for further research would be a larger collection of female samples to validate this study's results for both genders.

It must also be noted that online games are one aspect of many potential factors to influence one's leadership behaviors. Although these games may contribute to leadership development, it does not imply one will become a better leader merely by playing online games. Moreover, the most effective hours of video game exposure for leadership development requires further investigation. Excessive gameplay may lead to addiction and lead to irreversible side effects (e.g., [5–7]), whereas too little gameplay may not benefit leadership development at all.

10   Conclusion

This study has provided evidence of an intricate relationship between how games are played and the leadership characteristics that game players possess. Online games established a portal for game players to discover their potential leadership styles and work towards developing effective leadership in everyday life. Through the use of an elaborate theoretical framework with multiple leadership styles, this study also extended beyond the general concept of leadership as a singular definition within the virtual world. Each unique game role generates different leadership opportunities for individuals, and the way one acts in the virtual world reflect upon his/her potential in reality.

The most important aspect of this study comes with the confirmation that MOBA games such as DotA and HoN are in fact a didactic tool. This sheds light on new possibilities for enhancing leadership development for adolescents by incorporating these practices into video games that are already part of their lives. This study also provides a framework for developing better video games tailored for real-world leadership skills enhancement.

Acknowledgement. The author would like to express his appreciation to Hitoshi Mitomo, Atsuyuki Kato and Chutipong Keesookpun for their vast knowledge and generous advice. A sincere gratitude is extended to Ai Lu Wang for her insightful comments, support and motivation.

References

1. Harris, B.J.: Console Wars: Sega, Nintendo, and the Battle that Defined a Generation. HarperCollins, New York (2014)
2. Dyer-Witheford, N., de Peuter, G.: Games of Empire: Global Capitalism and Video Games. University of Minnesota Press, Minneapolis (2009)
3. Juul, J.: A Casual Revolution: Reinventing Video Games and Their Players. The MIT Press, Cambridge (2010)
4. Provenzo Jr., E.F.: Video Kids: Making Sense of Nintendo. Harvard University Press, Cambridge (1991)
5. Gentile, D.A., Saleem, M., Anderson, C.A.: Public policy and the effects of media violence on children. Soc. Issues Policy Rev. 1, 15–61 (2007)
6. Anderson, C.A., Gentile, D.A., Buckley, K.: Violent Video Game Effects on Children and Adolescents. Oxford University Press, Oxford (2007)
7. Fischer, P., Greitemeyer, T., Kastenmüller, A., Vogrincic, C., Sauer, A.: The effects of risk-glorifying media exposure on risk-positive cognitions, emotions, and behaviors: a meta-analytic review. Psychol. Bull. 137, 367–390 (2011)
8. Hull, J.G., Draghici, A.M., Sargent, J.D.: A longitudinal study of risk-glorifying video games and reckless driving. Psychol. Pop. Media Cult. 1, 244–253 (2012)
9. Chiang, O.: How Playing Videogames Can Boost Your Career. http://www.forbes.com/2010/07/19/career-leadership-strategy-technology-videogames.html
10. Barnett, J., Coulson, M.: Virtually real: a psychological perspective on massively multiplayer online games. Rev. Gen. Psychol. 14, 167–179 (2010)
11. Fiedler, F.E.: A contingency model of leadership effectiveness. Adv. Exp. Soc. Psychol. 1, 149–190 (1964)
12. Fiedler, F.E.: The contingency model: a theory of leadership effectiveness. In: Levine, J.M., Moreland, R.L. (eds.) Small Groups: Key Readings, pp. 369–382. Psychology Press, New York (2006)
13. Lofgren, E., Fefferman, N.: The untapped potential of virtual game worlds to shed light on real world epidemics. Lancet Infect. Dis. 7, 625–629 (2007)
14. Yee, N.: The demographics, motivations and derived experiences of users of massively multi-user online graphical environments. Presence 15, 309–329 (2006)
15. Reeves, B., Malone, T., Yee, N., Cheng, H., Abecassis, D., Cadwell, T., Abbey, M., Scarborough, J., Read, L., Roy, S.: Leadership in Games and at Work: Implications for the Enterprise of Massively Multiplayer Online Role-Playing Games. Seriosity Inc., Palo Alto (2007)
16. Jang, Y.B., Ryu, S.H.: Exploring game experiences and game leadership in massively multiplayer online role-playing game. Br. J. Educ. Technol. 42, 616–623 (2011)
17. Bandura, A.: Social Learning Theory. General Learning Press, Morristown (1971)
18. Nelson, L.D., Norton, M.I.: From student to superhero: situational primes shape future helping. J. Exp. Soc. Psychol. 41, 423–430 (2005)
19. Yoon, G., Vargas, P.T.: Know thy avatar: the unintended effect of virtual-self representation on behavior. Psychol. Sci. 25, 1043–1045 (2014)
20. Greitemeyer, T., Osswald, S.: Effects of prosocial video games on prosocial behavior. J. Pers. Soc. Psychol. 98, 211–221 (2010)
21. Fiedler, F.E.: A Theory of Leadership Effectiveness. McGraw-Hill, Urbana (1967)
22. Fiedler, F.E.: Situational Control and a Dynamic Theory of Leadership. In: King, B., Streufert, S., Fiedler, F.E. (eds.) Managerial Control and Organizational Democracy, pp. 107–131. Winston Wiley, New York (1978)

23. Dubin, R.: Human Relations in Administration: The Sociology of Organization, with Readings and Cases. Prentice-Hall, New York (1951)
24. Lewin, K., Lippitt, R.: An experimental approach to the study of autocracy and democracy: a preliminary note. Sociometry **1**, 292–300 (1938)
25. Lewin, K., Lippitt, R., White, R.K.: Patterns of aggressive behavior in experimentally created social climates. J. Soc. Psychol. **10**, 271–301 (1939)
26. Bass, B.M.: The Bass Handbook of Leadership: Theory, Research, and Managerial Applications, 4th edn. The Free Press, New York (2008)
27. Bandura, A.: Aggression: A Social Learning Analysis. Prentice-Hall, Englewood Cliffs (1973)
28. Bandura, A.: Self-efficacy: The Exercise of Control. W.H. Freeman, New York (1997)
29. Kriz, W.C.: Creating effective learning environments and learning organizations through gaming simulation design. Simul. Gaming **34**, 495–511 (2003)
30. Prensky, M.: Computer games and learning: digital game-based learning. Handb. Comput. Game Stud. **18**, 97–122 (2005)
31. Defense of the Ancients. http://dota2.gamepedia.com/Defense_of_the_Ancients
32. Defense of the Ancients. http://dota.wikia.com/wiki/Defense_of_the_Ancients
33. PlayDotA.com: Basic Survival. http://www.playdota.com/learn/survival
34. Hsu, S.H., Wen, M.-H., Wu, M.-C.: Exploring user experiences as predictors of MMORPG addiction. Comput. Educ. **53**, 990–999 (2009)
35. Yee, N.: Motivations for play in online games. Cyberpsychol. Behav. **9**, 772–775 (2006)
36. Aboukhadijeh, F.: Cheating in Video Games. http://feross.org/cheating-in-video-games/
37. Consalvo, M.: Cheating: Gaining Advantage in Videogames. The MIT Press, Cambridge (2007)
38. Information Solutions Group: 2011 PopCap Games Social Gaming Research. http://www. infosolutionsgroup.com/pdfs/2011_PopCap_Social_Gaming_Research_Results.pdf
39. Reuters: A New Type of Cyberbully Hits Online Gaming World. http://www.reuters.com/ article/2007/07/05/us-internet-bullying-idUSN0343424320070705
40. Mesch, G.S.: Parental mediation, online activities, and cyberbullying. Cyberpsychol. Behav. **12**, 387–393 (2009)
41. Przybylski, A.K., Deci, E.L., Deci, E., Rigby, C.S., Ryan, R.M.: Competence-impeding electronic games and players' aggressive feelings, thoughts, and behaviors. J. Pers. Soc. Psychol. **106**, 441–457 (2014)
42. Role (2015). http://dota2.gamepedia.com/Role#Main_Roles
43. Drakthul: Roles. http://www.playdota.com/guides/a-simple-guide-for-heroes-roles
44. Rodriguez, J.: Dota Roles| Explanations and Examples. http://itsme-gaming.blogspot.jp/ 2011/03/dota-roles-explanations-and-examples.html
45. Cabahug, P.: Top 10 Best DotA Players of All Time…(Countdown). http://www.sk-gaming. com/forum/16-DOTA/2298319-TOP_10_BEST_DOTA_PLAYERS_OF_ALL_ TIMECOUNTDOWN
46. Khor, E.: GosuAwards 2013 - Dota 2 Nominations. http://www.gosugamers.net/dota2/ features/3603-gosuawards-voting-closed
47. Khor, E., Kolev, R., Järvinen, J., Benjamin, F., Vitug, D.P.: GosuAwards 2013: Dota 2. http://www.gosugamers.net/390-gosuawards-2013-dota-2
48. Hero Classifications. http://honwiki.net/wiki/Hero_Classifications#Carry
49. FortyeniN: [PSA] So You Think You Can Carry Part 1. http://www.reddit.com/r/DotA2/ comments/nc9st/psa_so_you_think_you_can_carry_part_1/
50. SRKVEN: Dota 2: Hard Carry for Newer Players. http://team-dignitas.net/articles/blogs/ DotA/795/Dota-2-Hard-Carry-for-newer-players
51. Leech: Supports. http://www.dotafire.com/dota-2/guide/supports-108

52. tech-ladan: How to be a Pro-support. http://www.playdota.com/guides/how-to-make-a-good-support
53. Mayer, B.: A DotA 2 Guide for Support and Carry. http://www.team-dignitas.net/articles/blogs/DotA/851/A-DotA-2-guide-for-support-and-carry/
54. Rodriguez, J.: 10 Ganking and Supporting Defense of the Ancients Guide. http://itsme-gaming.blogspot.jp/2011/01/10-ganking-and-supporting-lessons-you.html
55. Ganking. http://dota2.gamepedia.com/Ganking
56. Rodriguez, J.: DotA Ganking Styles. http://itsme-gaming.blogspot.jp/2010/12/9-dota-ganking-styles.html
57. Goodnight, R.: Laissez-faire leadership. Encycl. Leadersh. **98**, 820–823 (2004)
58. Avolio, B.J., Bass, B.M., Jung, D.I.: Re-examining the components of transformational and transactional leadership using the multifactor leadership. J. Occup. Organ. Psychol. **72**, 441–462 (1999)
59. Derue, D.S., Nahrgang, J.D., Wellman, N., Humphrey, S.E.: Trait and behavioral theories of leadership: an integration and meta-analytic test of their relative validity. Pers. Psychol. **64**, 7–52 (2011)
60. Stewart, W., Barling, J.: Fathers' work experiences effect children's behaviors via job-related affect and parenting behaviors. J. Organ. Behav. **17**, 221–232 (1996)
61. Al-Khasawneh, A.L., Futa, S.M.: The impact of leadership styles used by the academic staff in the Jordanian public universities on modifying students' behavior: a field study in the northern region of Jordan. Int. J. Bus. Manag. **8**, 1–11 (2012)
62. Bhatti, N., Maitlo, G.M., Shaikh, N., Hashmi, M.A., Shaikh, F.M.: The impact of autocratic and democratic leadership style on job satisfaction. Int. Bus. Res. **5**, 192–201 (2012)
63. Caliendo, M., Kopeinig, S.: Some practical guidance for the implementation of propensity score matching. J. Econ. Surv. **22**, 31–72 (2008)
64. Rosenbaum, P.R.: Sensitivity analysis in observational studies. Encycl. Stat. Behav. Sci. **4**, 1809–1814 (2005)
65. Funk, M.J., Westreich, D., Wiesen, C., Stürmer, T., Brookhart, M.A., Davidian, M.: Doubly robust estimation of causal effects. Am. J. Epidemiol. **173**, 761–767 (2011)
66. Austin, P.C.: Balance diagnostics for comparing the distribution of baseline covariates between treatment groups in propensity-score matched samples. Stat. Med. **28**, 3083–3107 (2009)
67. Cohen, J.: Statistical Power Analysis for the Behavioral Science, 2nd edn. Lawrence Erlbaum Associates, Hillsdale (1988)
68. Normand, S.-L.T., Landrum, M.B., Guadagnoli, E., Ayanian, J.Z., Ryan, T.J., Cleary, P.D., McNeil, B.J.: Validating recommendations for coronary angiography following acute myocardial infarction in the elderly: a matched analysis using propensity scores. J. Clin. Epidemiol. **54**, 387–398 (2001)
69. Eagly, A.H., Johannesen-Schmidt, M.C., van Engen, M.L.: Transformational, transactional, and laissez-faire leadership styles: a meta-analysis comparing women and men. Psychol. Bull. **129**, 569–591 (2003)
70. Einarsen, S., Aasland, M.S., Skogstad, A.: Destructive leadership behaviour: a definition and conceptual model. Leadersh. Q. **18**, 207–216 (2007)
71. Goleman, D.: Leadership that gets results. Harv. Bus. Rev. **78**, 78–90 (2000)
72. Gackenbach, J., Bown, J.: Mindfulness and video game play: a preliminary inquiry. Mindfulness **2**, 114–122 (2011)

An Efficient Pose Tolerant Face Recognition Approach

Refik Samet$^{(\boxtimes)}$, Ghulam Sakhi Shokouh, and Kemal Batuhan Baskurt

Department of Computer Engineering, Ankara University, Ankara, Turkey
samet@eng.ankara.edu.tr,
{shokouh.sakhi,batuhanbaskurt}@gmail.com

Abstract. Face recognition is biometric pattern recognition, which is more acceptable and convenient for users compared with other biometric recognition traits. Among many problems in face recognition system, pose problem is considered as one of the major problem still unsolved in satisfactory level. This paper proposes a novel pose tolerant face recognition approach which includes feature extraction, pose transformation learning and recognition stages. In the first stage, 2DPCA is used as robust feature extraction technique. The linear regression is used as efficient and accurate transformation learning technique to create frontal face image from different posed face images in the second stage. In the last stage, Mahalanobis distance is used for recognition. Experiments on FERET and FEI face databases demonstrated the higher performance in comparison with traditional systems.

Keywords: Biometric pattern recognition · Face recognition · Principal component analysis · Feature extraction · Pose transformation learning

1 Introduction

Pattern recognition is a branch of artificial intelligence and machine learning concerned with the study of how the machine can observe the environment, learn to distinguish pattern of interest and make decision based on the classification or description of observations [1]. One of the most popular research areas in pattern recognition is face recognition in recent years. Recognition of human faces from still images and video frames is an active research area due to the increasing demand on human authentication and identification systems. Common application areas of face recognition other than biometric authentication are surveillance, human-computer interaction, multimedia management, law enforcement, smart cards and auto tagging of photos [2].

There are several biometric identification technologies like finger print, DNA, iris, voice, hand geometry, palm print or retina recognition. Almost all these technologies require some voluntary action by the user, i.e., the user needs to place his hand on a hand-rest for fingerprinting or geometry detection and has to stand in a fixed position in front of a camera for iris or retina identification. Iris and retina identification also requires expensive equipment and is too sensitive to any body motion. Voice recognition is susceptible to background noises in public places and auditory fluctuations on a phone line or tape recording. Signatures can be modified or forged. However, face

© Springer-Verlag Berlin Heidelberg 2016
M.L. Gavrilova et al. (Eds.): Trans. on Comput. Sci. XXVI, LNCS 9550, pp. 161–172, 2016.
DOI: 10.1007/978-3-662-49247-5_10

recognition can be done passively without any explicit action or participation on the part of the user since face images can be acquired from a distance by a camera. Among all biometric traits, face provides a more direct, friendly and convenient recognition method because it is non-intrusive and automatic pattern recognition can be performed without the cooperation of user [3].

Over the last decade, face recognition has become a popular area of research in pattern recognition, computer vision, and one of the most successful applications of image analysis and understanding. The problem in face recognition is the deformability of the face. The difficulty of this task comparing to other pattern recognition traits is the variation of the same face's form because of several environmental and temporal effects as inter-class variability (e.g., variation of pose, variation due to lighting condition, facial expression, scale, age, different skin, visual point, occlusion, make-up, glasses and orientation of image) and intra-class similarity (father and son, twins).

Among all problems in face recognition, pose problem is considered as one of the most challenging and difficult task to be solved. This is because of the facts that face appearance changes drastically with changes in facial pose, due to misalignment as well as hiding of many facial features.

In this paper, a novel face recognition approach is proposed in order to contribute to the solution of pose estimation problem. Proposed system is based on creating features of frontal face by transformation of the features extracted from different posed face images. Proposed system includes feature extraction, pose transformation learning and recognition stages. Firstly, 2D Principal Component Analysis (2DPCA) technique is used for feature extraction. Secondly, regression technique is used for transforming posed face image feature vectors to the frontal posed feature vectors [4]. This transformation is based on the theory of linear object class [5]. Finally, as recognition is concerned, Mahalanobis distance technique as simple and accurate classifier is used for matching the feature vectors and identifying the probes [6].

The content of this paper is organized as follows. In Sect. 2, the most relevant existing literatures are summarized. The design and methods of proposed system are presented in Sect. 3. Section 4 presents the implementation results and discussions. Finally, the paper is concluded in Sect. 5.

2 Related Works

The traditional solutions overcome face pose variation problem by keeping many different posed images of the same person in the database and then matching each coming probe face image with its corresponding poses stored in the database at the time of recognition. Recent works about pose problem of face recognition, which will be referred as "modern solution" in this paper, are to construct frontal pose out of different poses through some transformation techniques and artificial modeling.

Modern solution is more efficient in real-life applications, where normally limited face images in the database (gallery) per each person for matching are kept. Generally there are three main approaches for handling the pose transformation issues within the scope of this solution.

The first branch of the approaches is based on 3D modeling of frontal pose using different poses [7, 8]. The pose synthesis approaches synthesize images with different poses for each gallery image. Only virtual images with similar pose are used for matching the gallery and probe images. In spite of explicit geometric information contained in 3D face data, 3D data can hardly be processed in a convenient manner. This is because 3D face scans are commonly irregular in data representation. Different faces usually contain different number of vertices and inconsistent boundaries. Even with the same point number and consistent boundary, the vertices in two 3D faces can be scattered completely different. These approaches increase their popularity in recognition rate, but the major issue with them is that, in spite of requiring one training image for modeling, it has extensive computational cost which limits its application in real life condition [9].

The second branch is 2D modeling of face image through some geometric techniques, like Elastic Bunch Graph Matching [10], Active Appearance Model [11], Active Shape Model [12], and many more. Constructing a 2D model with specifying landmark on face area is also one of the effective methods for face detection under different pose. However major problem with these approaches is their fiducial feature point detection as locating exactly the land mark position is not easy task and it needs to be placed manually [9]. Both robust and automatic land mark positioning cannot be performed on real time. In [13], generating the frontal view face image using linear transformation in feature space is proposed. Since a face image has very high-dimensional data, they represented the face image in subspace not only for dimension reduction, but also for relevant feature extraction. Instead of linear feature extraction, they used Kernel PCA (K-PCA) which is non-linear to extract features from a posed face image. Then, they transformed the posed face image into its corresponding frontal face image using the transformation matrix predetermined by learning. The goal of transformation was to obtain a pose transformation matrix that could convert the posed face image into its corresponding frontal face image such that the converted frontal face image looked similar to the original frontal face image. Their system recognizes the face image by three different discrimination methods such as LDA, NDA, or GDA instead of using distance based metrics such as Euclidean distance. Through the experiment they proved their approach had better performance than the traditional face recognition system of without pose transformation. Since this approach uses the geometric features, it is very difficult to exactly locate the landmarks for feature extraction. Mostly it requires manual intervention to place the landmarks.

The third branch of the approaches relies on appearance or intensity based techniques. This approach is holistic approach, means it uses the intensity features extracted by some techniques like Principal Component Analysis, Gabor Wavelet and neural network, and perform the transformation techniques on intensity features [14, 15]. In one of the recent works, an automatic head pose estimation method from a pose face image is proposed [16]. The face image is divided into a regular grid and a representation of the image is obtained by extracting dense SIFT descriptors from its grid points. Dimension of the concatenated SIFT descriptor vector is reduced by applying random projection to obtain optimized significant data that can be processed in real time condition. Recently, [17] proposed Coupled Latent Space Discriminative Analysis which aims to maximize correlations between different poses of the face under the same condition to overcome the multiple pose face recognition problem. The model merges different techniques like partial least squares canonical correlation analysis and bilinear model into a hybrid one and considers small pose errors in the latent space for enhancing the performance.

In last branch of the modern approaches mentioned above, the features to be extracted or transformed are generally holistic intensity features. Using this approach, one needs to find the transformation more accurately, and since the conventional linear regression technique does not perform well in presence of multi-collinearity and hetero-scedasticity, ridge regression is used to overcome this shortcoming. Multi-collinearity arises when two or more predictor variables in a multiple regression model are highly correlated. Hetero-scedasticity arises due to variance of regression estimation error not being constant for all values of independent variable, that is, error term could vary for each observation [18].

Through the mentioned studies, geometric distance/angles computation of face common features, such as distance among eyes, nose, mouth, ears, is not an enough and efficient technique. Later on the idea of statistical analysis of multidimensional data such as whole face image proved to be efficient for feature extraction which both reduces the dimensionality of data at reasonable without useful data loss, and speeding up the performance of matching and recognition. PCA is a robust method for statistical analysis, dimensionality reduction and feature extraction of high dimensional data. Using PCA we can construct the face recognition system which is very efficient comparing to geometric model, and 3D modeling, which requires manual landmark positioning, and heavy computational efforts, respectively. This all make the system less useful in practical conditions.

After obtaining the low dimension feature vector, pose invariant face recognition system requires techniques to transform any arbitrary posed images to front pose images. This pose transformation is performed on feature vectors deduced from PCA, rather than performing the transformation on face image itself. As making appropriate tradeoff between different pose transformation techniques, based on the idea and requirement of automatic and non-intrusive face recognition system, intensity based transformation of features is proposed to be reasonable and practical for real life condition. Based on the idea of linear object class [5], and correlation analysis, there is close linear relationship between frontal posed images and different posed images. It means at least there are few shared features between posed and frontal images. Based on this mathematical relationship, an appropriate transformation can be performed for pose transformation.

3 Methodology

An efficient approach for pose tolerant face recognition system, which contains the feature extraction, transformation learning and recognition, is proposed. Figure 1 illustrates the proposed system architecture.

First of all, noise removal process is applied to ease the feature extraction and prevent detection of undesired poor features. Two-level Haar wavelet decomposition on face images has been used for this purpose. The Haar transform is the simplest one

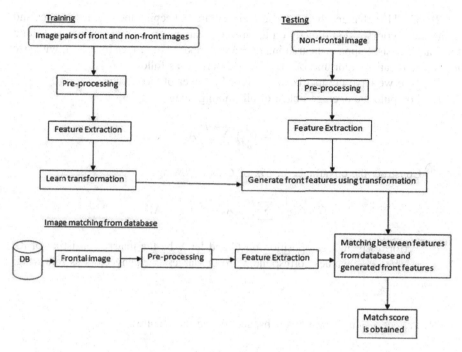

Fig. 1. Proposed system architecture

of the wavelet transforms which cross-multiplies a function against the Haar wavelet with various shifts and stretches, like the Fourier transform cross-multiplies a similar function against a sine wave with two phases and many stretches. After the transformation, smoother surfaces are obtained by compressing undesired noisy regions and the characteristic features of the face become dominant.

3.1 Feature Extraction Stage

Feature extraction is a special form of dimensionality reduction. When the input data to an algorithm is too large to be processed and it is suspected to be too much redundant, then the input data is transformed into a reduced representation asset of features (also named features vector). If a robust feature extraction operation is performed, it is expected that the feature set will extract the relevant information from the input data in order to perform the desired task using this reduced representation instead of the full size input. One of the powerful and efficient feature extraction techniques is Principal Component Analysis (PCA), which is used in the proposed approach. PCA is a way of identifying patterns in data, and expressing the data in such a way as to highlight their similarities and differences. Since patterns in data can be hard to find in high dimension data, PCA is a powerful method for analyzing the data. PCA allows us to compute a linear transformation that maps data from a high dimensional space to a lower dimensional sub-space.

2DPCA [19] changes the Eigenfaces algorithm by keeping the original images and doing the decomposition directly on the mean covariance matrix of the images to find the feature basis. Suppose the training data are composed of M face images A_i with size mXn. The detailed algorithm of 2DPCA is described as follows.

Suppose we have the matrix of A with M number of face images.

(1) Compute the average image of all training images.

$$\overline{A} = \left(\frac{1}{M}\right) \sum_{i=1}^{M} A_i$$

(2) Construct the covariance matrix of C as following:

$$C = \left(\frac{1}{M}\right) \sum_{i=1}^{M} (A_i - \overline{A})(A_i - \overline{A})^T$$

(3) Perform Eigen decomposition on C and let X be the matrix consisting of the selected eigenvalues corresponding to the largest k eigenvectors as following:

$$X = [x_1, x_2, \ldots, x_k]$$

(4) Project a sample into this subspace to find the features.

$$Y_i = (A_i - \overline{A})^T X.$$

3.2   Transformation Learning Stage

In transformation learning, transformation is performed based on the linear regression theory. The learning process is performed between the feature vectors of frontal face image and feature vectors of different posed face images.

Instead of traditional regression technique, robust and accurate regression technique called ridge regression with a new and accurate parameter estimator is used in proposed system [20, 21]. It is based on assumption of the Linear Object Class [5], and it also uses the modular Eigenspace concept [22]. The linear object class assumption is that transformation corresponding feature vectors of the given and the desired poses is linear, and a feature vector of a face image can be represented as a linear combination of corresponding training vectors of its related poses.

Face images also rely on the linear object class category. Once this linear transform is obtained, feature vectors of different poses can be obtained from one pose using corresponding transformation matrix between them. Modular Eigenspace concept states that corresponding to each "view" set, that is pose, there exists an Eigenspace. So, every face image can be written as a linear combination of basis vectors of its own vector space.

Let X and Y be the matrix containing the feature vectors of non-frontal and frontal face images of the training set respectively. Features vectors of corresponding poses are present as column vector in the matrix X and Y. For the posed face transformation to frontal face scenario, the linear regression model can be simulated as:

$$Y = X\beta + \varepsilon$$

Let T be the desired transformation matrix to be learn. Then we have:

$$Y = T \tag{1}$$

Common estimator for β is the least square estimator as following:

$$T = ((X^T Y)^{-1}) X^T Y \tag{2}$$

In the presence of multi-collinearity the least square solution is not considered as good solution [18], so a good solution is given by the ridge regression $(\widehat{\beta})$ as following:

$$\widehat{\beta} = ((X^T Y + \lambda I)^{-1}) X^T \tag{3}$$

λ is the ridge estimator and it defines degree of freedom or penalty for estimator. Suppose the degree of freedom $= d_f; \lambda_i, \ldots, \lambda_n$ are the eigenvalues of transformation matrix.

$$d_f \text{ Ridge } = \sum_{i=1}^{n} \frac{\lambda_i}{\lambda_i + \lambda} \tag{4}$$

Ridge regression shrinks the coefficients of low variance components and hence the parameter λ controls the degree of freedom, where $d_f = n$, at $\lambda = 0$ as normal regression, and where $d_f = 0$, at $\lambda = \infty$.

In our system for selecting ridge estimator we have used the best formulation in [21], which gives the lowest Mean Square Error (MSE), which is originally the extension of formulation in [18].

The ridge parameter is calculated iteratively such that the covariance of the error converges and

$$\varepsilon = Y - X\widehat{\beta} \tag{5}$$

Ridge regression deliberately introduces bias into the estimation of β in order to reduce the variability of the estimate. The resulting estimate has generally lower mean squared error than conventional approaches like the Ordinary Least Square (OLS) estimate. Equations (2) and (5) are used to get an OLS estimate and the estimation error matrix respectively. Covariance of this error matrix is found by taking the sum of squares of all elements in error matrix. This is the initial estimate of covariance of error thus an initial guess for λ is done. Now, the estimation is done using Eq. (3) and covariance of estimation error matrix is calculated, iteratively. Whenever the covariance is less than its present estimate, the values of λ and covariance are updated. Final estimate of λ is used to calculate the transformation matrix.

3.3   Recognition Stage

In recognition stage, the feature vectors obtained from previous step are matched with the frontal face feature vectors in the database. A distance based classifier has been proposed for matching, because for most of the practical applications, database generally contains only one image for a single person. As evaluation is concerned, better results are found using efficient distance based classifiers such as Mahalanobis distance.

Mahalanobis distance is based on correlations between variables by which different patterns can be identified and analyzed. Mahalanobis distance gauges similarity of an unknown sample set to a known one. It differs from Euclidean distance in that it takes into account the correlations of the data set and is scale-invariant. The Mahalanobis distance is a better distance measure when it comes to pattern recognition problems [6]. Smaller match score means that two vectors are closer in the Mahalanobis space and vice versa. If the match score is less than a threshold value, the two vectors are said to be matched or belonging to the same person.

4   Experimental Results

Firstly, training and testing protocol of proposed approach is described in this section. Like any other learning based approach we require training data to learn the model parameters. Thus some of the test images are used for training to obtain required information in order to synthesize frontal face from non-frontal ones. One frontal face for each subject is stored in database to compare with synthesized face image for recognition. Training images are shown in Fig. 2.

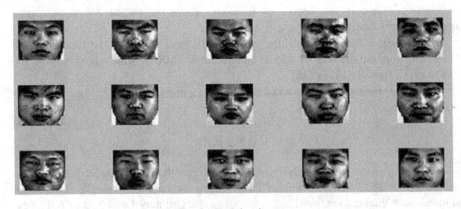

Fig. 2. Training images

Feature extraction and dimensionality reduction operations which create feature vectors (Eigenfaces) are applied to test images. These feature vectors are the mentioned lower dimensional sub spaces used for creating weight vectors for recognition step. The significant Eigenvectors are decided on the basis of Eigen vectors preserving the most of weight. Once the significant Eigen vectors are selected, the images are projected into the reduced vector space that is formed only by the selected significant Eigen vectors. Finally projection coefficients form the feature vector and the reduced vector space forms the feature space. Figure 3 demonstrates the eigenvectors of principal components.

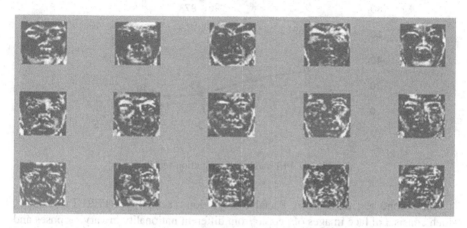

Fig. 3. Eigenfaces of training images

Then the image reconstruction process is performed. It is useful for illustrating that we reconstruct our old image from reduced dimensional feature vectors (principal components). Feature vectors of images in vector spaces of each pose are used to learn the linear transformation between the feature vectors of frontal and non-frontal face image. Then the final step of matching and recognition is implemented. The face images are classified heuristically according to the metric weight of feature vectors. Then the Mahalanobis distance is used for matching the probe images with reference images in the database.

Our experiment is performed on two databases: FERET [3], and FEI [16] databases. In FEI face database, 80 subjects, 4 different posed images, totally 320 images with the pose variation of +22.5, –22.5, +45, and –45 are selected and used. 80 frontal pose are kept in the database, remaining are used for training (learning) and testing. Table 1 and Fig. 4 illustrate the results.

Table 1. FEI database recognition results

Angle	Traditional approach		Proposed approach	
	Accuracy %	*Error %*	*Accuracy %*	*Error %*
+22.5	87	13	94	6
–22.5	90	10	95	5
+45	69	31	79.1	20.9
–45	75	25	81.6	18.4

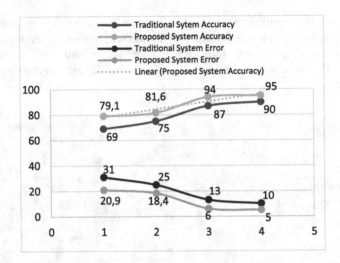

Fig. 4. FEI database recognition results

Our second test database is Facial Recognition Technology (FERET) database, which consists of face images of people from different nationality in varying poses and times. In our experiment we have used 270 images of 80 subjects in angle between +45 to –45. 80 frontal pose are kept in the database. Remaining 190 are used for learning the transformation matrix and testing. Table 2 and Fig. 5 illustrate our test results.

Table 2. FERET database recognition results

Angle	Traditional approach		Proposed approach	
	Accuracy %	Error %	Accuracy %	Error %
+15	92	8	95.6	4.4
–15	94	6	98.4	1.6
+45	69	31	78	22
–45	75	25	81.8	18.2

The test results are compared with the existing face recognition system with different poses [13]. The proposed face recognition system shows significant increase in performance over the compared system. This contribution arises from robust feature extraction and dimensionality reduction, better regression technique with accurate parameter estimation for transformation learning, and accurate distance classifier for recognition. Robust feature extraction techniques solve the deficiency of PCA, and a better regression technique helps in solving the problem of existing regression techniques. It is also noted that recognition accuracy decreases as pose angle increases. This is because of the fact that regression error increases for big pose angles, thus the system generates an inaccurate transformation matrix. Considering the pose angle, our proposed approach is found to be better than the system in [13].

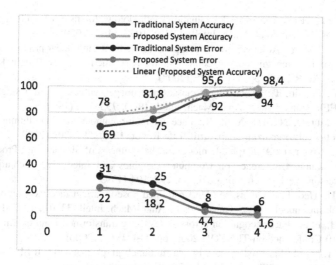

Fig. 5. FERET database recognition results

5 Conclusion

Amongst many problems of illumination, occlusion, facial expression, age and facial accessories; pose variation is more problematic due to misalignment and displacement of facial features. Among three different approaches for pose problem, intensity based approach has been preferred for its automaticity by the means of no need for any user interaction to select visual landmarks and its performance. Geometric and model generation approaches require user intervention, and have heavy computational cost which doesn't suit with performance requirements of practical applications. Proposed system makes use of 2DPCA to extract features and reduce the dimensionality. Then it uses robust regression techniques with accurate parameter predictor on the bases of linear object class to generate the feature vector of frontal face from the given face images. Finally, Mahalanobis distance technique is used for accurate recognition. The experiment on FERET and FEI face databases demonstrate that the proposed approach performs better than the existing system [13].

Finally, proposed approach is not resistant enough to illumination changes. Thus future work includes applying an illumination normalization operation to both training and test images and comparing result with the current approach.

References

1. Wee, W.G.: A survey of pattern recognition. In: Seventh Symposium on Adaptive Processes, 1968, pp. 25–25. IEEE (1968)
2. Choi, J.Y., et al.: Automatic face annotation in personal photo collections using context-based unsupervised clustering and face information fusion. IEEE Trans. Circuits Syst. Video Technol. **20**(10), 1292–1309 (2010)

3. Phillips, P.J., et al.: The FERET evaluation methodology for face-recognition algorithms. IEEE Trans. Pattern Anal. Mach. Intell. **22**(10), 1090–1104 (2000)
4. Wang, J., Chen, Y., Adjouadi, M.: A comparative study of multilinear principal component analysis for face recognition. In: 2008 37th IEEE Applied Imagery Pattern Recognition Workshop, AIPR 2008, pp. 1–6. IEEE (2008)
5. Vetter, T., Poggio, T.: Linear object classes and image synthesis from a single example image. IEEE Trans. Pattern Anal. Mach. Intell. **19**(7), 733–742 (1997)
6. Aly, S., Tsuruta, N., Taniguchi, R.: Face recognition under varying illumination using Mahalanobis self-organizing map. Artif. Life Robot. **13**(1), 298–301 (2008)
7. Blanz, V., Vetter, T.: A morphable model for the synthesis of 3D faces. In: Proceedings of the 26th Annual Conference on Computer Graphics and Interactive Techniques. ACM Press/Addison-Wesley Publishing Co., pp. 187–194 (1999)
8. Prabhu, U., Heo, J., Savvides, M.: Unconstrained pose-invariant face recognition using 3D generic elastic models. IEEE Trans. Pattern Anal. Mach. Intell. **33**(10), 1952–1961 (2011)
9. Zhang, H., et al.: Face recognition across poses using transformed features. In: 2006 IEEE Region 10 Conference on TENCON 2006, pp. 1–4. IEEE (2006)
10. Wiskott, L., et al.: Face recognition by elastic bunch graph matching. IEEE Trans. Pattern Anal. Mach. Intell. **19**(7), 775–779 (1997)
11. González-jiménez, D., Alba-castro, J.L.: Pose correction and subject-specific features for face authentication. In: 18th International Conference on Pattern Recognition, 2006, ICPR 2006, pp. 602–605. IEEE (2006)
12. Cootes, T.F., et al.: Active shape models-their training and application. Comput. Vis. Image Underst. **61**(1), 38–59 (1995)
13. Lee, H.S., Kim, D.: Generating frontal view face image for pose invariant face recognition. Pattern Recogn. Lett. **27**(7), 747–754 (2006)
14. Gross, R., Matthews, I., Baker, S.: Eigen light-fields and face recognition across pose. In: Proceedings of the Fifth IEEE International Conference on Automatic Face and Gesture Recognition, 2002, pp. 1–7. IEEE (2002)
15. Akimoto, T., Suenaga, Y., Wallace, R.S.: Automatic creation of 3D facial models. IEEE Comput. Graph. Appl. **13**(5), 16–22 (1993)
16. Ho, H.T., Chellappa, R.: Pose-invariant face recognition using Markov random fields. IEEE Trans. Image Process. **22**(4), 1573–1584 (2013)
17. Sharma, A., et al.: Robust pose invariant face recognition using coupled latent space discriminant analysis. Comput. Vis. Image Underst. **116**(11), 1095–1110 (2012)
18. Hoerl, A.E., Kennard, R.W.: Ridge regression: Biased estimation for nonorthogonal problems. Technometrics **12**(1), 55–67 (1970)
19. Yu, H., Bennamoun M.: A compact and complete AFMT invariant with application to face recognition. In: Proceedings of the 2nd International Conference on Machine Intelligence, ACIDCA-ICMI'2005 (2005)
20. Wang, J., et al.: Multilinear principal component analysis for face recognition with fewer features. Neurocomputing **73**(10), 1550–1555 (2010)
21. Dorugade, A.V., Kashid, D.N.: Alternative method for choosing ridge parameter for regression. Appl. Math. Sci. **4**(9), 447–456 (2010)
22. Pentland, A., Moghaddam, B., Starner, T.: View-based and modular eigenspaces for face recognition. In: 1994 IEEE Computer Society Conference on Computer Vision and Pattern Recognition, 1994, Proceedings CVPR 1994, pp. 84–91. IEEE (1994)

Author Index

Printed in the United States
By Bookmasters